AN ECONOMIC HISTORY
OF TROPICAL AFRICA

Volume Two

The Colonial Period

Z. A. Konczacki and J. M. Konczacki

AN ECONOMIC HISTORY
OF TROPICAL AFRICA

VOLUME ONE   : THE PRE-COLONIAL PERIOD
VOLUME TWO   : THE COLONIAL PERIOD

VOLUME THREE: AN ECONOMIC AND SOCIAL
HISTORY OF SOUTHERN
AFRICA

AN
ECONOMIC HISTORY
OF TROPICAL AFRICA

VOLUME TWO

THE COLONIAL PERIOD

Selected and Edited by
Z. A. KONCZACKI
Professor of Economics, Dalhousie University
and
J. M. KONCZACKI
Associate Professor, Mount St Vincent University

Routledge
Taylor & Francis Group

LONDON AND NEW YORK

First published 1977 in Great Britain by
Routledge
2 Park Square, Milton Park, Abingdon, Oxfordshire OX14 4RN
711 Third Avenue, New York, NY 10017

First issued in paperback 2014

Routledge is an imprint of the Taylor and Francis Group, an informa business

This selection and introduction Copyright © 1977
Z. A. Konczacki and J. M. Konczacki

ISBN 13: 978-0-714-62915-5 (hbk)
ISBN 13: 978-0-415-76111-6 (pbk)

Publisher's Note
The publisher has gone to great lengths to ensure the quality of this
reprint but points out that some imperfections in the original
may be apparent

CONTENTS

INTRODUCTION

This volume is a sequel to the Economic History of Tropical Africa: The Pre-Colonial Period. Like its predecessor it excludes the southernmost part of the Continent. The editors feel that differences in the nature of South African development call for a separate volume. Moreover the inclusion of Southern Africa would vitiate the uniformity of presentation by making it impossible to take the 'scramble' for African colonies as a convenient point of departure. However, convenience has its price: a conventional periodization may tend to obscure the continuity of the developments which were taking place in some parts of Africa throughout the nineteenth century and even earlier. For this reason the reader is asked to treat the two volumes as an inseparable whole.

The enormous diversity of the various economies encountered by a student of the economic history of sub-Saharan Africa poses special problems. We have attempted to overcome this by combining comprehensive and comparative studies with more detailed monographs dealing with particular countries. This approach we have adopted when dealing with the problems which cut across the boundaries of some colonial territories. Case studies concerned with particular countries are assigned a prominent place.

Nigeria and Ghana are chosen as representative of West Africa, and Uganda because of its unique developmental traits, as that of East Africa. Special attention is paid to Francophone Africa and to the territories under Portuguese rule. The absence of a separate paper on the former Belgian Congo (with the exception of the one on the Congo State) is compensated for by references made to that country in other papers included in this book.

We have decided to preserve the names originally used by the authors, even if post-independence names are applied to the colonial period.

The period of colonial economic activity covered in this volume begins with the partition of Africa at the Berlin Conference of 1884–5, and ends with the granting of independence to the former dependencies in the late 'fifties and 'sixties of the twentieth century. The years immediately following the partition produced little change in the economic life of the territories over which European rule was extended. Hopes that private investment by

Europeans would stimulate economic activity did not materialise. On the contrary, in many parts of the Continent the predatory activities of the early exploiters affected considerable numbers of people while the more constructive efforts leading to the development of cash crops and wage employment had little effect on the indigenous population. The ideal of a fiscally self-supporting colony, with regard to current expenditure, was in contrast to the public debt policy of the colonial governments which borrowed overseas to provide a rudimentary transportation network.

The period which followed the First World War was characterised by a tendency to closer economic cooperation between the metropolitan countries and their dependencies. Yet even then their main reliance was still placed on private investment. A new element was introduced when the former German colonies became mandated territories and the new responsibilities of the trustees led to the re-thinking of their attitudes towards the colonial question at large.

The efforts of the 'twenties were brought to a practical standstill by the Great Depression. Metropolitan governments, unable to deal effectively with the problems at home, were in no position to deal adequately with the question of colonial economic development.

The Second World War created a demand for resources which the African territories could partly provide. At the same time, it was realised how little had been done in the past to develop them, and efforts were made to avoid such mistakes in the future. Also, during the war years and immediately after the war, African territories managed to accumulate considerable foreign exchange balances which they were, at that time, unable to spend on imports. These, together with the meagre grants from the metropolitan countries, provided a financial basis for modest development plans.

The division of the subject-matter of this collection of readings tries to reflect this historical sequence, even if at times the approach is also influenced by other considerations. The purpose of Part One is to provide an outline of the various colonial economic theories and policies, as well as their evolution.

Part I begins with a paper on King Leopold's activities in the Congo. His dreams of a private empire contributed to the atmosphere of the 'scramble'. The predatory aspects of the economic policy of the Congo State were not uncommon in other parts of the Continent in the early stages of modern colonialism.

The change in the British attitude towards Africa had its

protagonist in Joseph Chamberlain, who became the Secretary of State for the Colonies in 1895. Chamberlain's concept of 'tropical estates' was hardly idealistic. Realising that private resources were incapable of further development of the Africa territories he evolved a plan for 'scientific' management, thereby reducing the function of government to that of a board of directors. The motivation for curbing the liquor traffic, abolishing the remnants of slavery, and eliminating forced labour was not humanitarian, but was largely pragmatic. There was supposed to be a goose laying golden eggs and it would have been foolish to kill it.

The excerpt on Chamberlain's doctrine is followed by a short paper on German colonial policy. The short-lived German experiment in colonialism is of particular interest because of the several distinct stages through which colonial policy passed in quick succession. Bismarck, in spite of his early image as a 'reluctant colonialist', established an empire in Africa. His amazing flexibility was shared by the framers of German strategies who succeeded him.

New opinions which dominated the approach to the colonial question after the First World War are presented in the excerpts from Lord Lugard's work *The Dual Mandate in British Tropical Africa* and S. H. Roberts' monograph on French colonial policy. There was a marked change in the spirit of the policy but, at the same time, there was no real departure from the formerly declared economic aims. Lord Lugard in Great Britain and Albert Sarraut in France differed little in their beliefs that the metropolitan countries had a dual obligation towards their overseas territories: first, to govern justly, and second, to promote the development of the dependent peoples. The philanthropic pretext was abandoned once it was realised that these two expressed aims were not in conflict. The benefit resulting from the presence of the Europeans in Africa was jointly shared by the rulers and their subjects. According to Lugard, this reciprocity should have been the aim and desire of any civilised administration. For Sarraut, the mutuality and the necessity of colonial aid were expressed as an idea of colonial co-operation aiming at a division of labour between the colonies and the mother country, which necessitated an ambitious investment programme.

A fragment from Sir Keith Hancock's monumental *Survey of British Commonwealth Affairs* concludes this part of the book. A critique of inter-war British economic policy, which impaired the principle of the dual mandate, is followed by his recommendations for a new approach. It is there that the student of the colonial period of the economic history of Africa will find one of the most forceful expressions of the principle of 'colonial development and welfare' which remained a guideline for the administrators of African territories until the end of the colonial era.

Part Two strives to show what were the results when some of the colonial theories and policies were put to the test vis-à-vis African reality. An attempt is also made to provide an overview of economic activities during the whole of the colonial period. Of necessity the treatment of the subject is rather fragmentary and the editors hope that the mere glimpse offered here will encourage the reader of this volume to go deeper into the subject on his own.

This part begins with a chapter on transportation in sub-Saharan Africa by S. D. Neumark. Provision of this basic service was a *sine qua non* of modern economic development, and for many decades of the colonial period the lack of it, and consequently the extremely high costs of carrying commodities, were the main impediments to material progress. It was, therefore, natural that the initial efforts and the bulk of the investment by the colonial administrations went mainly in this direction.

An essay by Catherine Coquery-Vidrovitch discusses the problems of economic development in French Equatorial Africa prior to 1920, and it contrasts the conditions in that 'poor relation among the French colonies' with those in the more prosperous French West Africa. Despoliation of the meagre natural resources, as well as the crude and the subtle forms of economic exploitation of the native people, is a recurring theme.

The paper by Robert E. Baldwin takes the reader to a British territory of what was formerly Northern Rhodesia. That country provides an outstanding example of the rise of the mining industry in the so-called Copperbelt and its impact on the local economy. Mining, as is well known, influenced the development of several African countries under colonial rule; but because of the need for economy of space, only this early case study has been included.

The prolonged presence of Portugal in Africa has attracted continuous attention amongst Africanists. A paper written after Portugal's withdrawal from the African scene attempts to reassess Portuguese economic policies in Angola and Mozambique. A tale of high hopes and deep disappointments is told against the background of the hard reality faced by an economically weak and underdeveloped country.

The concluding paper in Part Two discusses the issues arising out of the adoption by colonial authorities of the doctrine of 'colonial development and welfare'. A more systematic approach to planning became a necessity. The problems of the war economy underscored the need for efficient marketing. The fiscal role of the marketing boards in Nigeria is dealt with in a paper by G. K. Helleiner which discusses this important aspect of post-war development.

The remaining parts of this volume (Parts Three, Four and Five) follow the 'classical' division of the factors of production into land, labour and capital. This division reflected the structure of the pre-industrial or early industrial economies of Europe and it can be legitimately applied to the economies of colonial Africa.

Parts Three and Four pay special attention to the response of the Africans to the challenges created by the new situation which arose under the colonial administration. The editors believe that the economic history of the colonial period should not concern itself exclusively with narrowly understood European activity. To avoid such a distorted view answers have to be found to a host of questions. Were there any major areas where the colonial economy affected Africans in a significant way? If so, what was the nature and the strength of their reaction? What were the broad socio-economic results of the interaction between the foreign and the native elements? Was there any important economic change taking place in the areas not directly affected by European interference? If so, how did it originate and what sustained it?

It is scarcely necessary to say that an attempt to answer these questions would most likely lead a researcher into a multitude of by-ways, so far mostly unexplored. In this volume we can only endeavour to throw some light on the most basic problems. Thus in Parts Three and Four a considerable amount of space is devoted to an examination of the conflicting hypotheses of African non-economic versus rational economic behaviour. A more general approach by W. O. Jones in his paper on 'Economic Man in Africa' can be coupled with a more specialised article by M. P. Miracle and B. Fetter on 'Backward-sloping Labour-Supply Functions and African Economic Behaviour'.

Interactions between colonial policy and African economic behaviour as well as the phenomena of African entrepreneurship and peasantisation are the topics of C. Ehrlich's essay on paternalism in Uganda. Polly Hill's paper on Ghanaian capitalist cocoa-farmers draws attention to a minor agricultural revolution launched by African peasants.

Whereas the production of cash crops and the participation of Africans in export trade are related issues, their share in the import trade is dealt with separately in an excerpt from P. T. Bauer's well known book on West African Trade.

In Part Four, the immense problem of African labour is considered from both the economic and the social points of view. The latter can hardly be separated from the former. Migrant labour, productivity of the worker and the growth of an African proletariat are the topics which occupy a prominent place. A human touch is added by the inclusion of a chapter from *The African Labourer* by G. St. J. Orde Browne, whose great familiarity with the conditions of labour in British Africa during the pre-war period introduces an element of unique authenticity. His observations on the moral effects of wage-earning refer mostly to the way this form of employment affected family life and tribal relations.

The last part of this book (Part Five) is primarily concerned with the problems of saving and investment. It includes excerpts and articles by such well known writers as Sir Alan Pim, S. H. Frankel and W. O. Jones. It also presents an essay by T. R. de Gregori in which technological diffusion and foreign investment are linked together. It exemplifies the approach of a modern economic historian who, while fitting a set of relevant facts to a particular economic theory of long standing, finds that the theory does not stand up to the test.

The editors have deliberately devoted a considerable proportion of the limited space available to them to the excerpts from some of the older writings with which a present-day student may not be familiar. While presenting more recent works and opinions, they also wish to recall the views expressed by contemporaries on the problems with which they were faced and some first-hand impressions of the phenomena which now belong to a long-forgotten past.

A fair assessment of actions taken, or policies adopted, can only be achieved if the student familiarises himself with the thoughts and ideas which guided contemporary actions.

The editors were reluctant to include any of the existing overall evaluations of the colonial period. These are likely to undergo revision every few years as the results of new research become available. Instead, they felt that materials of a more lasting nature should be incorporated in this book of readings. It is this decision which prompts them to add a few comments with regard to the answer to a problem which was never meant to form part of this volume. It concerns an overall estimate and comparison of the costs and benefits of colonial development. Such a line of inquiry immediately generates a multiplicity of other important issues. What were these costs and benefits in the first place, and are they capable of quantitative expression? How were they shared between the Africans and the Europeans? How can colonial development be explained in relation to the pre-colonial period? Has colonialism thwarted the initiative displayed by the native would-be entrepreneurs? Was there no practical alternative to what colonial development offered Africa?

Attempts have been made to solve such questions, but they have not resulted in unequivocal answers. It is not possible to present a balance-sheet of the colonial period and attach to it a stamp of finality. Analysis of this kind is seldom free from arguments that enter it as a result of the intellectual background and the personal predilections of the analyst. An analysis of the past ought to be done dispassionately and rigorously if results of scientific value are to be gained. The issue is complicated by the fact that what has actually taken place in Africa in so far as colonial activities are concerned, has been the combined outcome of individual and collective value judgments translated into policies. Their implementation has been subject to the distorting influence of unforeseen circumstances, human passions, personal prejudices, and the subterfuges which were only too often employed to cover up vested interests.

There are many other topics of considerable importance which could not be dealt with in this book because of regrettable gaps in the existing literature. Such neglected topics could be listed *ad libitum*, but it is not the role of this introduction to suggest agenda for future research.

It is interesting to note that in recent times far greater emphasis has been placed on pre-colonial economic history rather than on the history of the years of colonial dependence. The obvious reason is that relatively little was known about the pre-colonial period and historians of Africa rightly turned their efforts to the reconstruction of its more distant past.

Now the time is ripe for conducting intensive research into the colonial period. There are already encouraging signs of this change of emphasis on the part of historically minded economists

and other social scientists who are conducting such studies. But
in spite of its fragmentary character and the presence of serious
gaps, the literature on colonial economic problems is far from
scanty, as there are many accounts written by contemporaries and
also works by more recent writers, whose interest in economic
history has been rather marginal. On the other hand there is a
distressing scarcity of studies written by economic historians with
sufficient knowledge of economics to permit them to formulate
hypotheses capable of being tested against the existing body of
economic theory or, alternatively, to contribute by formulating
new theories.

Finally, a modern economic historian of Africa should consider a number of factors that would stimulate his interest in the
colonial period. There are abundant archival data of a quantitative
nature available to the researcher. Also, it is still possible to
obtain direct information from the surviving former colonial
officials and from the Africans who were affected by their policies.
This oral evidence will be available only for as long as these
persons are alive and information should be recorded before it
is too late. A researcher must avail himself not only of the new
methods available in his own discipline, but also of the experience
of modern development economics, which will permit him to view
colonial economic policies and their results in a far more pene-
trating way than was possible a decade ago.

The study of the colonial experience will prove valuable for
present and future developmental efforts. An example of how
fruitful such revisions can be is provided by the changing views
on the rationality of African economic behaviour. There is a
growing body of opinion amongst the economists interested in
Africa that the hypothesis of the 'non-economic' African is largely
based on generalisations which have grown out of an uncritical
interpretation of opinions of contemporary Europeans living in
the colonies and the lack of independent and objective research.
If so, the assumptions made in modern development literature
about the importance of traditional attitudes would prove exaggerated and their value as an explanatory device should be subject
to scrutiny.

It is hoped that continuing efforts in the right direction will
reveal other areas of doubt and will eventually lead to
the correction of some of our erroneous opinions which dis-
tort views of the past and obscure the understanding of the
present.

Since practically all present developments have their roots in history, the study of the colonial period in Africa can fulfil a useful purpose by improving our ability to deal with today's problems. It cannot then be dismissed as the luxury of discovering new facts for their own sake.

It is partly with this thought in mind that the editors present this volume to the reader.

Z. A. KONCZACKI
J. M. KONCZACKI

PART ONE

Colonial Theorists and Pragmatists

1

THE ECONOMIC POLICY OF THE CONGO STATE*

Ruth Slade

King Leopold's attitude towards his African subjects can only be understood by reference to his economic policy, and to the financial difficulties which by 1890 were threatening to ruin him. His personal fortune had already been swallowed up by the State which he had acquired with such difficulty, and in addition to the burden of the everyday expenses of administration there was a costly and urgent programme to be undertaken, for vast areas of State territory remained unoccupied, the Arabs were advancing down the Congo, and the construction of the Matadi-Stanley Pool railway was essential if the Congo economy was ever to be put on a sound basis. In face of the tasks which lay before it, the revenues of the Congo State were pitifully small. Since the Berlin Act had forbidden the imposition of import duties within the conventional basin of the Congo, the State depended almost entirely upon export duties. Direct taxation would have discouraged European settlers, and they could not be expected to provide revenue sufficient for the administration of the State.

Leopold II had created the Congo Independent State by his own efforts, and borne the expense out of his own pocket. He had thus come to regard himself not only as the Sovereign, but also as the *owner* of the State. He considered himself, as he put it in 1909, as having the 'absolute ownership, uncontested, of the Congo and its riches'.[1] In 1906 he wrote:

> The Congo has been, and could have been, nothing but a personal undertaking. There is no more legitimate or respectable right than

*Reprinted by permission of the Institute of Race Relations, London, and Oxford University Press from Ruth Slade, *King Leopold's Congo*, (1962).

3

that of an author over his own work, the fruit of his labour.... My rights over the Congo are to be shared with none; they are the fruit of my own struggles and expenditure.[2]

And again in 1908 Leopold declared: 'The King was the founder of the State; he was its organiser, its owner, its absolute sovereign.'[3]

It was because the King's colonial doctrine was essentially economic that he was led to this conception of his 'ownership' of the Congo State. As it has been put, he was a great capitalist who 'possessed the Congo just as Rockefeller possessed Standard Oil'.[4] For Leopold, a colony existed for the sake of the material advantages which it could offer to the colonial power. He was not consciously insincere when he talked of suppressing the slave-trade and bringing civilisation to the Congo, but the economic aspect of his African venture was far more important in his eyes. So when in 1890 the King was faced by the fact that the Congo State could not maintain itself, he decided that the State must undertake commerce on its own account—and must create a monopoly.

Even before 1890 State officials were paid commission on the ivory which they bought and thus became the rivals of the European traders on the Congo; an English missionary wrote:

A matter causing heartburning among the ivory buyers on the river is the money interest that State officers have in the collection of ivory—whether as fines or by purchase . . . at present much ivory falls into the hands of the State. It seems to me to be a great mistake to give officers who possess almost absolute power a pecuniary interest in the collection of the principal product of the country.[5]

But before 1890 there had been no attempt to create a State monopoly. In 1891 the whole question was brought up by a dispute between the *Société Belge du Haut-Congo* and the Government; the *Société* objected to the State officials taking part in the ivory-trade, while the Government was beginning to consider that if the State's property were systematically exploited it might become possible for the State to pay its way.[6] For in 1885 the Congo State had claimed all 'vacant lands' within its territory, while Africans were to keep their rights over the lands which they occupied. Leopold decided that the State should profit from these 'vacant lands' which it had claimed, and in September 1891 a secret decree ordered State officials in the Aruwimi and Ubangi-Uele basins to secure all the ivory and rubber they could on behalf of the State. At the same time the

King encouraged the Englishman Colonel North and the brothers Browne de Tiège to found a new group of commercial companies at Antwerp, and to these the State gave large concessions of land.[7]

Thus the Leopoldian system was established in embryo; the State itself began to exploit some of its 'vacant lands' either directly or through concessionary companies. In 1892 several circulars forbade the Africans of these regions to sell ivory or rubber to private traders. Not all the Belgians who had hitherto collaborated closely with King Leopold in his African enterprise agreed with this policy; indeed, the Governor-General resigned in protest, and men like Banning and Beernaert made their disapproval known to the King. There were also protests from the commercial companies which were already established in the upper Congo. In spite of all this opposition, however, a decree of October 1892 was more explicit than that of the year before. Certain districts of the Kasai were left open to private traders, but about half the area of the State—to be known as its *domaine privé*—was reserved to the exclusive exploitation of the State itself. Almost all the territory above the Equator was closed to traders, while the Katanga was provisionally closed on the grounds that the State could not guarantee the safety of Europeans who might settle there. In fact, by the agreement which the State had made in 1891 with the *Compagnie du Katanga*, the whole territory had been divided between the two parties for administration and exploitation.

The King's policy resulted in a marked improvement in the financial position of the Congo State; this improvement began in 1892, was very noticeable in 1896, and steadily continued during the following years. This growing prosperity was largely accounted for by the exploitation of the *domaine privé*. In 1896 King Leopold went even further; he secretly added to the *domaine privé* the *domaine de la Couronne*, a large expanse of territory around Lake Leopold II.[8] This became the personal property of the King, to be exploited for the benefit of the extensive programme of public works which he had undertaken in Belgium.[9]

Exploitation of the State territory, either by the State itself or by concessionary companies, required African labour. This was obtained in two ways: a labour tax was imposed which would compel Africans to work, and a system was introduced by which it was hoped that they would be persuaded to work for remuneration. Unfortunately the State's policy towards its African subjects

became dominated by the demands which were made—both by
the State itself and by the concessionary companies—for labour
for the collection of the wild produce of the territory. The system
itself engendered abuses; State or company officials were left to
determine the amount of labour required and the remuneration
to be assigned to it, and they were paid commission on the ivory
or rubber which they secured.[10] It was difficult to recruit these
agents in Belgium, and often—with the exception of the Belgian
officers in the State employ—they were men who had already
shown their instability and lack of principles in Europe. Men
like these were all too easily tempted to apply extreme methods
for the sake of increasing production. Armed African soldiers
were employed to supervise the collection of rubber; thus a
widespread system of local tyrannies was established.[11] The primary
interest of the European officials lay not in securing a stable
administration, but in collecting as much rubber as they could;
in practice they were given almost unlimited power over the
Africans in their neighbourhood and it was inevitable that many
of them should abuse that power. State agents were poorly paid;
it was taken for granted that the commission they earned would
supplement their salaries, and the men who could expect promotion were those who obtained the most rubber and ivory from
their districts.

NOTES

1. J. Stengers, 'La place de Léopold II dans l'histoire de la colonisation',
La Nouvelle Clio, IX, 1950, p. 524.
2. P. Daye, *Le Congo Belge* (Bruges–Paris, 1927), p. 33.
3. Stengers, 'La place de Léopold II', p. 524.
4. Stengers, 'La place de Léopold II', p. 527.
5. George Grenfell, June 1890, in Slade, *English-Speaking Missions*,
p. 239.
6. Berriedale Keith, *The Belgian Congo*, p. 121.
7. A. Stenmans, *La reprise du Congo par la Belgique* (Brussels, 1949),
pp. 135–6.
8. J. Stengers, *Combien le Congo a-t-il coûté à Belgique?* (Brussels, 1957),
pp. 151 ff.
9. Berriedale Keith, *The Belgian Congo*, pp. 121–2.
10. Cattier, *Droit et administration*, p. 244.
11. Berriedale Keith, *The Belgian Congo*, p. 123.

2

CHAMBERLAIN'S DOCTRINE OF TROPICAL AFRICAN ESTATES*

R. Robinson, J. Gallagher, A. Denny

The coming of Joseph Chamberlain to the Colonial Office in 1895 opened a new era in west African policy. It was he who first tried to release expansion from the shackles of the old informal system. He was the first British statesman to prize west African territory highly enough to risk fighting France to get it. It was he who first called a halt to the long British retreat in the west. Chamberlain brought a new incentive to the British movement into tropical Africa. Its largest territorial claims hitherto had been collaterals of the supreme interests in the Mediterranean, in south Africa and in the Orient. Not until the eleventh hour did another, less sophisticated motive intervene: the aim of taking territory for its own sake as an estate for posterity. This was Chamberlain's special if belated contribution. It made little difference to the map of Africa by treaty, for most of that had been drawn already. Yet his radical approach to empire left a more lasting monument. Because he was the first Colonial Secretary to believe in the need for developing tropical Africa as a state enterprise, he set a new value on the possession of territory. He was too late to add much of it to the empire; but he inspired the beginnings of its modern administration and development.

The Colonial Secretary declared his doctrine as soon as he took office. Progress and prosperity in Britain, he preached, depended upon developing the empire.[1] But private enterprise had neglected its colonial opportunities in the tropics, particularly in the West Indies, Cyprus[2] and east and west Africa. The imperial government had also failed in its duty to improve the condition of its subjects. As Chamberlain put it to his colleagues:

*Reprinted by permission of Macmillan, London, from R. Robinson, J. Gallagher, A. Denny, *Africa and the Victorians*, (1961).

7

Up to the present time the Imperial Government has done hardly anything to aid our Colonies and Dependencies in opening up the Countries which are under the British Flag. We have trusted entirely to individual enterprise and capital . . . yet it is certain that in many cases progress has been delayed, and in some cases absolutely stayed, because the only methods by which improvement could be carried out were beyond the scope of private resources.[3]

Therefore, the Colonial Secretary argued, the state must take the lead in empire-building from the merchant and investor. If the vast 'undeveloped estates' claimed by Britain in tropical Africa and elsewhere were not to be liabilities on the Treasury, a new policy was needed. Imperial activity in tropical Africa had been restricted hitherto to the aim of excluding foreign rivals. Now it should urgently promote development 'by opening up new fields for private enterprise and new markets for British industry'.[4]

It was no longer enough for this purpose to rely on local revenues, on diplomacy and spheres of influence. The Imperial Treasury should provide loans to make the roads, railways and harbours, the lack of which had turned away the private merchant and investor.[5] The imperial government should bring its spheres of influence under effective rule, it should impose peace, encourage the African to contribute his labour and taxes, and hold even the balance of justice between European and African interests. 'Scientific' administration, Chamberlain hoped, would create wealth and engineer progress for the African, as for the British urban and agricultural poor. Like other nonconformist businessmen of conscience, he held that profit and social justice must go together. It was his special aim in tropical Africa to curb the liquor traffic, and to abolish slavery and forced labour. Otherwise he explained, '. . . We should kill the goose that lays the golden eggs—the people we want to be our best customers.'[6] Chamberlain brought colonial 'development' and 'welfare' into the vocabulary of policy toward the African tropics.

In some ways such an outlook was not new. Something like it had been applied to the Indian empire since the Eighteen forties; but there the British investor, not the taxpayer, had willingly supplied the capital, because the Indian government's revenue offered good security. Other ministers from 1889 onward had occasionally talked in Chamberlain's tones. Salisbury himself had spoken publicly of the government's duty to make smooth the path for the merchant, just as he had complained of foreign tariffs excluding British trade from Africa. In 1893 Rosebery had turned a gilded phrase for it when he spoke of 'pegging out claims for the future.'⁷ But hitherto the Victorians had paid only lip-service to the doctrine of tropical estates. It had sometimes helped in public to justify their advances in tropical Africa. It had rarely inspired them. To most ministers, talk of the prospects there was little more than sugar to help a trading nation swallow a sophisticated strategy. With Chamberlain it was not so. He meant to open the bolted Treasury and the closed minds of Parliament and the electorate to the need for state enterprise. He intended to make a business of the tropical African fields which others had staked out mainly with an eye to security.

In August 1895 the Colonial Secretary appealed to British opinion for support:

'I regard many of our Colonies as being in the condition of un-developed estates, and estates which can never be developed without Imperial assistance.'⁸
'I may submit to you . . . what is in a certain sense a new policy. . . . If the people of this country are not willing to invest some of their superfluous wealth in the development of their great estate, then I see no future for these countries, and it would have been better never to have gone there. I shall appeal to the opinion of the country, which is gradually ripening, and I think I shall meet with a satisfactory response.'⁹

Chamberlain admitted that the policy represented a radical de-parture. It is also notable that he spoke not as one representing a strong national demand for developing tropical Africa, but as one trying to evoke it. His tone and tenour confirm that hitherto no such demand had arisen in British opinion. In his opinion at least, the British investor, manufacturer and merchant generally had been hugely indifferent to the possibilities of the African tropics. Their need of markets and raw materials had played little part in instigating British claims.

But now, Chamberlain thought, the trend was more favourable. Imperial sentiment perhaps was rising. Sections of British business, beginning to feel the force of foreign tariffs and industrial com-petition, were turning toward protectionism, perhaps to imperial preference. Capital was cheap, and investors would welcome new outlets. Depression was lifting, and industrial growth meant a rising demand for tropical materials. Chamberlain hoped for sup-port, not from the few east and west African merchants alone, but from the many businessmen whom he envisaged as coming to see the importance of developing a specifically imperial economy. Perhaps the Colonial Secretary's impressions were to some extent true. Yet when he came to carry out his schemes, he found the nation's interest in turning tropical Africa into another India still dwarfed beside its objections to more taxation and state enterprise, its respect for *laisser-faire* tradition, and its scepticism about the region's resources in lands, minerals and labour. What was more, the stiffest opponents of a radical departure were among his own Cabinet colleagues.

In August 1895 the Colonial Secretary asked the Cabinet to turn the large profits of the government-owned Suez Canal shares into a colonial development fund. The money would be used for loans to build colonial railways and other public works.[10] His private argument for tropical estates however, suggests that he was more immediately concerned to avoid asking Parliament for grants-in-aid of the derelict colonies and unprofitable railway projects already on his hands, than with the long-term promotion of imperial trade. His plea to Salisbury was simply: . . . If I can get just a little money I believe something may be done to make Cyprus a paying proposition.'[11] There was a similar problem in the West Indies. In Chamberlain's proposal to the Cabinet, the whole cost of the Uganda railway which was vital to Salisbury's Nile Valley strategy, was to be the first charge on the proposed fund.[12] But Hicks Beach at the Exchequer and Sir Edward Hamilton strongly objected. As the British taxpayer had bought the shares, so the profits should be spent in the United Kingdom. Chamberlain's proposal was financial heresy. Parliament would reject it as a 'crooked expedient' to evade its control over expenditure. There was nothing in the plan which would justify such high political risks.[13] The Cabinet put Chamberlain's development fund into cold storage.

But the Colonial Secretary was freer in his own department. West African colonial trade and revenue were improving, especially in the Gold Coast which was enjoying a minor gold boom. Towards the end of 1895 he authorised the west African administrations to make a start with the inland railways which merchants and officials alike had been demanding since 1883.[14] At the same time Chamberlain, without consulting the Cabinet,[15] was able to clear the path towards the gold of Ashanti. For a decade Knutsford and Ripon had refused the merchants' petitions for this undertaking, waiting until the local Treasury could pay for it.[16] Chamberlain would wait no longer. He unleashed an expedition to bring Ashanti under control,[17] and advanced the Gold Coast administration the money to pay the cost.[18] In Sierra Leone, Cardew was allowed to bring the protectorate under closer administration, and in the Gold Coast, Chamberlain endorsed Maxwell's attempts to introduce land reform, to gain control of the chiefs and to levy a house tax on Africans.

These were the small beginnings of Chamberlain's large plan of 'scientific' development. Imperial control was to be extended; and the interior pacified; the chiefs were to be brought under official supervision. Railways were to open the interior, attract European capital and stimulate African production, before French and German railways could divert the inland trade to foreign ports. But the greatest difficulty was to make the railways pay. Each administration was to be equipped with a strong agricultural department which would at last persuade the African through the chiefs to grow cotton, kola nuts, fibres, cocoa and rubber.[19] Where necessary, tribal land tenures were to be reformed and the progressive peasants given a secure, individual title. Waste and unoccupied lands were to be brought under government's control. But the administrations could do none of these things without money. Chamberlain and his officials hoped to tax the African population directly, both as a spur to production and for revenue. European enterprise must also contribute a higher share of royalties on its concessions and trade. The remainder would have to be made up from imperial loans and grants-in-aid. Where the British merchant and investor, the African chief and the native economies had failed, the administrator was to organise African society for production and progress.

NOTES

1. Chamberlain to West African Railways Deputation, 24 Aug. 1895, Garvin, *op. cit*, III, 20.
2. Chamberlain to Salisbury, 1 Aug. 1895, S.P. (Chamberlain).
3. Cabinet Memo., enclosed in Chamberlain to Salisbury, 26 Nov. 1895, S.P. (Colonial Office, Private, 1895–1900).
4. *ibid.*
5. Cabinet Memo., 25 Nov. 1895, Garvin, *op cit.*, III, 177.
6. *Hansard*, 4th ser., XXXVI, col. 642.
7. Speech at the Royal Colonial Institute, 1 Mar. 1893, *The Foreign Policy of Lord Rosebery*, (1901).
8. *Hansard*, 4th ser., XXXVI, col. 642.
9. Speech to Deputation on West African Railways, 23 Aug. 1895. Garvin, *op. cit.*, III, 20.
10. Chamberlain to Salisbury, 1 Aug. 1895, S.P. (Chamberlain).
11. *ibid.*
12. Chamberlain, Cabinet Memo., enclosed in Chamberlain to Salisbury, 26 Nov. 1895, S.P. (C.O., Private, 1895–1900).

13. Hicks Beach, Cabinet Memo., 29 Dec. 1895; Sir E. Hamilton, Cabinet Memo., 14 Dec. 1895, S.P. (C.O., Private, 1895–1900).
14. *vide Construction of Railways in Sierra Leone, Lagos and the Gold Coast*, Cd. 2325, P.P. [1905], LVI, 361–410. *vide Correspondence on Proposed Concessions of Railways in the West African Colonies*, C.O. Africa (West), 448.
15. Chamberlain to Salisbury, 8 Nov. 1895, S.P. (Chamberlain).
16. Ripon to Hodgson, 30 Jan. 1894, C. 7917, P.P. [1896] LVIII, 613–4; Ripon to Maxwell, 15 Mar. 1895, C. 7918, P.P. [1896], LVIII, 761–2; *vide* C. 7917, C. 7918 *passim*.
17. Chamberlain to Maxwell, 22 Nov. 1895, *ibid.*, 847–9.
18. The charges of the expedition were regarded as a loan to the Gold Coast, which was expected to recover the expenses eventually from the Ashanti themselves. The expedition cost about £99,000. (Gold Coast Annual Report, 1902, Cd. 1768, P.P. (1904), LVI, 379.)
19. For a characteristic statement of west African development plans at this time, *vide* C.O. Memo. on the British Possessions in West Africa (HJR), 12 May 1897, C.O. African (West) 534.

3

GERMAN COLONIAL POLICY*

W. O. Henderson

The history of German colonisation, though it covers only a short period of time, is particularly interesting because German colonial policy quickly passed through several significant phases. Changes which in the overseas possessions of other countries were a matter of gradual evolution took place much more rapidly in the German colonial empire. The Germans were late-comers in the field of colonial expansion and it is not surprising that they made mistakes at first. But they learned quickly. Between 1884 and 1914 German colonial policy passed rapidly through several distinct phases.

The first six years (1884–90), when Bismarck was Chancellor, saw the establishment of the colonial empire and the attempt to administer it through chartered companies. This method of colonial government failed and the Reich had to shoulder the full responsibility for the administration of the colonial empire.

When the German colonial empire was established in 1884 Bismarck repeatedly expressed the view that chartered companies should be responsible for the administration of newly acquired overseas possessions. He argued that while senior Prussian civil servants and non-commissioned officers in the army performed their duties admirably at home they did not have the experience which would enable them to undertake the entirely different task of governing native peoples in Africa or the Pacific. Bismarck believed that it was merchants from Hamburg and Bremen—with their long experience of trading in the Cameroons, at Zanaibar and in Samoa—who should be prepared to shoulder the responsibilities of colonial administration because they alone had

*Reprinted by permission from W. O. Henderson, *German Colonial Policy*, Frank Cass, (1962).

13

the necessary knowledge of the territories in which protectorates were being established.

Bismarck declared that he was opposed to any adoption of French colonial methods which were, in his view, unsuited to German needs. The French system, according to Bismarck, consisted of taking possession of a piece of territory, subduing the natives, establishing first a military and then a civil administration and finally hoping that French traders and settlers would follow in the footsteps of the soldiers and the officials. Bismarck thought that this was putting the cart before the horse. In his opinion trade should not follow the flag. On the contrary the flag should follow trade and the traders themselves should administer the colonies.

Two explanations may be given to account for Bismarck's adoption of this point of view. In the first place Bismarck himself had never had any experience of colonial administration. He had to make use of the experience of others. The French system of colonisation—or what he thought to be the French system—did not commend itself to Bismarck. But the British system of chartered companies seemed to Bismarck to be admirably suited to Germany's needs in the 1880s. Britain had had three centuries of colonial experience and Bismarck argued that what was good enough for Britain should be good enough for the Reich. In view of Bismarck's professed admiration for British colonial methods it is a little surprising that in practice he did not devise colonial charters on the British model. The charter given to the German Colonial Society in respect of territories in East Africa bore very little resemblance to any charter granted to a British company.

The second reason why Bismarck favoured chartered companies concerned the financial aspect of colonisation. After 1871 the national finances of the Reich were based upon the principle that indirect taxes were levied by the Federal Government while direct taxes were levied by the individual States. Federal budget deficits were covered by grants from the individual States. Bismarck desired that the Federal Exchequer should be as self-supporting as possible and should not rely any more than was absolutely necessary upon the contributions of the separate States. This was one reason why Bismarck adopted a fiscal policy of Protection since additional revenues from customs duties would increase the funds under the direct control of the central Government. Unfortunately the Government's expenditure was increasing owing to the rising cost of the army and the social services.

Bismarck viewed with misgivings the possibility of incurring heavy expenditure in the establishment and maintenance of a colonial empire. In the circumstances it is not surprising that he should argue in favour of a system of colonial administration which would throw virtually the entire cost upon the shareholders of privileged chartered companies.

The second sixteen years in the history of Germany as a Colonial Power—between Bismarck's fall in 1890 and the crisis caused by the 'colonial scandals' in 1906—saw the establishment of the authority of the Reich in most of the interior of the overseas possessions. It was an era of 'little wars' against the natives. But it was a period that ended in disaster and disillusionment. There were serious revolts both in South West Africa and in East Africa and grave scandals in colonial administration were brought to light. The economic results of colonisation were disappointing. Bitter controversies on the colonial question heralded a 'new era' in the administration of the overseas territories. Between 1907 and 1914 a more enlightened policy was pursued and by the eve of the first World War there was much less to criticize in Germany's colonial rule than there had been only a few years before. Administrators such as Dernburg, Rechenberg, Solf and Schnee were men of ability, courage and integrity. The loyalty of the natives to the Germans during the colonial campaigns of the first World War suggests that there was no longer any serious discontent with German rule.

In theory no doubt, there were strong arguments in favour of the idea that commercial establishments which had been trading for many years on the African coasts had the experience necessary to undertake administrative functions in newly acquired territories. In practice the merchants of Hamburg and Bremen were unwilling to accept such responsibilities. New colonial companies established with the support of the big banks—such as the German S.W. Africa Colonial Company—were equally reluctant to shoulder administrative responsibilities.

4

THE DUAL MANDATE*

Lord Lugard

At the time of the first impulse of Imperial expansion in the reign of Queen Elizabeth, the small and chiefly agricultural population of these islands was able to supply its own essential needs in food and materials; by the time the second impulse came 240 years later, after the Napoleonic wars, the population had quadrupled, while in the next seventy-five years of the nineteenth century, 1816–91 (when the partition of Africa began in earnest), it again nearly doubled itself. The congestion of the population, assisted by the discovery of the application of steam to industrial uses, led to the replacement of agriculture by manufacturing industry, with the consequent necessity for new markets for the product of the factory, and the importation of raw materials for industry, and of food to supplement the decreased home production, and feed the increased population. The same phenomenon was to be seen in Germany and elsewhere in Europe.[1] I recapitulate these figures because their importance in this connection can hardly be over-estimated.

But mere increase in population alone, prodigious though it was, does not represent the full measure of the pressure on the Governments of the industrial nations of Europe. The standard of comfort, and what had come to be regarded as the absolute necessities of life by the mass of the population, had, during the nineteenth century, advanced in an even greater ratio. I cannot here attempt to depict the contrast. It is enough to recall the fact that 100 years ago a labourer's wage was 4s. to 6s. a week. He rarely tasted white bread, for the quartern loaf stood at 11d., and had been double that price a few years before. Still less could he afford to eat beef or mutton. Towards the close of the nineteenth

*Reprinted by permission from Lord Lugard, *The Dual Mandate in British Tropical Africa*, 1922. Frank Cass, (1965).

16

century, tea, coffee, and cocoa, previously unknown luxuries, were his daily beverages and white bread his daily food. Sugar was cheap, and rice, sago, and other tropical products were in daily use. If my reader will turn to the pages of Miss Martineau's history,[2] or to those of Carlyle, and contrast the condition of squalor and misery in which the bulk of the people of these islands lived in 1816 with the conditions prevailing in 1891, he will realise how insistent had become the demand alike for the food-supplies and for the raw materials which were the product of the tropics.

These products lay wasted and ungarnered in Africa because the natives did not know their use and value. Millions of tons of oil-nuts, for instance, grew wild without the labour of man, and lay rotting in the forests. Who can deny the right of the hungry people of Europe to utilise the wasted bounties of nature, or that the task of developing these resources was, as Mr. Chamberlain expressed it, a 'trust for civilisation' and for the benefit of mankind? Europe benefited by the wonderful increase in the amenities of life for the mass of her people which followed the opening up of Africa at the end of the nineteenth century. Africa benefited by the influx of manufactured goods, and the substitution of law and order for the methods of barbarism.

Thus Europe was impelled to the development of Africa primarily by the necessities of her people, and not by the greed of the capitalist. Keen competition assured the maximum prices to the producer. It is only where monopolies are granted that it can be argued that profits are restricted to the few, and British policy has long been averse to monopolies in every form. The brains, the research, the capital, and the enterprise of the merchant, the miner, and the planter have discovered and utilised the surplus products of Africa. the profits have been divided among the shareholders representing all classes of the people,[3] and no small share of them has gone to the native African merchant and the middleman as well as to the producer. It is true to say that 'a vast area of activity has been opened up to the British workman, in which he shares with the capitalist the profits of the development of tropical resources.'[4]

In accepting responsibility for the control of these new lands, England obeyed the tradition of her race. British Africa was acquired not by groups of financiers, nor yet by the efforts of her statesmen, but in spite of them. It was the instinct of the British democracy which compelled us to take our share. When Mr. Gladstone's Cabinet in 1893 had decided to evacuate Uganda, he

C

was told by his Scottish agent that if he did so he would have to evacuate Downing Street too. Even were it true—and I have shown that it is not—that we could do as lucrative a trade in the tropical possessions of other nations, there can be no doubt that the verdict of the British people has been emphatic that we will not ask the foreigner to open markets for our use, or leave to him the responsibility and its reward. Nor will tariff walls, like those of Jericho, fall flat at the sound of the trumpet of the new Labour leaders.

The general effects of European policy in Africa have been almost wholly evil,' says the Labour reporter, yet he admits that 'experience and temperament have made the rule of the British over non-adult races an example of everything that is best in modern imperialism.' The verdict of another of the prophets of Labour is to the same effect. The fundamental character of British official policy in West Africa, he says, has primarily been influenced by a desire to promote the welfare and advancement of the native races. England, he points out, led the way in the suppression of the overseas slave-trade, paying enormous sums in compensation to slave-owners in the West Indies, and at the Cape, and to Spain and Portugal, and in patrolling the seas. She espoused the cause of Congo reform, and of the indentured labour in Portuguese West Africa. The extension of British control in the Gold Coast hinterland was (he adds) to secure protection of the natives, and in Southern Nigeria to suppress war and human sacrifice.

The indictment against European misrule in Africa appears therefore to lack consistency, and to be directed chiefly against foreign Powers, though bitter charges, as we have seen, are made against some of the Eastern British dependencies in Africa, which have been fully discussed in these pages. In so far as they concern the territories of other Powers, this attitude of what Mr. Rhodes called 'unctuous righteousness', which has the appearance of assuming that others are actuated by less generous motives than our own, is more likely to promote resentment than reform. That the aims of these critics are good will not be denied, but they write without actual experience, and they create prejudice where sympathy and appreciation would be more promising of results.

Let it be admitted at the outset that European brains, capital and energy have not been, and never will be, expended in developing the resources of Africa from motives of pure philanthropy; that Europe is in Africa for the mutual benefit of her own industrial classes, and of the native races in their progress to a higher plane; that the benefit can be made reciprocal, and that it is the aim and desire of civilised administration to fulfil this dual mandate.

By railways and roads, by reclamation of swamps and irrigation of deserts, and by a system of fair trade and competition, we have added to the prosperity and wealth of these lands, and checked famine and disease. We have put an end to the awful misery of the slave-trade and inter-tribal war, to human sacrifice and the ordeals of the witch-doctor. Where these things survive they are severely suppressed. We are endeavouring to teach the native races to conduct their own affairs with justice and humanity, and to educate them alike in letters and in industry.

When I recall the state of Uganda at the time I made the treaty in 1890 which brought it under British control, or the state of Nigeria ten years later, and contrast them with the conditions of today, I feel that British effort—apart from benefits to British trade—has not been in vain. In Uganda a triangular civil war was raging—Protestants, Roman Catholics, and Moslems, representing the rival political factions of British, French, and Arabs, were murdering each other. Only a short time previously triumphant paganism had burnt Christians at the stake and revelled in holocausts of victims. Today there is an ordered Government with its own native parliament. Liberty and justice have replaced chaos, bloodshed, and war. The wealth of the country steadily increases.[5] The slave-raids and tyranny of the neighbouring kingdom of Unyoro have given place to similar progress and peace.

In Nigeria in 1902 slave-rading armies of 10,000 or 15,000 men laid waste the country, and wiped out its population annually in the quest for slaves. Hundreds of square miles of rich well-watered land were depopulated. Barth bore witness to a similar condition of things fifty years ago. Men were impaled in the market-place of Kano. I have described its dungeon. Nowhere was there security for life and property. Today the native Emirs vie with each other in the progress of their schools; the native courts administer justice, and themselves have liberated over 50,000 slaves. The Sultan of Sokoto and the other Emirs are keenly interested in such questions as afforestation, artesian well-boring, and vaccination. The native prisons have been pronounced by the medical authority to be a model for Government to imitate; the leper settlement in Bornu under purely native control is the most successful I know of.

I refer to these two countries because I happen to have personally witnessed their condition prior to the advent of British control, but similar results may be seen in every other British dependency in tropical Africa.

As Roman imperialism laid the foundations of modern civilisation, and led the wild barbarians of these islands along the path of progress, so in Africa today we are repaying the debt, and bringing to the dark places of the earth, the abode of barbarism and cruelty, the torch of culture and progress, while ministering to the material needs of our own civilisation. In this task the nations of Europe have pledged themselves to co-operation by a solemn covenant. Towards the common goal each will advance by the methods most consonant with its national genius. British methods have not perhaps in all cases produced ideal results, but I am profoundly convinced that there can be no question but that British rule has promoted the happiness and welfare of the primitive races. Let those who question it examine the results impartially. If there is unrest, and a desire for independence, as in India and Egypt, it is because we have taught the value of liberty and freedom, which for centuries these peoples had not known. Their very discontent is a measure of their progress.

We hold these countries because it is the genius of our race to colonise, to trade, and to govern. The task in which England is engaged in the tropics—alike in Africa and in the East—has become part of her tradition, and she has ever given of her best in the cause of liberty and civilisation.[6] There will always be those who cry aloud that the task is being badly done, that it does not need doing, that we can get more profit by leaving others to do it, that it brings evil to subject races and breeds profiteers at home. These were not the principles which prompted our forefathers, and secured for us the place we hold in the world today in trust for those who shall come after us.

NOTES

1. The population of the United Kingdom in 1816 was about 19,890,000, and in 1891 it had increased to 38,104,000. That of Germany was respectively 24,831,000 and about 50,000,000, and of France about 29,000,000 and 38,342,000. The pressure of population was thus not so great a factor in France, who was foremost in the scramble for Africa. Her motives, as I have said, were chiefly due to the belief that it was by expansion in Africa alone that she could hope to find means to recover from the effects of the war with Germany in 1870.
2. H. Martineau, 'The Thirty Years' Peace,' vol. i. chapters 4. 7, &c.
3. Lord Leverhulme lately stated that in his Company alone—which is largely concerned in the development of the African tropics—there were no less than 127,000 shareholders.

4. Bruce, Sir Charles, 'Broad Stone of Empire', p. 4. In view of all these facts I read with amazement the verdict of the Labour Research Committee, that it is doubtful whether the acquisition of territory in Africa has added to the power of the European States who have assumed it. It is certain that it has not added to their wealth.'

5. The last report, 1918–19, shows an export of cotton alone valued at close on a million sterling.—Cmd. 508/37, 1920.

6. 'I believe,' says Sir C. Lucas, 'that to our people has been given the work of carrying justice and freedom throughout the world. I do not claim for them any immunity from wrong-doing. Like other people, they have sought and found gain. But I find the weak peoples of the world looking to and trusting England. I find British justice a proverb among nations. . . . I believe the world to be a better world for the fact that the British have peopled some lands with their own race, and taken the rule of others into their own hands.'

'We of West Africa ought from our heart of hearts to thank Almighty God that we have been born into the British Empire,' says a Lagos paper on Empire Day 1920; while a Gold Coast journal observed that 'to us of West Africa Empire means a relation of goodwill between the Imperial unit and its links, harmonising all interests irrespective of race and colour.' West Africa, it adds, looks to Imperial Britain to lead the nations to a just recognition of Africa's claims.

Beaulieu pays a very generous tribute to England's success. 'La nation qui tient le premier rang dans la-colonisation, celle qui donne à tous l'exemples de vastes empire fondés au dela des mers, c'est l'Angleterre. . . . Mais le temps le grand maitre et ce juge impartial, qui met enfin de compte chaque peuple à la place que ses qualités ou ses défauts lui assignent sédormé à l'Angleterre pour ne plus le lui reprendre le premier rang parmi les nations colonisatrices.'—Loc. cit., vol. ii. p. 246. See also vol. i. p. 92.

5

THE SARRAUT PROGRAMME*

S. H. Roberts

Albert Sarraut—the Radical deputy who has already come into this survey, as a successful Governor-General of Indo-China, and as the leading exponent of the *association* theory—outlined his policy in Indo-China in the French Senate as early as February, 1920, and in the Deputies in July of the same year.[1] But it was not until 12 April, 1921, that the scheme was put forward in its final form—in that form of a general programme which has since been accepted as the basis of colonial development.[2] He commenced his exposition by showing how the general colonial question had been metamorphosed by the conditions of the War. Until then, the image had been blurred: but, by 1920, he argued, the pressure of economic facts had given it definiteness. The theory of the day was that French destinies depended on increased production. To do this, colonial and metropolitan action had to dovetail in to each other, and the colonies were to become reservoirs of raw material and emporia for home manufacturers. But the striking feature, as he emphasised it, was the mutual interdependence of France and the colonies, and the realisation that the former depended on the latter as much as the latter did on the former. A new interpretation was given to this interaction. 'Here again,' said Sarraut, 'and the phenomenon is of a relatively recent date, the image of colonial reality comes to adapt itself as a necessary complement to that of metropolitan existence'; and this realisation on the part of French politicians was something entirely new.[3] Instead of the improvised empiricism of pre-war years, there was to be what Sarraut called 'colonial incorporation', a term which in itself expressed the mutualism and the necessity of colonial aid.[4]

*Reprinted by permission from S. H. Roberts, *The History of French Colonial Policy 1870–1925*, 1929. Frank Cass, (1963).

To realise this new objective, Sarraut held that all colonial efforts had to be co-ordinated. The earlier policy of *petits paquets* —of desultory and discontinuous schemes, was anathema to the reformers. The Millerand Ministry stood for the elimination of such policies from national existence, and nowhere had they been more noticeable in the past than in the colonies. There, a fixed plan was needed above all things. A division of labour was necessary, if the maximum output was to be obtained, and this meant specialisation. Each colony, therefore, had to confine its development to those particular directions that would strengthen the general structure: the older notion of an attempt to secure something like colonial self-sufficiency was definitely discarded. Colonisation had to become specialised. 'Our colonies must be centres of production and no longer museums of specimens,'—development had to be made efficient and co-ordinated. Mass-effort on the best factory-principle was the word of the day—in short, the application of the principles of modern industry was to transform the colonial *régime*.

The new method of colonisation was thus to impose a division of labour on the colonies as a whole, and to introduce efficiency-methods in each part. Sarraut in this much was extending the newer Belgian theory. Lucien Franck, who had been the Belgian Minister of the Colonies since 1919, had consistently urged this 'policy of industrialisation', and had said that colonisation was only a synonym for industrial modernisation under post-war conditions.[5] A leader of industry, Lippens, had been appointed Governor-General of the Belgian Congo, and was to manage the colony as he would a huge industrial undertaking. Sarraut readily adopted this idea. Despising what he dubbed *colonisation en jardinets*, he turned to a huge programme of imperialistic specialisation. The colonial world was roughly divided up into groups, each of which was assigned a certain range of products and provided with facilities for an intensive and efficient development. That, in brief, was the Sarraut method. West and Central Africa had to give oils and timber: West Africa had also to follow the Gold Coast in providing cocoa and had to stress cotton in the Niger valley: North Africa had to concentrate on food-stuffs and phosphates: Indo-China, in addition to its rice, was to provide cotton and silk and rubber: Madagascar had to give meat and grains, and the Antilles sugar and coffee. The products of each were to go into the great national pool. Work was apportioned so that it would produce the maximum result, and, really the whole

Empire was to become a huge factory, using every device of in-dustrial specialisation.[6]

The first step in securing this increased output was in providing facilities for the development of the wealth that was latent in nearly every colony. The Sarraut programme, as translated into practice, thus came to mean a scheme of public-works, empire-wide. He took the general principles of his predecessors, Simon and Hubert, and gave them a definite practical expression. Above all, he wanted a development that was practical and that would secure the most return. Therefore, he invoked the aid of the specialists. In February, 1921, he appointed a Commission of technicians to outline a plan for the scientific development of the colonies, in particular by picking out those nerve-centres which could serve as the principal centres of production. On these strategic points in the economic world, his State efforts in the direction of communications and other facilities were to centre. Commissions had previously been instituted in each local group of colonies: now, their findings were co-ordinated, and the whole resolved into what is known as 'the Sarraut Plan'. This was to construct public works to the value of four milliards of francs and allow future colonial development to take place round these pivots. The North African possessions, being under other Mini-stries, did not come under the scheme, but every other colony was to benefit.[7]

The main works were naturally in the larger colonies, especially those which, like Indo-China and West Africa, produced the most. For instance, in West Africa, the Dakar port was to be extended and the Thiès-Kayes railway completed; and development in general was to centre as far as possible on the Niger irrigation-scheme. Equatorial Africa, the most backward of the French colonies was to be released from its dependence on the Belgian Congo by the construction of a railway from Brazzaville to the sea, and the Cameroons were to have their economic future, already a bright one, enwidened by the extension of the central railway-line to Yaundé.

The execution of the project, therefore, went on at different rates in each colony, and its main features were soon secured in the larger ones. The railways in West Africa and Indo-China were finished by 1925, and that in the Congo was progressing. Works on the ports in each of these places were in progress. The irrigation-scheme for the Niger was approved and missions sent out to investigate, and a start was made in the direction of con-trolling the water-supplies of Indo-China. Even in the poorer colonies—Tahiti, for instance—the works went on to some degree, the harbour-improvements of Papeete being recommenced. But the lesser parts of the project had to be postponed, because the position changed. The prevalence of high prices up to 1922 meant a considerable degree of colonial prosperity and a general growth of prosperity; and this in turn led to a greater budgetary stability and a general spirit of optimism. Reaching its height—a somewhat hysterically dizzy height—at the Colonial Exposition of Marseilles in 1922, this optimism failed to survive the reaction, because the stagnation of European markets reacted on the colonies and budgetary deficits reappeared.[8] Moreover, the financial embarrassment of France, coupled with the expenditure of at least 5 milliards in Moroccan and Syrian wars, turned attention away from the *mise en valeur* scheme;[9] and under the circumstances, the wonder was, not that the project was not carried out in its entirety, but that even its major lines should have been sketched. The metropolis could afford practically no aid, because, although most of the colonies paid their civil expenses and the larger even made grants towards their military charges, the great bulk of the Minister of Colonies' appropriation was already earmarked.

Sarraut's successors, Daladier and André Hesse, performed yeoman service in continuing his work, but it was a new theorist with an executive mind who was needed, rather than loyal henchmen.

The general problem remains the same as when Sarraut commenced his labour. There has been little increased production, and France received only 10 per cent of her colonial goods from her own lands in 1925.

Since the War, France has constantly been slipping back in the import trade of her colonies and has not be able to command any more of their exports; and the old policy of tariff-assimilation, self-annulling though it might almost be termed, has increased in proportion to the loss of colonial trade by France. This, when joined to the actual diminution of colonial production, led to a new lethargy—a lethargy accentuated by the national financial crisis of 1925–1926. The *mise en valeur* project was thus of necessity swept into the background.

NOTES

1. E.g. in *Journal Officiel*, Deps., 3/7/20; Senate, 28/2/20.
2. *Ibid.*, Deps., 13/4/21, 19/6/21. Compare *Colonies et Marine*, August 1921, p. 481.

3. Speech at Brussels Colonial Conference, in *L'Afrique Française*, May 1923, p. 247.
4. A Sarraut, *La Mise en Valeur des Colonies Françaises*, (1923) p. 316.
5. *L'Afrique Française*, Feb. 1922, p. 113; compare May 1921, p. 162.
6. Sarraut (1923), *op cit.*, pp. 339–341.
7. For details, see Sarraut (1923), *op, cit.*, p. 342 *et seq.*
8. For analysis see Besson in *L'Afrique Française*, July 1921, p. 233.
9. Cachin in *Journal Officiel*, Deps., 7/12/24.

6

DEVELOPMENT AND WELFARE*

W. K. Hancock

In conformity with its double parentage in the evangelical and free-trade movements the theory of colonial trusteeship has two sides. The mandate is a 'dual' one; the trusteeship is exercised for the sake both of the 'backward' peoples and 'the commerce of the world'. Under the conditions from which the theory arose each of the two elements in it appeared to reinforce and support the other. By granting equal commercial opportunity to the traders of all nations the imperial power drew the sting from sovereignty and assuaged the international jealousies which inevitably arise when empire connotes economic monopoly or privilege. By the same policy the imperial power safeguarded its colonial subjects against the evils of economic subservience to a single European nation. The open competition of traders from many nations assured to colonial producers the fair market price for their exports; the same competition was a guarantee to colonial consumers that they would not be overcharged for their imports. Thus, to all seeming, Great Britain's colonial system fitted perfectly into that programme of 'the harmonisation of interests' which, according to Sir Eyre Crowe, was a necessity of imperial policy. It enabled the British Empire to erect its defences, not merely upon the foundation of armed power, but on the foundation of consent—consent of the people in whose interest, and with whose increasing participation, it governed: consent of the whole society of nations who were free to share the material advantages created by just government and impartial commerce. ... This, at any rate, was the official doctrine.[1]

In the late nineteenth and early twentieth centuries this conception of commerce and colonisation enjoyed high international

*Reprinted by permission of Oxford University Press from W. K. Hancock, *Survey of British Commonwealth Affairs*, Volume ii, (1942).

prestige. Its first embodiment was in the free-trade policy which
Great Britain by unilateral decision adopted for herself and her
colonies; but it grew into a European conception and embodied
itself in international conventions. Even at the time when conti-
nental nations were surrendering to the 'nation system of political
economy' the ideal of commercial impartiality found expression
in the most-favoured-nation treaties which mitigated the excesses
of protectionist conflict. In mitigation of commercial rivalries
overseas the 'open door' treaties went a good deal farther. They
aimed at keeping tariffs impartial and also low. Some of these
treaties represented a one-sided and impermanent imposition of
force; but others—and particularly those instruments in which
the European powers pledged themselves to grant to each other
equality of trading opportunity over a large area of Africa—did
create a real and substantial measure of European solidarity in
the colonial world. In the vast region known as the conventional
Congo River Basin this solidarity was affirmed in 1885, and
reaffirmed in 1890 and 1919. The year 1919 also witnessed the
establishment of the mandates system. This marked an important
forward move of liberalism in the colonial sphere. The early
experience of frustration in the Congo area had borne fruit: the
terms in which the African mandates were drawn and the supervision exercised by the Permanent Mandates Commission ruled
out of possibility the evasion which King Leopold had employed
to defeat the intentions of the Act of Berlin. In form, Great
Britain's conception of the relationship between sovereignty and
commerce seemed to be establishing itself as international practice.

In fact, the trend of development was less encouraging. The
movement towards freedom and equality in colonial trade was
the continuation of an impulse which arose in the nineteenth
century and was seriously challenged even then: in the twentieth
century a very different impulse became dominant. Even in the
areas of positive international agreement the movement was away
from freedom, if not from formal equality of trading opportunity.
In 1885 import duties were altogether forbidden in the Congo
area; in 1890 10 per cent *ad valorem* duties were permitted; in
1919, by the Treaty of St. Germain-en-Laye, all limitations upon
tariffs, excepting only the proviso against formal discrimination,
were removed.[2] Outside the area of international agreement tariffs
became increasingly formidable and discriminatory: the imperial
preference systems of France and Portugal showed how colony-
owning powers intended to act when their freedom was unfettered.
France also revealed a determination to enlarge the area of her

unfettered imperial decision. In 1898 France and England had by mutual agreement extended into West Africa the system of commercial equality which prevailed in the Congo basin; but in 1936 France denounced this agreement and brought her West African possessions into the preferential system of the French Empire.

By this time Great Britain herself had turned her back on the policy which she had originated, and set her feet along the path of imperial privilege which other colony-owning nations were following. The British Dominions had long since been urging her along that path, and one of the great parties in the British State had made their arguments its own. This story, and its culmination in the Ottawa Conference of 1932, has been told in an earlier part of this volume from the Dominions' point of view. But the Colonies were also affected by Great Britain's undertakings at Ottawa. The 'open door' of the dependent Empire was now closed, except in those territories where the closure was prohibited by international stipulation. In 1932 the British revolt against trade impartiality took the form of preferential customs duties. In 1934 it took the new form of import quotas, directed principally against the Japanese.[3]

How far has this revolution in commercial policy impaired the principle of the dual mandate? Can Great Britain still claim that she harmonises her imperial interests with the interests of other nations and those of the colonial peoples for whose well-being she is responsible? It can hardly be disputed that foreign nations now challenge Great Britain's imperial position far more vehemently than they ever did in the day when she remained constant to the principle of the open door. Admittedly it would be unjustifiable to assume that this new challenge has been wholly or even primarily a consequence of the change in British policy. The very nations which have trumpeted abroad their grievances against the British Empire have openly advertised the most extreme programmes of monopolistic exploitation in the colonial empires which they hope to acquire for themselves. Moreover, the damage which they have suffered is incomparably less than that of which they complain: critical study of the 'colonial question' had made it clear that only a small proportion of the foodstuffs and raw materials consumed by industrial countries is of colonial origin.[4] Despite all this it cannot be denied that the new preferential tariffs and quotas are intended to penalise foreign trade for the benefit of British trade. The extent of the benefit, and the measure of foreign losses, are in all likelihood both exaggerated. There can, however, be no doubt that the new policy has not altogether missed its aim, and that foreign traders have as a consequence suffered.[5] Under these circumstances it would be rank hypocrisy for the British Empire to pretend that it has no responsibility for the new discords which have invaded international economic relations, or that it remains, in the old sense of the phrase, 'trustee for the commerce of the world'.

In the nineteenth century it was generally assumed that free trade benefited colonial peoples as exporters no less than as importers, because it assured them the boon of a competitive world price. But nowadays this competitive world price is more often a bane than a boon. Glutted markets, falling prices, and restriction schemes have become familiar features in the economic life of primary producing countries. The circumstances amidst which Great Britain turned her back upon nineteenth-century policies were circumstances which men in the nineteenth century could hardly have anticipated; none of the trade depressions which they experienced could compare with the ferocious spin dive into ruin which began at the end of the nineteen-twenties. Surely it is perverse to discuss Great Britain's change of policy without paying any attention to the economic blizzard in which the change took place, and without observing the steady deterioration in the economic climate of which this blizzard was a portent? And surely it is myopic to ignore the part which the self-governing Dominions played in effecting the change? Their attitude gives flat contradiction to the notion that imperial preference is necessarily an act of oppression committed by a sovereign industrial metropolis against helpless agricultural dependencies. It was their persistent initiative which prepared the change in British policy. They knew their own interests, or rather they thought they did. What they wanted was a shelter in British markets for their exports of food and raw materials. They were prepared to pay for this boon by giving increased shelter in their own markets to British exports of manufactured goods. From the economic point of view, as an earlier chapter has made abundantly clear,[6] this bargain was not precisely a mountain peak of human wisdom; but from the moral point of view it could hardly be described as an abyss of human depravity. At the very lowest it represented the morality of *do ut des*. Despite all the wrangling and haggling which went to the making of it, it represented also the genuine desire of sister nations to give each other mutual aid. If pressures and aspirations of this nature induced the self-governing nations of the Commonwealth to combine in a system of imperial preference, how can the inclusion of the other parts of

the Empire be ascribed altogether to sinister motives? Admittedly
there is a very great difference between the voluntary give and
take of self-governing nations and the unilateral decisions by
which a sovereign nation judges, not only its own interests, but
those of its dependencies. But it cannot be assumed that the
judgement is wholly biased. In 1932 Great Britain gave to the
colonies the same privilege which the Dominions demanded—
sheltered markets. Was it inequitable to expect that the colonies,
like the Dominions, should undertake some obligations of reciprocity? This line of thought is not merely a plausible justification
of British policy; it did really play a considerable part in determining the policy. To cite but one example: the supplementary
preferences granted to colonial (and particularly West Indian)
sugar were granted as a sequel to Lord Olivier's report on the
parlous state of the colonial industry, and even then fell considerably short of what Lord Olivier advocated. Anyone taking
the trouble to go through the Ottawa schedules could make
an impressive list of similar preferential advantages granted to
colonial producers who badly needed help.

The story of imperial preference, it is now clear, cannot be
told simply as a dirge for free trade and a lament for departed
virtue. Rather should it be told as the story of commercial policy
in the Old Empire is now told. Historians once believed that they
explained this policy adequately when they denounced British
selfishness and greed. The researches of George Louis Beer,
thirty or more years ago, proved that the reality was more complicated: if Great Britain imposed restrictions upon American
industry and trade, she also imposed them upon her own people:
if she demanded privileges for her own production and commerce, she also granted privileges to the colonists. Every reputable
American historian since Beer has admitted that there was an
element of genuine reciprocity in the 'old colonial system'. But
recent historians have carried the matter considerably farther.
Their researches have revealed the unequal incidence of the burdens which this system imposed, and the unequal distribution of
the favours which it granted. Ideally the system may have been
reciprocal; but some colonies did very well out of it, whereas
others did impossibly badly.[7] . . . May it not be similarly necessary
to pass into this third phase of judgement upon the resurrected
protectionist and preferential policies of the contemporary British
Empire? It is not enough to denounce British policy as egotistical.
It is only just to recognise that there is a sharing of burdens and
an exchange of favours. But it may well be that some colonies,

or some sections of colonial producers, get more than their fair share of the favours, whereas others bear more than their fair share of the burdens.

Are there any new standards to set up in place of the old? The changes in commercial policy have already been examined from this point of view. Their inadequacy has also been made plain. Sheltered imperial markets are an aid to some producers and some colonies, but are no aid to others. The reciprocal shelter given to British exports imposes burdens on colonial consumers. It also reverses the open-door policy and brings the two sides of the mandate into conflict.

However, there have been other methods of reaction to the new situation. The colonial governments have reviewed their agricultural policies. Monoculture has fallen out of favour, and production for export is no longer regarded as the dominating consideration. A more balanced system of agriculture is favoured— both as a means of raising nutritional standards and as an insurance against depressions transmitted through world markets. Governments which have regarded commerce simply as the outflow of exports and the inflow of imports have now begun to envisage the great possibilities of an internal exchange of goods. There are also a few signs of official interest in the possibilities of simple manufacturing development. All these plans and prospects are hopeful. But quick results can hardly be expected. In particular it cannot be expected that these new developments will in the immediate future enable colonial governments to finance the public works and social services which they know to be essential.

If the admitted need is to be met, the imperial government must come forward with direct aid. This is now official doctrine. In the White Paper published in February 1940 the British government assumed direct financial responsibility for a new drive to develop colonial resources and raise the standard of the social services. Here is a radical and striking adaptation of policy to meet the needs of a new time. It contradicts the traditional wisdom of the Treasury, which—except for reluctant relief granted from time to time to the hopelessly indigent—has persistently demanded that each dependent territory shall be financially self-sufficient and content with the services it can pay for.

It will be prudent to remember that the new policy is so far no more than promise; it is not yet performance. It may be prudent—or it may be unduly cynical—to remember that the promise has some immediate propaganda value. Nevertheless, the White Paper is a notable document.

There is at first sight something paradoxical in its timing. Throughout all the successive decades when the British government and people had plenty of money to spare, the traditional wisdom of the Treasury prevailed—only to be overthrown at a time when Britain's financial prospects were extremely uncertain. Year after year throughout the previous decade the annual balancing of account had failed to show a surplus for overseas investment. The best expert opinion inclined to the belief that Great Britain was suffering an absolute diminution of the resources which in more prosperous times she had accumulated abroad.[8] And what would the coming time bring forth? What efforts, what privations would be demanded of the British people in their struggle for survival, in their struggle to repair the destruction of war? Was it prudent for them to assume, at this juncture of their history, an obligation which they had never assumed before—the obligation of expending their own treasure in an attempt to raise to a new level of welfare the backward populations of more than two score colonial territories?

The present age no longer accepts Adam Smith's equation of private interest and public good: in rebellion against the careless and uneven scattering of rewards and deprivations which is the result of 'free' economic activity, it has summoned public authority to assume direct responsibility for transmuting wealth into welfare. But this public authority has been hitherto the sovereign state: its watchword has been, 'The welfare of *our* nation'. If the sense of community has deepened, it has also narrowed. From this narrowing, frustration has been born. From the frustration there may in turn be born a blind revolt, or a new effort of thought and will. May it not be sound, both in ethics and economics, to alter the watchword once more so that it shall read —'the welfare of nations'?

This revision of Adam Smith, it may be argued, will fit the facts of the twentieth century as closely as his conception of 'the wealth of nations' fitted the facts of the nineteenth century. That century witnessed a geographical expansion of material civilisation on a scale which was unprecedented in human history. The economic frontiers of the western world advanced to the farthest limits of the new continents. Today there is no longer any room for advance. The frontiers are fixed. The direct opportunity of new land and life which the New World offered to increasing millions in the Old World exists no longer. At the same time, the

D

productive energies liberated by the settlers and traders and investors who responded to New World opportunity now find themselves constricted by the diminution of population-increase in Europe and by the policy of European governments. An economic order which at the very roots of its nature is expansionist[9] has been compelled to run inwards. It can no longer sprawl; in some fashion or other it must plan. Throughout the past decade the conception of armed power has increasingly dominated its planning. This conception has flourished amidst economic crisis and spiritual despair; its fruits are destruction, poverty, and a deeper despair. But in the conception of the welfare of nations there is hope. It offers a new stimulus to take the place of the moving frontiers; it promises to an expansionist society the means of living in harmony with its own nature, even in an age when geographical expansion has reached its limits. A struggle to raise the standard of the depressed classes and the depressed areas of the world could have a dynamic effect comparable with the discovery of a new America. Your America, Goethe said, is at home; this is an economic truth today, if 'home' is taken to mean not merely the soil of Europe but the whole area of economic collaboration and human need in which Europe is implicated. The America of an earlier hope no longer exists today—that empty America remote from Europe, the land of promise, of escape from European evil. For good or ill, the whole society of nations has become 'home'. Here, among the slums of western Europe and the crowded peasantries of eastern Europe, in backward Africa and impoverished China, a vast work of development and welfare is waiting to be done: here are the markets to be opened: here is the new way to wealth. If the new way is resolutely followed, the door of equal opportunity will open once again; for the multitudinous tasks which challenge effort—tasks of soil conservation and agricultural training, medical service and nutrition, education and transport and industrial development—call for an expenditure too large for the resources of a single imperial nation. Trusteeship on behalf of backward and neglected people, when it is given a positive economic content, will demand for its effective exercise positive international collaboration. Once again those nations which have no 'possessions' will find the doors of opportunity opening to them.

This is the new conception into which the British White Paper of 1940, with its programme of colonial development and welfare, naturally fits.

NOTES

1. See prefaces to vols. i and ii.

2. *Informal* discrimination has been dealt with in vol. ii, part i, pp. 78–9.

3. The new policy expressed itself in British West Africa as follows: Sierra Leone and the Gambia were at once brought into the preferential system: the Anglo-French convention of 1898 kept Nigeria and the Gold Coast outside it. Even when the French denounced this convention in 1936, very strict obligations of tariff impartiality remained incumbent on Great Britain in virtue of a treaty made with Holland in 1871, when Dutch possessions in the Gulf of Guinea were transferred. Nations enjoying under treaty M.F.N. rights shared the advantages conferred on the Dutch; but the extent of the geographical area was dubious. The British government maintained that not only Gambia and Sierra Leone, but even Nigeria, lay outside the Gulf of Guinea. It did not, however, press the contention about Nigeria, and it never questioned its obligation with regard to the Gold Coast. The Gold Coast could not give preferences, but it could and did receive them. All the West African colonies have adopted the system of quota regulation; but the Gold Coast has worked out a unique system under which it assigns import percentages, not only to foreign countries, but to Great Britain also.

4. See particularly the League of Nations *Report of the Committee for the study of the problem of Raw Materials* (Geneva, 1937) and the text and references of two Information Papers issued by the Royal Institute of International Affairs: No. 18, *Raw Materials and Colonies* (1936); and No. 23, *Germany's Claim to Colonies* (1938).

5. This can be very clearly seen by comparing the national origin of imports into a territory within the preferential system and an adjacent territory still under the open door. The *Trade Reports* of the Gold Coast (e.g. for the year 1938, pp. 13, 15, 17) show how the quota policy adopted there was in danger of being defeated by the flow of Japanese goods through British Mandated Togoland.

6. See this *Survey*, vol. ii, chap. iii, sec. 4. Reference may also be made here to the restriction schemes. These also hardly represent 'a mountain peak of human wisdom'; but, like the preferential duties, they represent a departure from *laissez-faire* principle, undertaken under the pressure of necessity with the intention of benefiting producing interests.

7. See this *Survey*, vol. ii, part i, pp. 38–40.

8. See above, vol. ii, part i, pp. 181–3.

9. See above, vol. i, part i, pp. 41–3.

PART TWO

From the Scramble to Independence:
A Survey of Economic Development

7

TRANSPORTATION IN SUB-SAHARAN AFRICA*

S. D. Neumark

Head Porterage

In Negro Africa man was his own beast of burden. In tsetse infested areas most domestic animals could not survive, and even in areas where cattle did survive they were not trained for transport or draught. In North-West Africa, as in North Africa, the ass, the horse, the camel, and possibly the ox, were used as beasts of burden. Horse-drawn chariots may have traversed the Sahara in prehistoric times, but in historic times, except during the Roman era in North Africa, wheeled transport, if not unknown, seems to have been unused until the advent of Europeans.[1]

There were thus hardly any roads, for they were not needed by human porters. In fact, surfaced roads would have been harder on the feet of man and beast than dirt trails (1, p. 179). In the greater part of Africa goods were almost universally carried by the most expensive mode of transport—the human head. As Sir Gerald Portal, speaking of the East African carrier, observed more than half a century ago, 'As an animal of burden man is out and out the worst. He eats more, carries less, is more liable to sickness, gets over less ground, is more expensive, more troublesome, and in every way less satisfactory than the meanest four-footed creature that can be trained, induced, or forced to carry a load' (2, p. 139). Lord Lugard calculated the cost of head porterage, including subsistence on the return journey and a margin for sickness and supervision, at 3 shillings per ton mile. 'It follows,' Lugard says, 'that produce worth £30 a ton at the

*Reprinted by permission of Stanford University from S. D. Neumark, *Foreign Trade and Economic Development in Africa; A Historical Perspective*, (1963).

port of shipment will have cost its full value to transport over a
distance of less than 200 miles, leaving nothing for original cost
of production and profit to the producer, (3, p. 461, n.). As late
as 1926 the cost of transport per ton mile by head porterage in
Northern Nigeria, where labour was plentiful and cheap, worked
out at 2s. 6d., as compared with 1s. by motor transport, 9d. and
10d. by camel transport, and 2d. by railway (5). In short, the high
cost of head porterage not only limited the distance over which
bulky produce could be conveyed but also inhibited the development of natural resources.

Navigable Waterways

Except for West Africa, there are relatively few navigable waterways from the coast to the interior. The seaboard of Nigeria has
the most extensive network of waterways in Africa. The Lower
Niger, together with the Benue, is navigable by shallow-draught
barges for more than 1,000 miles, though the Benue is only
navigable for six months in the lower stretches. The Gambia, 'the
best river of western West Africa' (7, p. 18), is navigable all year
for launches and canoes for a distance of 292 miles, while ocean-
going vessels drawing up to 13 feet can reach Kuntaur, 150 miles
from Bathurst, and small vessels can go 228 miles up-river, to
Fatoto (7, pp. 216–17). Had the territory of Gambia been a French
possession, the Gambia River would have given the French much
better access to the interior than the Senegal River. As it was, the
course of French penetration into the interior savanna regions
was up the Senegal River, from St. Louis, established at the mouth
of the Senegal in 1659, to Kayes, and from there, following a
trail for over 300 miles, to the Upper Niger at Bamako (8, pp.
52–53). From Bamako to Kouroussa the Upper Niger is navigable
between the months of July and October, while below the rapids
of Bamado, from Koulikoro to Gao, a distance of about 756
miles, the Middle Niger is usable between mid-July and mid-
December.

   This river-and-trail combination to Gao, aggravated as it was
by the seasonal flow of the river, made the Senegal a difficult
means of access to the interior,[2] and the spit in the estuary and
the offshore bar made St. Louis a bad port. In fact, the St.
Louis-Dakar line, the first railway in West Africa, and the line
from Kayes to Bamako and Koulikoro were built with a view to
overcoming these difficulties.[3] Finally, a through railway from
Dakar to Bamako and Koulikoro was established in 1923 when

the railroad link from Thiès (on the St. Louis-Dakar line) to Kayes was opened. As a result, traffic on the Senegal River has now become of local importance only.

The Congo River is navigable from Stanleyville to Leopold-ville, a distance of over a thousand miles. The Ubangi, the great tributary on the right bank of the Congo River, is navigable for 400 miles from the point of confluence with the Congo to Bangui, while the Kasai, the principal tributary of the left bank, is navig-able for a distance of 378 miles to Port Franqui, the head of navigation of the Kasai River. However, for a distance of about 200 miles from the sea the Congo river is not navigable. At several other critical points, too, navigation on the Congo and its tributaries is interrupted by rapids. Railways had therefore to be constructed to carry traffic around these obstacles, for without the railways links the Congo system could at best be of limited use. In fact, the Congo River only began to assume economic importance after the construction of the railway line from Matadi to Leopoldville.

In East Africa, the Great Lakes—Victoria, Nyasa, Tanganyika, and Albert—offer facilities for water transport. However, it was not until the extension of the railway network to East Africa, which formed a link between the lakes and the Indian Ocean, that the Great Lakes began to play an important part in the economic development of the lake regions.

The Arrival of the Steamship

The evolution of the steamer and the transition from sail to steam proceeded at first very slowly. But in the course of the second half of the nineteenth century the carrying power and the reliability of the steamer led to a considerable reduction in ocean freights and thus narrowed the margin between prices of raw materials in exporting and importing countries. This was particularly true in the case of bulky commodities such as timber, grain, palm oil, copra, and oil seeds.

What was the impact of steamship development on the expan-sion of trade in Africa? In general, a reduction in the cost of ocean freight will benefit mostly the importing countries, while a reduction in the cost of transport from the interior to the coast will benefit mainly the raw material producers. In the United States, an extensive network of waterways had been created be-fore the advent of the steamship, and railway development went hand in hand with the development of steamships. By contrast,

Africa lacked simultaneous development of inland and sea transport. As a result, the arrival of steamships, which in Africa long
preceded that of railroads, had in most cases very little effect on
the cost of transport from the interior to the coast. It has been
suggested that following the drop in sea transport cost alone, a
number of bulky commodities, formerly debarred from the export
market by a combination of high costs of land and sea transport,
could now be tapped for export (10, p. 71). Although information
on this point is very scanty, it is difficult to see how the cheapening of sea transport alone could have tapped an increased volume
of bulky commodities unless there was also a commensurate
rise in their price in Africa. But there is no evidence of such a rise
in price. On the contrary, as far as palm products were concerned,
the available evidence points in the opposite direction. It therefore seems that the expansion of exports from West Africa was
due not so much to the cheapening of sea transport as to the
revolution in river transport brought about by small, shallow-
draught steamboats, specially constructed for this purpose by
Macgregor Laird in the 'fifties. Indeed, as McPhee points out,
unlike the sailing ships, these shallow-draught steamers 'could
be manoeuvred round sandbanks and past snags'. It was also
these boats that opened up the 'Nigerian hinterland' to direct
commerce with the coast (10, pp. 71–72). But, as noted earlier,
such favourable transport conditions as presented by the lower
Niger, the Gambia, and the Senegal were rare.

Railways and Mining Development

The first railways in Africa south of the Sahara were built in the
Cape. Although construction had begun in 1859, progress was
slow, and by 1873 the Cape had only a total of 64 miles of
railway. It was only after the discovery of the Kimberley
diamond-fields in 1870 that the era of railway construction in the
Cape began in earnest.

In the Rhodesias and the former Belgian Congo, as in South
Africa, the main railways lines were determined by discoveries of
mineral deposits (6, p. 374). The Rhodesias owe their first railways to Cecil Rhodes who, having obtained from Chief Lobengula
a mineral concession covering the immense area of what is now
Southern and Northern Rhodesia, persuaded the chartered British
South Africa Company, whose chairman he was, to assume 'heavy
obligations in the field of railway development' (11, p. 1550). The

railway line traversed Bechuanaland and reached Lobengula's kraal, on the site of the modern Bulawayo, in 1897. At the same time communication was being established with the Indian Ocean from the eastern side, with the line from Beira reaching Salisbury in 1899. Three years later a connection was established between Salisbury and Bulawayo at a point 50 miles east of Bulawayo (12, p. 565). From there the line was continued north to the Wankie coal fields. Victoria Falls were reached in 1904, and Broken Hill, where lead and zinc deposits had been discovered, in 1906. The railway finally reached the Katanga mines in the Belgian Congo in 1910, thus providing an outlet for Katanga copper to the Indian Ocean.

In 1931, completion of the Benguela Railway across Angola from Lobito Bay provided a more direct route from the Katanga to Europe by way of the Atlantic Ocean. The link with the Benguela Railway was made possible by the construction of the *Chemin de Fer du Bas-Congo au Katanga* (the B.C.K.), the most important railway system of the Belgian Congo. Like the Benguela Railway, this line, too, was designed to serve the mineral areas of the Katanga.

Southern and Central Africa are not the only territories in which main railway lines were determined by mineral deposits. In the former British colony of the Gold Coast, gold mining was responsible for the construction in 1898–1901 of the first railway line from Sekondi to Tarkwa, for its extension to the Obuasi gold mines in 1902, and for a branch to Prestea in 1912 (7, p. 142). In Nigeria, the Bauchi Light Railway (2 feet, 6 inches gauge) was opened in 1914 to link the Jos tinfields with the Lagos-Kano line at Zaria. In 1916, the Nigerian Eastern Railway from Port Harcourt to Enugu was opened to serve the Enugu coalfield. In Sierra Leone, a private railway, built by the Sierra Leone Development Company Limited, was opened in 1933 to link the rich iron-ore deposits at Marampa with the port at Pepel, fifteen miles up-river from Freetown, while Liberia's first railway, 45 miles in length, was opened in 1951 to connect the iron-ore mines in the Bomi Hills with the port of Monrovia. Similarly, in east Africa, an extension of the Uganda Railway from Kampala to Kasese, 209 miles in length, was opened in 1956 to serve the Kilembe copper mine.

This is not to say that the impetus to railway construction in Africa came exclusively from mining interests. In fact, some railways were built for political, strategic, and administrative purposes, or even to promote the production of export crops. For instance, the main line of the Government Railway in Sierra Leone was built mainly to serve the oil palm areas, the Accra-Kumasi line to serve the cocoa areas of the Gold Coast, the Kano-Lagos railway in Nigeria to facilitate the export of cotton and the import of building materials and trade goods (13, p. 72); and, as mentioned earlier, some railways were built to supplement the navigable sections of the Senegal, the Niger, and the Congo rivers. Nevertheless, it is significant that before World War II the length of the main railway lines serving the mineral territories in South Africa, Rhodesia, Bechuanaland, the Belgian Congo, Angola, and Mozambique, which amounted to 21,000 miles, comprised roughly 66 per cent of the total railway length (32,000 miles) of sub-Saharan Africa (6, p. 374). But what is even more significant is the fact that the railways in the mineral producing territories could easily pay their way, while the railways of most of the remainder of sub-Saharan Africa proved a financial burden to the governments concerned.

Indeed, the maintenance of the Sierra Leone Railway during 1899 to 1935 involved the Government in a net loss of nearly £2 million, an amount exceeding the whole of the capital cost of the line (6, p. 405). In Nigeria, the railway system had by 1936 become a heavy burden on the general revenues of the country (14, pp. 1561–62). In French West Africa few of the railways were self-supporting up to 1934, and the railways of the non-mineral areas of the Belgian Congo were little better off (6, p. 416).

One of the chief reasons why railways in the non-mineral areas of Africa proved a financial burden is that these areas were not able to provide the railways with sufficient traffic. Indeed, as Lord Hailey has observed (14, pp. 1538–39)

in the United States an extensive network of waterways and roads had opened up large fertile areas for settlement, and a considerable local industry had been created before the beginning of railway transport; while in Canada and Australia the building of trans-continental lines was undertaken in the expectation of attracting to rich agricultural areas large numbers of European settlers whose activities would rapidly provide an adequate volume of remunerative traffic. In Africa it has not been possible to base the transport system upon a large internal crosswise traffic, and the first stage of development has been to provide means of conveying raw produce from the interior to the coast for export, and bringing manufactured imports back to the inland dweller. Not only, however, is the building of a main line running inland from the coast expensive in relation to earnings, because of the long distance to be covered and the sparseness of the population, but the further development of connexion through branch lines and roads with surrounding districts is made uneconomic because African crops are frequently of small value, and available only in small quantities.

This is also the reason why railways in Africa, in contrast to other parts of the world, did not attract private enterprise, except where mineral exports promised early returns. In some cases, such as in the Belgian Congo, companies were offered large mineral and land concessions as an inducement to railway construction, but in the long run the system proved wasteful and ineffective (6, pp. 375-76).

Nevertheless, the important part played by railways in the non-mineral territories can hardly be exaggerated. Indeed, the railway often transformed the lands through which it passed, irrespective of the purpose it had been designed to serve. The history of the Uganda railway may be cited as a case in point. In 1896 the British Parliament sanctioned the construction of the Uganda railway, which six years later linked Mombasa on the Indian Ocean with Kisumu on Lake Victoria, a distance of 587 miles. The motives for building the railway were primarily philanthropic and strategic: to counteract the persisting slave-trade in the interior and to check German ambitions in that part of Africa. The commercial advantages of the railway or of retaining Uganda were none too clear at that time. In fact, all the Opposition in parliament was prepared to allow was the possibility of a trade in white donkeys and rattraps (15, p. 111). As it was, the railway turned out to be the making of Kenya, and the economic development of Uganda really began with the completion of the railway to Lake Victoria.

A vivid account of the changes that took place in parts of Kenya immediately after the arrival of the railway is given by Sir Harry Johnston (16, pp. 40-42):

I have had the privilege of seeing this country just in time—just before the advent of the railway changed the Rift Valley, the Nandi Plateau, the Masai countries, from the condition at which they were at the time of Joseph Thomson (1882) to one which day by day becomes increasingly different. On grassy wastes where no human being but a slinking Andorobo or a few Masai warriors met the eye; where grazed Grant's gazelle, with his magnificent horns, and the smaller but more gaily coloured *Gazella thomsoni*; where hartebeests moved in thousands, zebras in hundreds, ostriches in dozens, and rhinoceroses in couples; where, in fact, everything lay under the condition of Britain some 200,000 years ago; not only do trains puff to and fro (the zebras and antelopes are still there, accepting the locomotive like a friend, since it drives away the lions and ensures the respect of the Game Laws), but alongside the railway are springing up uncounted hideous habitations of corrugated iron and towns of tents and straw huts.

The solitude of the Rift Valley has gone. Thousands of bearded Indians, hundreds of Europeans and Eurasians, Negroes of every African type (from the handsome Somali to the ugly Mudigo), Arabs and Persians trudge to and fro on foot, ride donkeys, mules, and horses, pack the carriages like herrings, set up booths, and diverge far and wide a hundred miles in each direction from the railway line, trafficking with shy and astonished natives, who had scarcely realised the existence of a world outside their own jungle, for the beef, mutton, fowls, eggs, and vegetable food-stuffs which are to assist in feeding this invasion. Faraway on Baringo natives are extending their irrigation schemes and planting twice as much as they planted before, knowing that there is a market where their spare food can be exchanged for rupees. Farther north still, in the Suk countries, Englishmen, Scotchmen, Goanese, Arabs, Swahilis, and Baluchis are pushing into deserts to buy donkeys, are trading for ivory which the railway will carry to the coast at a rate less than the cheapest porter caravan. The Nyando Valley, for years without human inhabitants other than the shiftless Andorobo, is filling up with Masai, Swahili, and Nandi immigrants; while for twenty miles at a stretch on the beautiful heights and happy valleys of Mau you are in the presence of an unintentioned European colony, some of which no doubt will melt away with the completion of the railway, but much of which must be the nucleus of the great white colony one may hope to see established on the only land really fitted for its development in Equatorial Africa. The Kavirondo, alas! are wearing trousers and 'sweaters'; the sacred ibises have left Kisumu, for its swamps are drained. Piers and wharves, hotels and residences in corrugated iron, are springing up at Port Florence, destined, no doubt, to be a great emporium of trade on the Victoria Nyanza. The dirty brown waters of Kavirondo Bay, a gulf of the great lake that was only properly mapped last year, are now daily navigated by sailing boats and steamers.

Roads

Great as the impact of the railway has been on the economic development of Africa, it must be borne in mind that in the pre-automobile age this impact did not extend beyond a limited distance from the railway line. Indeed, in order to attain a wider impact, not only do railways need feeder roads, but roads also need wheeled vehicles. As noted earlier, tropical Africa had neither roads nor animal transport. It was only after the arrival of the automobile and the truck that there arose a demand for roads in tropical Africa. It can therefore be said that, until that time, the railways, owing to the lack of animal-drawn wheeled transport and feeder roads, could only provide a limited system of communication. In fact, as far as low-value, bulky commodities were concerned, a radius of 30 to 40 miles from a railway, or from a navigable waterway for that matter, was the extreme limit of profitable production for export under conditions of head porterage.

The nature of those difficulties was clearly demonstrated in the early days of cotton growing for export in Uganda. Cotton became Uganda's most valuable export following the arrival of the Uganda Railway from Mombasa to Kisumu in 1902. However, cotton cultivation was confined to areas within 30 to 40 miles of the ports of Lake Victoria from where the cotton was transported across the lake to the railway terminal at Kisumu and thence by railway to Mombasa. Beyond that area expansion of cotton growing was impeded by the lack of animal transport to the lake ports. Thus Sir H. Hesketh Bell, the Governor of Uganda who played a leading part in the early development of Uganda, reported in 1909 (17, p. 12):

> Up to the present the cultivation of cotton has been restricted to the districts that lie within a moderate distance of the ports on the shore of Lake Victoria. The native of Uganda is very willing to grow cotton, or, indeed, any other product which fetches a reasonable price, but he detests having to carry his crop to market, on his head, over a long distance. A journey of thirty to forty miles is the outside limit he is willing to travel with a load of his own produce. A radius of forty miles from a market may be taken as the extreme limit of area of profitable production under existing conditions.

To drive home his point, Sir Hesketh Bell related the following incident (17, p. 13):

> A few weeks ago I was travelling through some districts in the Kingdom of Buganda, distant about ninety miles from Kampala. Small plantations of cotton were to be seen dotted all about the country, and I was informed by the chiefs that at least 6,000 plots could be counted in those districts alone. To my surprise I found

that although nearly all the little plantations were giving a fair yield of cotton, which was already almost over-ripe, no attempt seemed to be made to gather the produce, and it was beginning to rot on the bushes. In answer to my enquiries, I was informed by some of the peasants that they had planted the cotton some months before in deference to the advice or orders of their chiefs, and that they had properly cultivated the plots. The idea of having now to carry their crops on their heads all the way to the ginneries at Kampala, ninety miles off, was, however, much more than they were prepared to do, even to please their chiefs or the Government, and they declared that they would far sooner let the cotton rot on the bushes than be put to such intolerable trouble. I was further-more assured that the price which the produce would fetch at Kampala would hardly pay for its transport, calculated at the current rates paid for porterage.

'The arguments of the peasants,' Sir Hesketh added, 'were unanswerable, and it was evident that a deaf ear would be turned to the chief if he attempted again to counsel his people to grow cotton' (17, p. 13).

It was under Bell's leadership that a definite plan was adopted for building 'good solid roads', fit for the use of 'light motor lorries'. Bell, in fact, was responsible for the introduction of the first motor car and the first truck into Uganda in 1908. 'During the last three or four years,' Bell wrote in January 1909. 'a number of roads have been improved to such an extent that it is now possible to supplement human transport to a considerable extent by wheeled traffic. . . . I am happy to be able to report that the experiments that have been made during the past year in the use of motor cars and lorries have exceeded our most san-guine hopes.' (18, p. 105).

It should be added, however, that, apart from the vision and initiative of Sir Hesketh Bell, roadbuilding in Uganda was also greatly helped not only by an abundant supply of laterite iron-stone, which provides an excellent material for roads (19, pp. 238–39), but also by the application of the traditional custom of *Luwalo*, one month's unpaid labour a year for public works (15, p. 124). In other territories, notably in British West Africa, partly owing to the scarcity of good road material, but largely owing to the high cost of labour, road construction was more difficult and more expensive.

NOTES

1. On the little island of Pemba, north of Zanzibar, ox carts have been used for a very long time. For several centuries the Arab landowners of that island have imported large numbers of Africans drawn from tribes who live as far inland as the southern shores of Lake Victoria. 'Many hundreds if not thousands of such people, having seen the amount of labour which can be saved by a wheel, returned to their own people, but not one seems to have imitated the device'. (4, p. 2).

2. Had Nigeria belonged to the French, the Niger river would have been used for trade with the interior of French West Africa.

3. The St. Louis-Dakar line was opened in 1885; the link between the Senegal and Niger rivers (Kayes-Koulikoro line) was completed in December 1904 (92, p. 220).

REFERENCES

(1) Benjamin E. Thomas, *Trade Routes of Algeria and the Sahara.* Berkeley: University of California Press. 1957.

(2) Sir H. Clifford, *Gold Coast Regiment*, p. 151, cited by L. C. A. Knowles, *The Economic Development of the British Overseas Empire.* London: George Routledge and Sons, Ltd. 1924.

(3) F. D. Lugard, *The Dual Mandate in British Tropical Africa*, reprinted by Frank Cass London, 1965.

(4) E. B. Worthington, *Science in the Development of Africa, A Review of the contribution of physical and biological knowledge South of the Sahara.* Prepared at the request of the Commission for Technical Co-operation in Africa South of the Sahara (C.C.T.A.) and the Scientific Council for Africa South of the Sahara (C.S.A.), 1958.

(5) *Report by the Hon. W. G. H. A. Ormsby-Gore on his visit to West Africa during the year 1926.* Cmd. 2744, 1926.

(6) S. Herbert Frankel, *Capital Investment in Africa.* London: Oxford University Press. 1938.

(7) R. J. Harrison Church, *West Africa.* London: Longmans, Green and Co., 1957.

(8) B. E. Thomas, 'Transportation and Physical Geography in West Africa,' Department of Geography, University of California, Los Angeles, 1959 (mimeograph).

(9) Eugene Guernier, *Afrique Occidentale Francaise* II. Paris: Encyclopedie Coloniale et Maritime. 1949.

(10) Allan McPhee, *The Economic Revolution in British West Africa.* London: George Routledge and Sons, Ltd. 1926, reprinted by Frank Cass, 1971.

(11) Lord Hailey, *An African Survey.* London: Oxford University Press, under the auspices of the Royal Institute of International Affairs. 1957.

(12) Southern Rhodesia, *Official Yearbook of Southern Rhodesia*, 1952, No. 4.

(13) R. J. Harrison Church, 'The Transport Pattern of British West Africa,' in *Geographical Essays on British Tropical Lands*, edited by R. W. Steel and C. A. Fisher. London: George Philip and Son, Ltd. 1956.

(14) Lord Hailey, *An African Survey.* London: Oxford University Press. 1938.

E

(15) Sir Alan Pim, *The Financial and Economic History of the African Tropical Territories.* London: Oxford University Press, under the auspices of the Royal Institute of International Affairs. 1940.

(16) Sir Harry Johnston, *The Uganda Protectorate*, Vol. I. London; Hutchinson and Co. 1904.

(17) Sir H. Hesketh Bell, Governor of Uganda, *Report on the Introduction and Establishment of the Cotton Industry in the Uganda Protectorate.* Colonial Reports—Miscellaneous—No. 62. Presented to Parliament by Command of His Majesty. November 1909.

(18) *Papers Relating to Mechanical Transport in the Colonies.* (Presented to both Houses of Parliament by Command of His Majesty. May 1909). Colonies—Miscellaneous, Cmd. 4589. The Governor to the Secretary of State, No. 41. January 6, 1909.

(19) H. B. Thomas and Robert Scott, *Uganda.* London: Oxford University Press. 1935.

8

ECONOMIC DEVELOPMENT IN FRENCH WEST AFRICA*

Catherine Coquery-Vidrovitch

In French Equatorial Africa, the poor relation of the French colonies, the system of concessions was soon found to be a failure. Hence efforts were made from 1910 onwards to formulate a new economic policy. In 1898 the state had in effect abandoned the greater part of the territory to businessmen, in the mistaken belief that they would by themselves undertake the necessary investment. However, the businessmen contented themselves with extracting from the jungle the maximum of advantage in the minimum of time, when they did not confine themselves merely to speculating on the stock exchange.

The Policy of Concessions

The idea of a concessionary policy went back to P. Leroy-Beaulieu, an economist who played a major role in the genesis of French imperialism. The policy was defended enthusiastically by Eugène Etienne, who was Under-secretary of State for the Colonies in 1891. Etienne proposed to concede to giant companies for ninety-nine years 'the fruits of the soil, of hunting and fishing ... the rights of police and of justice', the privilege of levying taxes and even that of making treaties with neighbouring states.[1] This idea, inspired more or less by the chartered companies of the *ancien régime*, meant imitating the Royal Niger Company, Cecil Rhodes's Chartered Company, and above all the Congo Free State. The latter, however, was still in financial difficulties, and Prime Minister Freycinet did not dare to create states within

*Reprinted by permission of Cambridge University Press from L. H. Gann and P. Dingnan, eds. *Colonialism in Africa 1870–1960*, Vol. I, (1969).

a state by simple decree. The project therefore fizzled out in the Chamber.

The Colonial Party was to gain an unexpected ally in the person of Brazza. The Commissary-General had no connexions or interest in the world of colonial capitalism. It was no accident that the year of the decree of concession was also the year of his resignation, which showed how far he disagreed with the mercantile community. But he was largely responsible for the illusions that were prevalent in French Equatorial Africa about 'its riches in men and its economic future . . . false notions that did a lot of harm'.[2] Brazza believed that a régime of free competition would bring about disastrous overbidding. He therefore favoured prematurely, and before French interests were ripe for it, the formation of great companies: the CPKN and the SHO (C° Propriétaire du Kouilou-Niari and Société Commerciale, Industrielle et Agricole du Haut-Ogooué).

From the time of his second voyage (1880-2) Brazza had dreamed of a railway that should link Stanley Pool with the sea. When the state refused to pay the very considerable cost, he made an agreement, in 1890, with the Governor of the Crédit Foncier; but Belgian pressure caused the enterprise to be abandoned. The idea was taken up again in 1892 by A. Le Châtelier, a businessman, who obtained a concession to 'study the means of communication between the sea and the Congo across French territory'.[3] The funds available for the purpose, a total of 600,000 francs, appeared ridiculously small compared to the 25 million francs raised at the same time by the Belgian Thys-Urban group. Although the building of the Belgian railroad meant the ruin of these projects, the company nevertheless had a brilliant future before it. Under the name of CPKN it passed in 1899 into the hands of Lever Brothers of Liverpool and was to become one of the components parts of the powerful firm of Unilever.

The failure of this initiative might well have served as a warning. But Brazza, and with him many sincere colonialists, believed in the primary role of trade as a weapon of penetration and a means of 'civilization'. The exaggerated nationalism of the Commissary-General made him believe that only a company that was powerfully protected by the state could drive out the dominant foreign traders, be they Dutch or Belgian as in the Congo, or English or German as in the Lower Ogooué. About 1882 he sent to Marius-Celestin Daumas, the only businessman of real substance in the colony, a plan for a vast monopolistic company that would cover the country with a close network of its factories.[4]

But it was not until 1893 that he succeeded in getting Delcassé to grant him the concession of a large quadrilateral in the Upper Ogooué, including 11 million hectares of jungle and 700 km of river. The exorbitant powers of the company, to which the state had delegated sovereign rights of police and of patronage, aroused its competitors and public opinion. The concession was withdrawn in 1896, but this decision was reversed on appeal to the Conseil d'Etat.

The SHO, which began its activities in 1897, was the first and the greatest of the concessionary companies, and also the best endowed. Complete master in its domain, it was not constrained in the matter of native reserves, nor was it obliged either to pay rent or to make plantations. Envied and soon imitated, it contributed powerfully towards developing in the Congo, a new and exclusive system of monopolistic commerce.[5]

In the following year the Colonial Party triumphed. Forty-one companies shared 70 per cent of the territory. The state issued decrees giving the companies for a period of thirty years all rights of enjoyment and exploitation, with the exception of mining, in return for a fixed annual rent and payment to the state of 15 per cent of the profits. The smallest of these concerns, the Knémé-Nkéni, received 1,200 sq. km, the largest (the Company of the Sultanates of the Higher-Oubangui) 140,000 sq. km. In relation to the immensity of these territories, the capital investment was insignificant—varying from 300,000 francs (for the Compagnie Bretonne du Congo with 3,000 sq. km) to 3 million (for the Compagnie Francaise du Congo with 55,100 sq. km). The Company of the Sultanates with a capital of 9 million francs was an exception.

If the state had hoped to develop the country at the least possible expense by eliminating competition, its hopes were doomed to disappointment on several counts. In order to encourage investment on the part of the companies, the decree granted them freehold rights over any territory they developed, but the definition of 'development' was derisory. It amounted, for example, to a harvest from rubber trees at the rate of twenty trees to the hectare, or buildings on one-tenth of the area. The domestication of an elephant would give a right to 100 hectares! Hence the companies did nothing except to engage in commerce.

The greater part of the territory belonged to the conventional basin of the Congo, where free trade was guaranteed by the powers. Thus the government could not use customs duties as a device for driving out foreigners. A subterfuge was resorted to in the creation not of companies with a commercial monopoly such as the SHO, but of companies that would have exclusive use of the products of the soil. Nevertheless, the trade of the metropolitan country did not gain a decisive advantage from this device. Most foreign firms concealed themselves under cover of a company registered in Paris. The Dutch company NAHV (Nieuwe Afrikaansche Handels Vennotschap) became the 'Brazzaville' company and stood behind the CCCCF (Compagnie Commerciale de Colonisation au Congo Français), which received a concession of 12,400 sq. km. Moreover, a number of French administrators lent their names as cover for foreign enterprises: the Alkélé group (Lefini, Nkémé-Nkéni, and Alima) was in fact under Belgian control.[6]

The Wretched Conditions in French Equatorial Africa

The companies, whether French or foreign, met with the same disappointments: the country was poor and the government ineffective. The savannah in the north was barely known and out of reach. It might take three months to reach Chad, and development was impossible as long as transport depended on human porterage. In the south there was jungle, impenetrable as far as the eye could reach, inhabited only along the waterways, an insalubrious region where many whites died of fever. The rain-forest zone proved little healthier to Africans who were weakened by malaria or decimated by sleeping-sickness that spread with the extension of trade.

The country produced practically nothing but ivory and wild rubber. Ivory production, worth 1·4 million francs in 1896, was declining. The stores laid up in the villages were exhausted, and the elephants were being wiped out. The height of the trade was reached in 1905, when 210 metric tons worth 4 million francs were exported; by 1920 exports had fallen to 97 metric tons. As for wild rubber, the record export of 1906 (1,950 metric tons, equal to half the production of French West Africa) was unequalled before the war. In 1920, for want of any product to replace it, the export exceeded 2,000 tons. The export of wood had barely started. For a long time the only species sought were ebony and a red wood used for dyestuffs. However, since 1893 Daumas had set great hopes on *okoumé*, 'this new business which has just started and which is not yet in the hands of everyone'.[7] An initial sample of 7 or 8 tons sent to the metropolis sold well, but the Havre merchants, who were accustomed to the northern woods, ganged up

against it. Hence trade in *okoumé* wood was for a long time
retarded in France, while in Hamburg it suffered from a glut on
the German timber market. Nevertheless, production rose from
7,000 tons in 1905 to 91,000 tons in 1911. It was a kind of rose-
wood, but soft and close-grained, whose low specific gravity made
it float easily. It served first as a cheap substitute for mahogany,
but did not come into its own until after the war, when the sheet
and plywood industry was set up. Although the total exportation of wood jumped from 2,000 metric tons in 1898, to nearly
150,000 tons in 1913, a survey of the forest riches of Gabon
remained to be made.

French Equatorial Africa was the poor relation among the
French colonies. Its total trade in 1920 was estimated at only 146
million francs, compared to 1·2 billion francs for French West
Africa and 2·2 billion for Indochina. The country found itself
in this invidious position not so much because of the poverty in
resources, but because of its economic system. The concessionary
companies limited themselves to trade even more rigorously than
in French West Africa. They considered themselves to be pro-
prietors of the product, and paid the grower only a paltry price
for gathering and transporting the product. They paid for merchandise preferably in kind, or even in a private currency accepted
only in their own stores.[8] They charged more for their merchandise
than was justified even by the high risks and considerable distribution costs of the colonial trade. The Company of the Sultanates,
for instance, exchanged a kilogram of salt (whose cost price
amounted to 25 centimes in France and to 1·25 francs after
delivery to Oubangui) for goods worth 5 francs. The general
manager of SHO calculated his sale price by adding a preliminary
profit of 40 per cent to the cost price. The heads of the trading
stations then tacked on another 40 to 60 per cent, according to the
distance involved; in addition they charged still another 25 per
cent for their private profit. The traders in turn took their cut.
Hence it is not surprising that 1 kilogram of rubber (worth about
15 francs in Europe) should have been exchanged for 1 kilogram of salt or two needles. The trade goods included powder
and flintlock (until the protocol of 1909 definitely stopped the
sale of these items), cloth, salt, canned goods, knives, beads, and
spirits in abundance. The SHO alone boasted of having forbidden
the entry of spirits into its territory.[9]

Control by the state was nonexistent. The native reserves envisaged around the villages were never delimited. A circular in
1902, which stipulated a reserve amounting to 25 hectares per

person on the average, aroused a general outcry. The minister himself had to give an assurance that these restrictions 'had nothing absolute about them'.[10] The Colonial Inspectorate, which was in charge of a special commissary, appeared illusory. From time to time tours of duty would reveal some crying abuses. An inspector in 1906 described a company of native carriers of SHO as 'unfit, puny, eaten up with ulcers . . . some moved along on their knees, others could not stand upright . . . children had large bald patches as a result of carrying loads; [out of] twenty men, the group had lost, in the course of its first voyage to Haut-Scoi, four men dead of fatigue, weakness and privation'.[11]

But the government had no power to punish or to control these abuses. In 1905, in the whole of the Middle Congo it had only 100 civil servants, of whom 54 were at Brazzaville and 12 at Loango. It was obliged to leave to the companies not only the policing of the territory but also the collection of taxes. On the very eve of Brazza's mission, the authorities were about to legalise a system whereby the agents of the concessionary companies received contributions in kind and turned over the proceeds to the colonial government.[12] Not surprisingly, ill-paid, ill-instructed and often unscrupulous traders committed abuses in order to secure workers, carriers or produce. There were low wages, broken contracts, camps for hostages, trails or timberyards lined with corpses. The mounting mortality among the natives and the rate of desertion diminished dividends year by year.

From the outset, some ill-informed concessionaries had been brutally disillusioned: though ten companies in 1905 could count profits totalling 10 million francs since their formation, the total deficit of the other twenty-one exceeded 9 million. After 1903 there were no more than twenty companies, some of which existed only on paper. The most scandalous case was that of Ngoko-Sangha concern, which in 1908 took advantage of the frontier rectification in favour of the German Cameroon to claim an indemnity. Only energetic action on the part of a group responsible for publishing the 'Cahiers de la Quinzaine',[13] supported by the socialists, prevented the company, in 1911, from obtaining 150,000 hectares in freehold by way of compensation for fictitious damages suffered in a territory that had been left uncultivated.

The Turning-Point of 1910

After Brazza's mission of inspection in 1905 had revealed the abuses of the system, the concessionary régime stood condemned.

Having decided to get rid of it, the state authorized the amalgamation of firms that were losing money. Many concerns combined with others in order to reduce their high overheads. Eleven companies merged into the Forestière Sangha-Oubangi. Another group was formed on the Gabon coast on condition that the interested parties should restore free trade in part of their territory or limit their monopoly to wild rubber. A more rigorous control was set up in the ministry, though there may be some doubt as to its efficacy in view of the fact that the departmental representative with the Compagnie Forestière entered the service of that company in 1913 and shortly afterwards became its president and director-general.

In setting up a federation on the model of French West Africa, the authorities sought to give the country the political structure required for the large-scale investments from which the concessionary régime had hitherto abstained. Having laboured for fifteen years and having expended 1·5 million francs, the SHO had only managed to create a road 100 km long in Middle Ogooué, so wretched that it was soon abandoned. In 1909 parliament voted a loan of 21 million to finance preliminary studies for a great development loan. On 13 July 1914 French Equatorial Africa was authorised to borrow 171 million to pay for a series of railroads that would free the country from the burden of porterage (Congo to the ocean with branches from Ogooué to Ivindo and Oubangui to Chari). This project was delayed by the war and it was only in 1934 that the scheme was partly inaugurated.

Under such conditions, the least economic disturbance was liable to bring on catastrophe. Between 1915 and 1916 a terrible famine broke out when the people, in addition to meeting habitual demands on them, had to contend also with the seizure of their food and the impressment of carriers for the use of troops attacking the German Cameroons. The system of monopolistic exploitation, brutally carried out in a poor and sparsely populated country, led to an intolerable situation. In the aftermath of the war, the companies prepared to reform themselves. From 1919 on, the SHO resolved to extend its activities to 'negotiation . . . of all businesses or enterprises whatsoever, agricultural . . . financial, forestry, mining . . ., of importation, and of exportation . . . of every sort of industrial and commercial establishment . . . and to take in all products'.[14] The time had come for the appearance in French Equatorial Africa of great trading companies, constituted on the model of those in the neighbouring federation (SCOA, DFAO).

From 1900 to 1920 French Equatorial Africa and French West Africa contrasted in every respect. The sole feature common to both was their unconditional devotion to trade; but French West Africa appeared relatively prosperous, while French Equatorial Africa suffered bitter distress. French West Africa had been able to evolve in an empirical fashion by reason of given historical or economic conditions. French Equatorial Africa, on the other hand, poor as it was in goods, in money and in men, could never do more than imitate its neighbours. French West Africa developed relatively harmoniously, around a long-standing colonial nucleus that was well-organised administratively and economically. French Equatorial Africa, made up of bits and pieces, without a model or centre of attraction, was a permanent field for abortive experiments. Its unity, tardily achieved, was always more apparent than real. French West Africa was the uncontested domain of free trade, tempered by a relatively strong administration. The conjunction of these two elements created the infrastructure necessary for its later development; in French Equatorial Africa, on the other hand, the monopolistic chartered companies managed for a long time to check any serious attempt at reform.

On the eve of war, however, both federations had come to a turning-point. The French had begun to understand that the principle of government hitherto relied upon for developing the wealth of the country had proved ineffective. Taxes and forced labour had discouraged or even reduced the population, ignorance of natural conditions or the absence of adequate means of transport had caused the failure of the first European plantations (cotton in Sudan, bananas in Guinea, coffee or cocoa in the Ivory Coast). It was in West Africa, more attractive to enterprise and better organised, that a real effort for economic development was first made. This attempt led to the extraordinary growth of the trading economy (predominance of the companies, and extension of export crops), and rested on a thorough acquaintance with the people, their aspirations and their needs. Following the example of a few great forerunners ('The hour is past, in Africa as in the other continents of the world, where orders can be imposed and maintained against the wish of the people.')[15], the rulers understood 'the need to understand men in order to direct their future'.[16] Native policy, less devoted to assimilation than hitherto, would now hinge on the study of local civilisation, and would work for the benefit of Africans by the employment of technicians and the creation of new rural types of organisation to even out the ups and downs of traditional economic society.

Revealing in this respect was an attempt made in the years after 1910 by two administrators in Senegal. By grouping peasants into *Sociétés de prévoyance*, which were at the same time buying co-operatives and credit organisations, and which the Africans administered themselves without French control, the founders attempted to ensure not only the education of the Africans, but their protection against the snares of private trade. All too often the experiment merely led to a more subtle form of exploitation. Nevertheless it did achieve considerable success. After the war the scheme developed to a remarkable degree and came to represent a turning-point in history. Hitherto the French had been content to exploit black Africa; now at last they thought in terms of accepting the local people as partners in a common enterprise.

REFERENCES

1. Henri Brunschwig, *La colonisation française du Pacte colonial à l'Union française* (Paris, 1949), p. 101.
2. R. Pasquier, 'Chronique d'histoire d'outre-mer: l'Afrique noire d'expression française', *Revue Française d'Histoire d'Outre-Mer*, 1963, no. 178, p. 78.
3. Alfred le Châtelier was the son of an engineer and the brother of a famous chemist. Himself an unsuccessful man of affairs but well educated, he published the first notable work on black Islam (*L'Islam dans l'Afrique occidentale*, Paris, 1899), and from 1903 onwards occupied the chair of Moslem sociology at the Collège de France.
4. Brouillon, undated, *Fonds Brazza*, 3rd mission, IV.
5. *Concessions AEF* L, Archives Nationales, and Archives de la Société.
6. *AEF* XI, B (2).
7. Daumas to Sajoux, resident director in Africa, 9 Feb. 1893, *AEF* L(I).
8. The SHO imposed the so-called *neptunes*, large plates of copper used for the payment of dowry; the Compagnie Française du Haut Congo used pieces minted with the effigies of their directors, the brothers Tréchot, a method comparable to the British truck system.
9. Note of 3 Feb. 1913, *AEF* L (3).
10. Circular of the Commissioner-General, 7 March 1902; circular of the Minister, 11 Sept. 1902, *AEF* XIII, A (1).
11. Dec. 1906, cercle de Samba, Archives de la Société.
12. Circular of Commissioner-General Gentil, 27 April 1905.
13. A review started in 1900 by the poet Charles Péguy after his breach with the socialists; Pierre Mille and above all Félicien Challaye, a young philosopher who accompanied Brazza in 1905, campaigned in the periodical against the scandals in the Congo.
14. Extraordinary general meeting of 1919, for the revision of the statutes, Archives de la Société.
15. *Une âme de chef, le Gouverneur général J. Van Vollenhoven: à la mémoire du capitaine J. Vollenhoven, Gouverneur général des colonies, tué à l'ennemi.* (Paris 1920), pp. 38–50.
16. Hubert Deschamps, *Les méthodes et les doctrines coloniales de la France du XVIe siècle à nos jours* (Paris 1953), p. 167.

9

THE NORTHERN RHODESIAN ECONOMY AND THE RISE OF THE COPPER INDUSTRY*

R. E. Baldwin

A worldwide ranking of countries for the early 1920s, starting with the most economically backward, would certainly find Northern Rhodesia near the beginning of the list.[1] Economic life tor most of the nearly one million Africans was not too different from the primitive state that David Livingstone observed during his famous journeys through the territory seventy years earlier.[2] Europeans (only 3,000 lived there in 1921) had achieved remarkable results in eliminating the slave trade, preventing tribal wars, and spreading Christianity, but the economy was still such that more than 96 per cent of the population lived in the rural subsistence sector.

Economic Activity in the European Sector

The European population was very small in number and concentrated in area. For example, in 1921, 82 per cent of the Europeans lived in the country's southern and central districts where the three main towns—Livingstone (the capital at that time), Lusaka (the capital since 1935), and Broken Hill—were located.[3] Furthermore, most of those who did not actually live in these three towns resided within only a few miles of the railway line connecting them.[4] The railroad, which ran from Livingstone in the south, through Lusaka and Broken Hill, to the Congo border in the north, was the artery of European economic life. It was constructed shortly after the British South Africa Company was given the power to administer the area in 1899 and 1900.[5] The railroad reached Livingstone in 1905 and Broken Hill in 1906.

*Reprinted by permission of the University of California Press from R. E. Baldwin, *Economic Development and Export Growth*, (1966).

The 506-mile-long line was finally completed to the Congo border in 1909.[6] Except for an insignificant distance of macadam all-weather roads (42 miles in 1925)[7] it was the only reliable means of transportation in the territory for many years.

The main non-tertiary economic activity undertaken by Europeans was agriculture.[8] One-third of the European males listing an occupation in the 1921 census were farmers. Most of these 504 farmers lived along the line of rail south and north of Lusaka, and cultivated maize (corn) as their main crop. The only other significant European farming area was around Fort Jameson where in 1921 there were 30 tobacco farmers.

Mining activities engaged only 133 Europeans in 1921 and involved mainly the production of lead and zinc at Broken Hill. The 1924 export value of metals (mostly lead) was £161,000. This sum, plus the £153,000 of agricultural exports, constituted about 70 per cent of the total export value of £456,000 in that year. Copper production was very small, contributing only £7,000 to total exports. The Bwana Makubwa mine near the Congo border produced a modest amount of copper during World War I, but extraction difficulties forced its shutdown from 1920 to 1926.

Manufacturing and construction were even less important than mining as industries of European employment. The former industry employed 58 Europeans and the latter 52 at the 1921 census date. The Zambezi Sawmills near Livingstone was the only significant manufacturing establishment.[9]

Tertiary activities, consisting of administration and defence, transportation, trade, and other services, actually represented the main category of economic activity for Europeans. Fifty-four per cent of those gainfully occupied were involved in these pursuits.[10]

Even though the European population was small and mostly confined to a small geographical area, a not insignificant number of Africans participated in the European directed and financed economic activities just described. By this time, the migration system, under which Africans sought employment for short periods, for example, a year, on European farms or in urban areas, was well established.[11] In 1921 36,000 African men worked for wages.[12]

Besides obtaining employment within Northern Rhodesia, large numbers of Africans accepted jobs outside the territory. For example, in 1921 the Rhodesian Native Labour Bureau recruited 13,000 individuals for employment in Southern Rhodesian mining and farming, and Robert Williams and Company recruited 7,260 for employment in the Katanga copper mines in the Congo.[13] A small number were also hired by recruiters for work on the sisal plantations in Tanganyika. On their own initiative, many more workers migrated to these same countries without a labour contract.[14] A total of 36,000 adult males—about the same number as those working in urban areas within the country—were known to be at work outside the country in 1921, and the census-takers believed this number to be an underestimate of the actual figure.

African agriculture, in the early twenties, was non-market oriented in all but a few areas. Africans rarely dealt with the money economy, but there were some market-oriented activities.

The largest and most remunerative cash activity in the country was the fishing industry.[15] It was centred in in the north-east along the Luapula River and around Lakes Mweru and Bangweulu and found its market outlet in the Katanga mines of the Congo. The district commissioner at Fort Rosebery estimated that 800 tons of dried fish were exported to the Congo in 1926.[16]

A smaller fishing industry flourished on the Kafue River in the vicinity of the railway line and in the Zambezi Valley. Trade in grains was confined to those Africans who lived in the vicinity of mines, plantations, or government stations.[17] The almost complete lack of suitable transportation facilities to the line of rail prevented any other markets from developing.[18]

The African cattle industry was of some importance, although the existence of the tsetse fly confined it mainly to Barotseland. In 1926 the number of African-owned cattle was estimated as 289,000.[19] Cattle were the only important liquid asset that an African could accumulate in the subsistence economy and were regarded as the main measure of wealth. Bride payments and other contractual obligations were made in cattle, and in earlier years apparently were slaughtered for food only at the time of special occasions or famines. By the twenties they were raised more and more frequently for sale in the monetary sector,[20] and by 1930 half the cattle sold were African owned.[21]

The Rise of the Copper Industry

From the backward, rural territory just described. Northern Rhodesia was transformed, within two decades, into one of the most rapidly growing economies in the world. Since 1945, for example, real gross domestic product (in the monetary sector) has grown at an average annual rate of 8·5 per cent (table 2-1).

and for the period 1938 (the first year for which national income estimates exist) to 1961 the growth rate averaged 5·8 per cent.

COPPER AS A NATURAL RESOURCE

The impetus for this outstanding growth performance came almost entirely from the creation of a large-scale copper industry.[22]

TABLE 1

Northern Rhodesia's Gross Domestic Product and Gross Capital Formation in the Money Economy, 1938–1961 (in millions of pounds)

	(1) Gross domestic product (current prices)	(2) Gross domestic capital formation (current prices)	(3) Percentage (2) (1)	Gross domestic* product (1949 prices)
Year				
1938	12·7	6·0	47·2	30·3
1945	15·0	1·6	10·7	28·6
1946	17·6	2·2	12·5	29·2
1947	27·2	4·4	16·2	32·1
1948	34·1	8·7	25·5	39·8
1949	43·9	12·0	27·3	43·9
1950	58·7	15·1	25·7	48·1
1951	85·7	19·3	22·5	55·1
1952	96·7	26·8	27·7	59·8
1953	112·4	28·9	25·7	72·9
1954	126·5	42·1	33·3	80·1
1955	154·9	47·5	30·7	76·5
1956	174·3	59·6	34·2	90·5
1957	137·3	60·1	43·8	95·1
1958	117·0	51·9	44·4	87·2
1959	164·2	43·7	26·6	106·2
1960	184·3	40·7	22·1	116·2
1961	175·3	41·2	23·5	116·1

a There is no satisfactory deflator of gross domestic product available for Northern Rhodesia, and the figures can only be regarded as rough estimates. The method used here was to deflate that portion of gross domestic product attributable to the mining industry by an appropriate index of mineral prices. The rest of the domestic product was deflated by an index of prices for domestic expenditure in the federation for 1954–1961, and by an index of consumer prices in Northern Rhodesia for the other years. The difficulty with this procedure is that prices of imported commodities enter into the deflator. For example, in view of a worsening in the terms of trade of about 25 per cent between 1939 and 1945, it is difficult to judge whether the apparent decline shown in the table in real gross domestic product between these years is in fact significant. Copper production was 9 per cent less in 1945 than in 1938 (the latter year was not surpassed in the post-war period until 1949), but a careful analysis is needed to determine whether the decline was enough to decrease the overall product figure.

Sources: Figures for 1938 taken from or estimated on the basis of Phyllis Deane, *The Measurement of Colonial National Incomes*, National Institute of Economic and Social Research, Occasional Paper, no. 12 (Cambridge: Cambridge University Press, 1948), chap. 3, and *Colonial Social Accounting* (Cambridge: Cambridge University Press, 1953) chap. 5. An estimate of depreciation allowances was added to the figure covering the monetary sector in these sources; data for 1945–1953 from *The National Income and Social Accounts of Northern Rhodesia, 1945–1953*, Federation of Rhodesia and Nyasaland, Central Statistical Office (Salisbury: Government Printer, 1954), table 2; the 1954–1959 figures are from *National Accounts of the Federation of Rhodesia and Nyasaland, 1954–1959*, Federation of Rhodesia and Nyasaland, Central Statistical Office (Salisbury: Government Printer, 1960). Gross domestic product data (1960 and 1961) and gross domestic capital formation (1954–1961) estimated from *National Accounts of the Federation of Rhodesia and Nyasaland, 1954–1960*, Federation of Rhodesia and Nyasaland, Central Statistical Office (Salisbury: Government Printer, 1961). Except for minor differences, the figures from all sources are based on similar methods of calculation. African subsistence output is excluded from total gross domestic product to obtain gross domestic product in the monetary sector.

The existence of copper was known, of course, long before the present industry developed. For centuries Africans worked the copper deposits of Northern Rhodesia and those just across the border in the Katanga Province of the Congo Republic. One of the main uses of copper was to fashion crosses and bars for use as mediums of exchange. It was not until around the turn of the century that European prospectors entered the area and discovered several of the ore bodies that are now mined. But even the extension of a railroad from Broken Hill to the Congo border in 1909 did not stimulate production on a large scale. Only one mine, Bwana Makubwa, was at all significant before the 1930s, and it never sustained a profitable level after World War I. The high costs of extracting copper from the comparatively low grade of oxide ore finally forced its closure in 1930.

The apparent existence in Northern Rhodesia only of oxide ores, averaging but three to five per cent copper, meant that prospects were poor for the development of a copper industry. In Katanga, a copper industry developed rapidly because of the presence of large supplies of oxide ores that averaged around 15 per cent copper. Ores of six to seven per cent copper actually were discarded in the Congo at this time as too poor to treat.[23] What was not realised was that, unlike the Katanga ore bodies, the deposits in Northern Rhodesia changed to copper sulphides of about three to five per cent at moderate depths. Sulphide ores can be fed directly into smelting furnaces after the crushing and concentrating process, whereas with oxide ores a leaching process is necessary to extract the copper. In the twenties the cost of processing sulphide ores was much lower than handling oxide ores of equal copper content. Thus, the discovery of extensive sulphide ores opened up a highly lucrative investment opportunity in Northern Rhodesia.

EXPLORATION AND GROWTH

Several factors were responsible for the intensive copper exploration that began in 1925. In 1923 the British South Africa Company, in contrast to its policy in Southern Rhodesia, decided to grant exclusive prospecting rights over large areas. This policy, in conjunction with a rise in copper prices during the twenties, as the electrical and automotive industries expanded throughout the world, attracted powerful financial companies who were prepared to undertake exploratory drilling on a large and systematic scale. The perfection of the flotation process during the second decade also gave a boost to the entire industry. This method of concentrating copper ore was much more economical than the use of vibrating tables. Another factor especially important for Northern Rhodesian development was the great improvement in methods of malarial control. Malaria and black-water fever were rife on the Copperbelt, and without the control knowledge obtained by Sir Ronald Ross and Sir Malcolm Watson in the Malay Peninsula of Southeast Asia, it would have been difficult to attract a sizeable European labour force.

Development work on four mines—Roan Antelope, Mufulira, Rhokana, and Nchanga—began in the late twenties. The first two are controlled by Rhodesian Selection Trust (now Roan Selection Trust), a holding company in which the American Metal Climax Company of New York has a 50·6 per cent ownership interest. Rhokana and Nchanga, on the other hand, are controlled by the Anglo-American Corporation of South Africa. Despite its name, this is a British and South African firm that also controls large mineral interests in the Republic of South Africa. Roan Antelope and Rhokana began operations in 1931, but the depression postponed the opening of Mufulira until 1933, and Nchanga until 1939. Additional mines were put into operation in the 1950's. Chibuluma, a Rhodesian Selection Trust mine, started production in 1956, and Bancroft, an Anglo-American firm, opened in 1957.

F

The latter mine soon closed because of the depressed copper market and technical difficulties, but re-opened in 1959. In 1963, Rhodesian Selection Trust announced the start of development work on still another new mine in the area, Chambishi.

The rapid growth of Northern Rhodesian copper production is shown in table 2. Output rose from a negligible quantity in 1930 to 138,000 long tons in 1934, and then remained approximately at this level through 1937. Production rose sharply thereafter, reaching a peak of 251,000 long tons in 1943. Technical difficulties in the mines and a decline in wartime demand for copper gradually reduced production to 182,000 tons in 1946. A slow

TABLE 2

Northern Rhodesia Copper Production for Selected Years

Year	Thousands of long tons	Percentage share of free-world market[a]
1926	1	—
1930	6	·56
1934	138	13·38
1938	213	13·42
1942	247	9·92
1946	182	11·05
1950	276	13·21
1954	379	16·16
1958	374	13·23
1960	579	15·68

[a] Free-world production defined as total world less U.S.S.R. and Yugoslavia.

Sources: Copper production for Northern Rhodesia from Annual Reports, 1926, 1930, 1934, 1938, 1942, 1946, 1950, 1954, Northern Rhodesia, Mines Department (Lusaka: Government Printer); *Year Book*, 1958, 1960, Northern Rhodesia Chamber of Mines (Kitwe, Rhodesian Printers); free-world production from *Mineral Resources of the United States*, 1926, 1930, U.S. Department of Commerce, Bureau of Mines (Washington: Government Printing Office); *Minerals Yearbook*, 1934, 1938, 1942, 1946, 1950, 1954, 1958, 1960, U.S. Department of the Interior, Bureau of Mines (Washington: Government Printing Office).

recovery took place after the war, but not until the devaluation of the pound in 1949, when the pound price of copper increased 44 per cent overnight, did another rapid expansion occur. From a level of 213,000 tons in 1948, output rose to 379,000 tons in 1954. Between 1954 and 1958 the general level of production changed very little, and it was not until 1959 that further significant growth began to take place.

As the percentage figures on the Northern Rhodesian share of the world copper market indicate, the territory has continued to grow in relative importance as a world supplier since the early thirties. Only the United States, with a production of about 1,100,000 long tons, exceeded Northern Rhodesia's output of 566,000 long tons in 1960. Following Northern Rhodesia in order of importance were Chile (497,000 long tons), Canada (364,000 long tons), the Congo Republic (296,000 long tons), and Japan (184,000 long tons). Total free-world production in that year was 3,594,000 long tons.[24] In recent years the Rhodesian share of the free-world market has averaged about 16 per cent.

THE DOMINANCE OF MINING

The domination of the Northern Rhodesian economy by the mining industry manifests itself in almost every aspect of the economic structure. For example, an average of 46·5 per cent of the territory's gross domestic product originated in this one industry between 1954 and 1961 (table 3). Although her figures

TABLE 3

Industrial Origin of the Gross Domestic Product of Northern Rhodesia, 1954–1961
(*percentage distribution*)

Industry	1954	1955	1956	1957	1958	1959	1960	1961
Agriculture								
Non-African	2·0	1·6	1·8	2·7	2·1	2·4	2·1	2·8
African	11·0	8·8	8·4	10·6	11·2	9·5	9·3	9·8
Mining and quarrying	52·4	56·8	54·0	39·0	32·6	45·4	47·5	44·1
Manufacturing	4·0	3·9	4·4	6·4	7·1	5·6	5·5	5·9
Building and construction	6·1	6·2	6·7	8·6	9·7	5·8	4·5	4·1
Electricity and water	0·4	0·4	1·6	1·9	2·5	2·0	2·3	2·2
Transport and communications	3·4	3·4	3·7	5·2	5·3	5·0	5·1	5·1
Distribution	5·7	5·1	5·1	6·5	6·4	5·2	5·4	5·6
African rural household services	6·6	5·4	4·9	6·4	7·9	7·0	6·2	6·9
All other	8·4	8·4	9·4	12·7	15·2	12·1	12·1	13·5
Total	100·0	100·0	100·0	100·0	100·0	100·0	100·0	100·0

Source: *National Accounts of the Federation of Rhodesia and Nyasaland, 1954–1961*, Federation of Rhodesia and Nyasaland, Central Statistical Office (Salisbury: Government Printer, 1962), p. 72.

are not strictly comparable with those of the Central Statistical Office, Phyllis Deane found that in 1938, 54·8 per cent, and in 1948, 47·4 per cent, of net domestic product was attributable to the mining industry.[25] Still another sign of the great importance of the mining industry appears in the export statistics of the economy. Between 1945 and 1953 copper exports accounted for an average of 86·5 per cent of the value of all exports. Other mineral exports added another 8·8 per cent to total exports. The fact that exports of mineral commodities equalled 69·3 per cent of Northern Rhodesia's gross domestic product during these years demonstrates the importance of the copper industry in the entire economy.[26]

NOTES

1. The term 'backwardness' is used as a description of the economic characteristics that affect the productive efficiency of a country's people. It denotes that levels of technological knowledge, general education, health, basic diet, and so on among most of the people are low in comparison with the so-called advanced countries, such as the United States and Great Britain.

2. Livingstone was by no means the first non-African to explore the region, but his travels provided the rest of the world with the first authentic information on Northern Rhodesia. From the 1790's onward. Portuguese explorers and traders travelled through parts of the country and Arab slave traders also operated in the northeastern part of the country. See Gann, *The Birth of a Plural Society*.

3. The two administrative districts (out of a total of ten in the territory at that time) were Batoka and Luangwa (*Blue Book for the Year Ended 31 December 1924*, no. 1, Northern Rhodesia [Livingstone: Government Printer, 1925], p. 2). Forty-one per cent of all the European population in the country resided in Livingstone, Lusaka, Broken Hill, and Fort Jameson—a community of 66 Europeans located near the Nyasaland border ('Census of Northern Rhodesia Taken 3 May 1921.' Northern Rhodesia [National Archives of Rhodesia and Nyasaland, Salisbury. Item No. A 3/19/2/5], p. iii).

4. One other group in the economy that should be mentioned is the Indian population. Although very small in numbers (56 in 1921), this group played an important role as storekeepers, traders, and hawkers who dealt primarily with the African population.

5. The charter of the company issued in 1889 dealt mainly with Southern Rhodesia and did not specify a northern boundary. The Barotseland North-Western Order in Council of 1899 and the North-Eastern Rhodesia Order in Council of 1900, however, explicitly extended the company's sphere of administration north of the Zambezi River. In 1911 North-Western and North-Eastern Rhodesia were combined into Northern Rhodesia.

6. *Mining Developments in Northern Rhodesia*, Rhodesian Anglo-American (London, 1929).

7. *Northern Rhodesia Report for 1926*, Colonial, no. 1380, Great Britain, Colonial Office (London: H.M.S.O., 1928), p. 18. There were only 1,875 miles of road suitable for motor traffic in 1924, and there were no bus or trucking companies (*Blue Book . . . 1924*, Section F.3).

8. 'Census . . . 1921,' table 16.

9. This firm mainly produced railway sleepers.

10. Trade (mostly in transit) with the Congo was especially important. In 1924 the Beira and Mashonaland Railway and the Rhodesia Railways, whose 2,462 miles of line ran from Vryburg in the Union of South Africa and Beira in Mozambique through Southern Rhodesia up to the Congo, earned half of its revenue from this traffic (*Report of the General Manager for the Railway: Financial Year Ended 30th September 1925*, Beira and Mashonaland and Rhodesia Railways [Bulawayo, 1926], p. 6).

11. This migration system will be discussed extensively in chapter 5.

12. 'Census . . . 1921,' pp. 74–75. The number of women accompanying the men was only 1,200.

13. 'Annual Report for the Year Ended 31st March 1922,' Northern Rhodesia, Secretary for Native Affairs (National Archives of Rhodesia and Nyasaland), pp. 5–6.

14. The term of the labour contract under the recruiter arrangement was 1 year in Southern Rhodesia and 6 months in Katanga. Deferred wage payments and repatriation were parts of both contracts. It was estimated in 1926 that about £54,000 was brought back in cash to Northern Rhodesia by recruited workers and another £25,000 by those returning independently ('Report upon Native Affairs for the Year 1926,' Northern Rhodesia, Native Affairs Department [Livingstone], p. 10). The Secretary for Native Affairs described the employment-seeking trip of these Africans as follows: 'The Native inhabitant of the Tanganyika Plateau today walks three hundred miles or more to find employment at sixpence a day rather than be content with twopence nearer home whether it be Northwards to the sisal plantations of Tanganyika Territory, Westwards to the Katanga, or Southwards to the Mines at Bwana M'Kubwa or Broken Hill. It takes him three weeks or more to complete his journey and with a scant and uncertain supply of food on the way he not seldom arrives and engages upon labour to which he is utterly unaccustomed in a half starved and emaciated condition' ('Report upon Native Affairs for the Year 1927,' p. 23).

15. 'Report upon Native Affairs for the Year 1928,' p. 13.

16. 'Report upon Native Affairs for the Year 1927,' p. 15.

17. 'Report upon Native Affairs for the Year 1926,' p. 13.

18. *Annual Report for the Year 1929*, Northern Rhodesia, Department of Agriculture (Livingstone: Government Printer, 1930), p. 5.

19. 'Report upon Native Affairs for the Year 1926,' Appendix I.

20. Audrey I. Richards, *Land, Labour and Diet in Northern Rhodesia* (London: Oxford University Press, 1939), p. 195.

21. *Milligan Report*, p. 19.

22. To supplement the brief account in the text of the history of the copper industry, consult these selected sources: Kenneth Bradley, *Copper Venture* (London: Mufulira Copper Mines, 1952); L. H. Gann, 'The Northern Rhodesian Copper Industry and the World of Copper: 1923–1952,' *Rhodes-Livingstone Journal*, XVIII (1955), 1–18; Sir Ronald L. Prain, *The Copperbelt of Northern Rhodesia* (London: Royal Society of

Arts. 1955) The *Rhodesian Mining Journal* also contains a number of articles in its 1929 volume which deal with the early history of the mines.
23. *Mining Developments in Northern Rhodesia*, p. 11.
24. *Year Book*, 1961, Northern Rhodesia Chamber of Mines (Kitwe: Rhodesian Printers), p. 18.
25. Phyllis Deane, *Colonial Social Accounting* (Cambridge: Cambridge University Press, 1953), p. 67.
26. Export statistics from A. G. Irvine, *The Balance of Payments of Rhodesia and Nyasaland, 1945–1954* (London: Oxford University Press, 1959), pp. 223–224; gross domestic product data, including an estimate for the African subsistence sector, from *National Income and Social Accounts of Northern Rhodesia, 1945–1953*, Federation of Rhodesia and Nyasaland, Central Statistical Office (Salisbury: Government Printer, 1954), pp. 23–25.

10

PORTUGAL'S ECONOMIC POLICY IN AFRICA: A REASSESSMENT*

Zbigniew A. Konczacki

The Growth of Modern Colonialism

At the time when Britain, France and Germany 'scrambled' for Africa, Portugal extended her effective occupation of the interior of Angola and Mozambique. Military campaigns putting down sporadic uprisings were carried on well into the twentieth century. As late as 1917, there were disturbances in Angola's region of Moxico, and in the Mozambique's region of Barué.[1]

At the turn of the century a new approach to colonial policy began to emerge. The highly centralised and restrictive system of military government was to give way to a civil administration which was more conscious of the economic interests of Portugal's African territories. Budgetary deficits were endemic in Angola. For over fifty years military and naval expenses were included in the colonial budget, and their accumulated total amounted to some 20,000 contos (over four million pounds sterling). In this respect Portugal differed from the other European colonial powers whose metropolitan budgets covered this type of expenditure. Over the same period, the amount allocated to public works, public health and education barely exceeded 8,000 contos. Critics in Angola were justified in identifying centralisation with exploitation.[2]

Mozambique's experience was different, in that there were budgetary surpluses, which were remitted to the mother country in addition to the subsidies, open or concealed, paid by the

*This paper, revised by the author, was originally published under the title 'Portugal in Africa: The Economics of the Decline and Fall' in *Co-operation and Conflict in Southern Africa, Papers in a Regional Subsystem*, edited by T. M. Shaw and K. A. Heard, (Washington: The University Press of America, 1976).

71

colony to the national shipping line, the Empresa Nacional de Navegacâo. It was obvious that Portugal was living at the expense of her two African possessions while at the same time neglecting their development. Mozambique's income came mainly from the earnings of the Lourenço Marques railways and the remittances of the migrant workers employed in the Witwatersrand gold mines. The economic policy represented the line of least resistance. Mozambique's development was tied to the destinies of the Transvaal and it relied on the growth of commercial enclaves, in an otherwise undeveloped country.[3]

During the 1890s, governmental indifference to colonial matters was largely responsible for the granting of considerable areas of land in Mozambique to chartered companies. Two of these, the Niassa and the Mozambique Company, financed by British capital, were controlled by their London office.[4]

Eduardo Costa was responsible for carrying out the basic work of the administrative reform of the colonies as embodied in the Colonial Reform Act of 1907.[5] The change in colonial policy introduced by the new legislation came three years before the fall of the monarchy in Portugal. As a result of the liberalisation of the attitude of the republican government towards the colonies, Angola and Mozambique pursued new development projects and began to borrow heavily during the decade of semi-autonomy which followed, resulting in serious trade deficits. The financial plight had to be remedied through considerable loans from the metropolitan government which, at that time, could ill afford such assistance.

The Portuguese colonies were considered the worst administered territories in Africa. The frequent changes of the Governor-Generals often led the newcomers to abandon projects initiated by their predecessors resulting in the increase of financial burdens. Mismanagement and corruption at all levels of administration were the bane of the colonies.[6]

Political and economic difficulties within Portugal itself led to a coup in 1926. The dictatorship which emerged relied on the advice of Antonio de Oliveira Salazar who became first the Minister of Finance and in 1932 Prime Minister. The need for stringent economic policies was used as a pretext by the new government to cancel most of the autonomy enjoyed so far by the colonies. The Colonial Act of 1930 became a framework for the policy of the 'New State'. Unlike the frequently ignored past legislation, the new colonial laws became a dogma which for the next thirty years governed Portuguese colonial policy.[7]

Salazar adopted the principle of balanced budgets. The policy of extreme financial austerity, the elimination of wastefulness and the reduction of governmental expenditure to a minimum, became his 'credo'. The most pressing needs had to await better times when the necessary funds became available. Priority was given to stability rather than to expansion.

In addition to Portugal's economic problems, which were of her own making, hardships caused by the Great Depression of the 'thirties were also responsible for lack of investment and immigration. Yet this state of affairs was consistent with the government's aim of stability and was preferable to the risks of development.[8]

It is not the intention of this paper to dwell on the ideology that lay behind the policy of the 'New State'; however some explanatory remarks are necessary. In the absence of resources to implement the material progress of the colonies a substitute had to be found which would have at the same time a propaganda value. It was readily found in a vague, mystical idea concerning Portugal's civilising 'mission' in Africa. This concept was hard to interpret and few outside Portugal viewed it seriously. The new rulers of Portugal tried to create a colonial mentality which recalled the traditions of the golden age of Portuguese expansion while at the same time incorporating both the heroic elements of Lusitanian overseas policy and the material elements of the present.[9]

The Constitution of 1933 embodied strong feelings regarding territorial integrity. Some thirty years earlier the inalienability of African possessions was hardly a dogma for some of the leading Portuguese statesmen. At that time many of the Portuguese doubted their country's ability to stay in Africa.[10] In 1891, Minister Ferreira d'Almeida went even so far as to propose, in the Cortes, that Mozambique and Goa be sold and the proceeds used to develop Angola.[11] This suggestion would have been anathema to a man like Salazar, who framed the Constitution of 1933, the terms of which prevented the State from alienating any part of its colonial lands. The Portuguese-controlled territories in Africa and Asia ceased to be regarded as colonies and were granted the status of provinces subject to direct rule from the central government.

There is no point in trying to answer the question whether members of the now defunct government genuinely believed in Portugal's special mission in Africa, or whether the concept was merely a smoke screen for other policy goals that were never

officially disclosed.[12] What is striking, however, is the obvious dis-
crepancy between the declared ideology of action and the actual
results.

Internal pressures and foreign criticism led to policy re-
evaluations. In James Duffy's words, the Angolan uprising which
started in 1961 meant 'the death of the dream'.[13] Portugal was
faced with a choice of either accepting the reality of the situation
or paying a price which it could ill afford in the long run. Under
these conditions, revisions of the old legislation became inevitable.
Adriano Moreira, who was appointed Minister for Overseas
Affairs in 1961, carried out these revisions aimed at administrative and economic decentralisation. Realising that the policy of
African assimilation was a failure, the government abolished the
native statute thereby ending the legal distinction between 'natives'
and 'assimilados'. A free movement of goods among the various
national territories was to be permitted. In 1962 Moreira was dismissed due to strong opposition from within the government. His
reformist policies, challenging the old order, failed, as under the
existing dictatorial system their implementation was an impos-
sibility. The new legal status of Africans remained a dead letter
of the law.[14]

It seems now highly anachronistic, that throughout the 1960s
right up to mid-1970s Portugal held on to her African territories
while the other colonial powers divested themselves of theirs.

Salazar gave reasons for this policy in his speech 'The decision
to stay', delivered in 1966.[15] 'The African peoples' he said 'sought
to de-colonise themselves either by liberally receiving their independence from the nations that held sovereignty over them, or
by claiming it until they got it', and he pointed out that in
reality, due to conditions existing in most African territories,
neo-colonialism merely replaced colonialism.

In Salazar's mind there seemed to be no other alternative.
Consequently, it was better for Portugal to continue its presence
in Africa as the latter could only benefit through the Portuguese
civilising mission within the framework of the multi-racial
approach.[16]

African nationalists and Marxists of all denominations were
ready to concede that the only alternative to colonialism is neo-
colonialism, but in contrast to Salazar and his followers they
could not agree with his reason which lay behind this statement.
Apart from being a politician Salazar was also an economist. He
began his career as a Professor of political economy at Coimbra
and no matter how outmoded his economics may have been, he

certainly took economic factors into account when he decided to keep Portugal in Africa as a full-fledged colonial power.

The Rationale of Portuguese Colonialism

An analysis has now to be made of the economic factors governing the relations between Portugal and her African possessions— Angola and Mozambique. Although economic factors were of great importance, political considerations cannot be minimised or overlooked, but they are outside the scope of this paper.[17]

The historical patterns of the economic development of Portugal and her colonies and the resulting structural characteristics indicate, quite clearly, that the relationship between these economies was not typically colonial in the accepted sense. It differed significantly from the mature colonialism evolved by Britain, France and even Belgium. Mature colonialism possesses three distinctive features which relate to trade, capital investment and labour relations.

With regard to trade generally two features emerge: Firstly, in a given colony's foreign trade, imports from and exports to the mother country predominate; secondly, imports consist mainly of manufactured and capital goods produced by the metropolitan industry and exports consist chiefly of raw materials, the demand for which is often inelastic. The conditions of dependence are usually strengthened by various institutions controlling the exchange. Their activities centre on production, marketing, transportation and finance. Monopolistic or oligopolistic market structures are often created. Most of these characteristics of external trade are likely to continue after political independence is achieved.

Capital investment in a colony is, as a rule, determined by the trading interests of the mother country. Investment funds originate primarily in the metropolis and are used to finance productive activities which concentrate on the industrial enclaves producing for export. The output of such enclaves seldom includes manufactured commodities. Such capital investment is mostly in the hands of large companies whose activities are spread over a number of different countries. Frequently they form interlocking groups. The degree of dependence created by this form of investment is related to the proportion of the economy subject to the continuing control by the investor.

Independent countries defend themselves against exploitation by foreign capital by nationalising the expatriate assets. However the real issue at stake is not the ownership of the assets, but the control over them. In the context of a neo-colonial relationship, foreign control is likely to continue for a considerable time. The shortage of local managerial and technical skills makes the reliance on foreign assistance inevitable even if the expatriate assets are nationalised. Hence the new type of dependence assumes the form of 'technological' dependence based on 'intellectual' imports. It often overlaps with particular forms of trade or direct investment dependence but it may be present even when other forms of dependence are relatively low.[18]

Native labour is exploited in a more subtle way. The labour market is determined, among other things, by some inherited factors beyond the control of the legal system. Low wages (in a relative sense) are not only a reflection of low productivity but also of prevalently monopsonistic powers exercised by employers. Also there is usually an ample supply of labour which far exceeds the demand. Low productivity is mainly the result of the lack of training and this, in turn, is largely due to discrimination. As a rule, skilled jobs are reserved for the people from the mother country.

Metropolitan countries which were in the stage of mature colonialism viewed the transition to neo-colonialism without apprehension. A crude cost-benefit analysis, based on both economic and political data, indicated that the future gains would exceed losses. This relationship is typical of the economically more developed countries, on the one hand, and the less developed ones, on the other. Portugal did not fit that mould. Until recently she displayed numerous characteristics of a less developed economy vis-à-vis her underdeveloped colonies and, to this day, she remains one of the least developed countries of Europe. Her own position in the world economy determined the manner in which she exploited her colonial territories.

Let us consider the most essential features of Portugal's underdeveloped economy. Portugal still has a relatively low per capita income, placing her merely on the threshold of the more developed world. In 1970 with US.$660 per annum, she was ahead of only two countries in Europe: Yugoslavia and Albania.[19] Furthermore, Portugal's income distribution is far more uneven than that of many European countries. This is not an unequivocal indicator of lagging development,[20] but it gives some support to the hypothesis that the Portuguese colonial policy was dominated by the vested interests of the powerful upper income group.[21] It was achieved at the expense of a large segment of low-income population.

A study of income distribution in fourteen selected European countries, in the early 1950s carried out by Professor S. Kuznets, shows that Portugal's income distribution was far more unequal than was the case in most other countries dealt with in the survey.[22]

The proportion of economically active population in agriculture tends to be high in the less developed countries and in the case of Portugal it is one of the highest in western Europe. In terms of percentages, Portugal's economically active population in agriculture was 43·9 per cent in 1959, 33·6 per cent in 1965, and 27·6 per cent in 1972. Comparable percentages for 1972 for Germany, Canada, the U.S.A. and the U.K. were 7·5, 6·9, 4·2 and 3·1.[23]

Agriculture's contribution to Gross Domestic Product in 1960, 1965 and 1971 amounted to 23·4, 19·4 and 15·0 per cent respectively.[24] This shows that in the mid-1960s roughly one-third of the economically active population was needed in the agricultural sector to produce about one-fifth of the GDP. As a result of primitive agricultural methods and low productivity of labour in that sector, Portugal was forced to import substantial quantities of foodstuffs.

The relative underdevelopment of Portuguese economy is also revealed in her relationship with England, showing a classic example of semi-colonial dependence.[25] This commercial dependence began in the seventeenth century and the Methuen Treaty, concluded with Britain in 1703, had far-reaching consequences. During the nineteenth century Portugal failed to create an industrial economy and was unable to establish a complementarity between the metropolis and her colonies in the absence of exportable manufactures and capital for overseas investment.[26] Since the middle of the nineteenth century a rapidly growing external debt was a striking feature of Portuguese dependence. In recent years, Portugal continued to rely heavily on foreign sources of capital and her external trade consisted largely of imports of manufactures and exports of primary products. Her commercial relations continue to be dominated by Great Britain.

Being herself economically dependent on other countries, Portugal exerted an even more direct control over her overseas territories. A more thorough study of the economic aspects of Portugal's colonialism was seriously thwarted by the paucity of information. Probably only a fraction of the data known to the previous regime was made available to the public. Even these statistics were edited and presented in such a way that no meaningful conclusions could be arrived at on their basis. The tendency to camouflage goes back to the 1930s, when all goods brought to Africa on Portuguese ships were listed as Portuguese exports, irrespective of their place of manufacture. Since such imports were subject to comparatively low customs duties, foreign exporters were encouraged to trans-ship them via Lisbon.

The existence of the escudo zone payments system offered another opportunity to camouflage the true picture. This zone covered both Portugal and her overseas territories making it difficult to distinguish between the separate monetary flows. One could cite many more such instances.

Some light must now be thrown on the crucial elements of Portugal's colonial relationships with her African possessions in the field of trade, capital investment and labour.

Trade Relations
Portugal's position in the overseas trade of Angola and Mozambique was predominant.

TABLE 1

Angola and Mozambique: Percentage of trade accounted for by Portugal, 1938–1970

Year	Imports (cif)		Exports (fob)	
	Angola	Mozambique	Angola	Mozambique
1938	41	20	43	41
1948	47	29	24	39
1955	47	29	22	44
1960	47	28	24	48
1965	39	36	35	37
1970	35	28	34	38

Source: United Nations *Yearbooks of International Trade Statistics.*

Table 1 indicates that in 1938 roughly two-fifths of Angola's imports came from Portugal and a similar proportion of her exports was absorbed by the metropolitan market. In the case of Mozambique, the corresponding proportions were about one-fifth and two-fifths respectively. The proportions of imports from Portugal rose considerably during the war years, as most other trade outlets were blocked. In 1943 it reached nearly three-quarters of

Angola's total import value.[27] In the post-war years, Angola's imports from Portugal continued to be proportionately higher than her exports to the metropolis. The opposite trend was discernible in the case of Mozambique. In 1970, Portugal's position in the trade of Angola and Mozambique was still predominant. In the same year Angola's total imports from the metropolis were in the region of 35 per cent and her exports amounted to 34 per cent. In the case of Mozambique, the percentages were 28 and 38 respectively.

Exports from Portugal to her African territories included a large proportion of re-exports of manufactures and capital equipment from other countries. The origin of these goods was disguised by official statistics. Consequently the foreign trade pattern could not be considered as typical of a more developed country which would be in a position to produce most of these exports.

On the other hand, neither Angola nor Mozambique held a predominant position in Portugal's distribution of trade. (See Table 2)

TABLE 2

Portugal: Percentage of trade accounted for by Angola and Mozambique, 1938–1970

Year	Imports (fif)		Exports (fob)	
	Angola	Mozambique	Angola	Mozambique
1938	4·9	3·3	5·4	5·0
1948	2·6	4·4	11·7	10·1
1955	5·6	7·4	13·3	7·4
1960	5·4	7·0	13·1	8·9
1965	7·7	5·0	14·1	8·8
1970	9·6	4·2	12·5	9·0

Source: United Nations *Yearbooks of International Trade Statistics.*

Prior to the war, Portuguese imports from and exports to the two African territories were even less significant than they were in more recent years. In 1938, Angola and Mozambique accounted for only 8·2 per cent of the total value of Portugal's imports and 10·4 per cent of her exports, whereas in 1970 the corresponding percentages were 13·8 and 21·5.

If a distinction is made between the two African territories, it would become apparent that in the 1960s the percentage of Portuguese imports accounted for by Angola showed a rising trend and in the case of Mozambique a falling trend. On the other hand, throughout the period under review, the proportion of exports from both territories was far more stable.

It can be assumed that trade transactions were used by the metropolitan country to exploit her privileged position. The tariff structure favoured exports and re-exports from the metropolis. Furthermore, reserve funds for external transactions were first made available to the firms doing business with the mother country and only what remained could be used to pay for imports from other markets.[28] There were also hidden subsidies benefiting Portugal. This was true in the case of rough diamonds imported from Angola and in the case of sugar from Mozambique.

Nothwithstanding the small proportion which colonial trade occupied in the total value of Portuguese trade, the metropolitan Government, being committed to the support of the narrow commercial vested interests, was loath to lose its privileged position which was likely to happen should independence be granted to Angola and Mozambique. It is almost certain that both these colonies would have taken the first opportunity to substitute direct and cheaper imports from the industrialised countries for the expensive Portuguese re-exports of manufactures and capital goods, thereby frustrating any attempts on the part of Portugal to practise neo-colonialism. The policy of an underdeveloped metropolis to keep her African dependencies in a state of under-development, permitting primitive exploitation, could only continue under a colonial regime.

Capital Investment

Substantial foreign investment helped neo-colonialism. Portugal's position differed from that of the other colonial powers. Portuguese territories in Africa were always grossly undercapitalised and a considerable proportion of investment was made by foreign countries.

Professor S. H. Frankel estimated in 1936 that a large part of capital invested in the Portuguese colonies was supplied by the British investors.[29] For example, the Benguela Railway, completed in 1936-37 was largely built with British capital with some participation by German and Portuguese investors. This railroad was intended to serve the copper belts of the then Belgian Congo and Northern Rhodesia. Another early example of foreign investment based on the British and French capital was the Mozambique Company, active in the districts of Manica and Sofala.[30]

Prior to the Second World War the Portuguese methods of stimulating exports from the metropolis to the colonies were in direct conflict with the industrial development of the latter. For many years Portugal's economic policy was strongly mercantilist. For example, a regulation of 1936 prohibited the existence of identical industries in the metropolis and in the colonies. This led to a paradoxical situation. Angola, which at that time was producing considerable quantities of wheat, had to export her grain to Portugal and to import wheat flour, as she was prevented from operating flour mills. Mercantilism was practised, in its various forms, until recently.

It is still true that Angola and Mozambique are largely under-capitalised and that a considerable proportion of investment capital is of foreign origin. More recently, in addition to the British investments, a considerable amount of capital came from the U.S.A., South Africa and some European countries.

Prior to 1962, the Portuguese government was suspicious of and opposed to foreign investment. The change in policy was prompted by the heavy costs of counter-insurgency which Portugal had to bear. At the same time, Portugal was experiencing a deterioration in the long-standing pattern of trade deficits with countries outside the escudo zone. Added to that she suffered from a serious lag in productive capacity of her economy.[31] In 1964–65 investment laws were modified in order to create conditions favourable to foreign investors.[32] Foreign firms were allowed to transfer full profits abroad, whereas Portuguese firms could only remit one-fifth of their profits to the mother country. Soon the results became visible. Foreign capital investment rose from 10·5 per cent in 1962 to 26·7 per cent in 1966 of the total annual investment in Portugal alone. In 1969 out of 1·8 billion escudos invested in the escudo zone by foreign firms, 60 per cent of that amount went to the colonial territories.[33]

The Gulf Oil Corporation is the best example of massive American investment. Gulf Oil developed a major new field in Cabinda with a capital of some $150 to $250 million. Other American investors moved into extractive, capital-intensive exploitation of Angolan diamonds, sulphur and phosphates.[34]

On the other hand, American capital stayed out of the huge Cabora Bassa Dam project in Mozambique which was financed by the West German, French, British and South African interests. A very sizeable South African investment took place in the Kunene River Development project on the border of Angola and Namibia.[35]

G

As a result of the national emergency, Portugal was forced to accept the dreaded foreign neo-colonialism in the form of heavy capital investment, not only in the metropolis itself, but also within the borders of her African possessions. It is clear that the foreign capitalist is the main beneficiary of this neo-colonialism as he is in a better position to survive the surgery of independence. Portugal has to pay a price for her state of relative economic underdevelopment.

The Question of Labour

One of the pillars of the Portuguese colonial system was the exploitation of labour. Portugal relied on the direct method of forced labour. Also she relied on the indirect method of taxation in order to obtain supply of cheap labour. The most effective means, in the latter case, was the collection of the head tax in Angola, and the hut tax in Mozambique.[36]

Forced labour was used to provide manpower for plantation owners. A circular letter issued by the Governor of Angola in 1921 recommended that at least fifteen per cent of men perform work on plantations. The employers had to pay contractual wages.

Although the other colonial powers abandoned widespread use of forced labour, Portugal continued to take advantage of this form of modern slavery. The Forced Labour Convention of 1930 was ratified by Portugal only in 1956. But even then the Portuguese legislation preserved certain provisos which in fact violated the terms of the Convention. Forced labour was allowed to be used in both governmental and municipal public works.[37]

In 1954, in the Department of Native Affairs in Luanda (Angola) the number of 'contract labourers' was 379,000. A labourer had to work for three to four months each year for the colonial administration.[38]

The existing legislation did not permit private employers to use forced labour. In practice, the authorities often went beyond these legal limits. Compulsory cultivation schemes of cotton and castor oil plants served as a pretext to use this kind of labour. These schemes were undertaken by European planters who held concessions from the government.[39]

The institution of forced labour had a great impact on the African. It meant a separation from his family as well as a certain stigma. Consequently the acceptance of low wage rates offered by private employers was preferable. It is, therefore, wrong to presume that these workers responded to normal economic incentives; they were rather victims of reckless recruiters.[40]

In the post-war years the practice of recruitment was still widespread. Restrictions were placed on the movements of Africans who could not leave the areas of their domicile unless they concluded a service contract through a recruiter. In Angola these restrictions were in operation till the end of 1956. In Mozambique recruiting was done on a large scale to satisfy the South African and Rhodesian demand for labour.[41]

The system, as outlined above, permitted widespread exploitation of labour giving rise to either additional tax revenue accruing to the government through the extensive use of forced labour,[42] or to abnormal profit rates in the case of private entrepreneurs through the various forms of illegal employment.

Recent Developments

Until fairly recently Portugal and her colonies created the impression of a closed system, impervious to the impact of the 'winds of change' blowing from outside with increasing force. But this image of colonial exploitation of underdeveloped Angola and Mozambique by their economically and politically backward 'master' had to change drastically when the liberation wars started. The acceleration of economic growth in the African territories in the 1960s can be attributed to a number of factors. By far the most important were major mineral discoveries in Angola which by the mid-1960s began to contribute greatly to the Angolan economy. Needless to say, the opportunities created by these discoveries, coupled with the new investment laws, encouraged the inflow of capital on an unprecedented scale.

Under the impact of the unleashed economic forces, some of the most anachronistic mercantilist restrictions had to be modified, a move which formed part of Moreira's reforms initiated in 1961. Angola and Mozambique were permitted to industrialise even in the areas where Portugal herself was developing, namely in the fields of light engineering, textile, clothing and footwear industries.

In the post-World War II years, Portugal encouraged a policy of assimilation in her African possessions, the failure of which provoked criticisms from abroad. Portugal decided instead on a new policy of intensified colonisation by white settlers from the mother country. Due to this policy, by 1970, the permanently settled white population of Angola reached the mark of 350,000, while the total African population was over five million.[43]

In Mozambique the ratio between the whites and the blacks was 150,000 to 8 million.

All these events, involving resource discoveries, influx of capital and immigration, point to an unprecedented acceleration of the development process in the African territories with Angola in the forefront. Between 1969 and 1972 Angola's industrial production doubled, rising from just over 6,000 million to 12,000 million escudos.[44]

In Portugal, meanwhile, priority was given to war effort and the development in Africa. In the late 1960s the cost of defence and security reached 45 per cent of total government expenditure or 9 per cent of national income.[45] The need for new sources of revenue led to substantial tax increases and heavy reliance on foreign credits. Portugal's foreign debt rose from 1,839 million escudos in 1961 to 8,665 million escudos in 1969.[46]

Another factor which adversely affected the economy was an increase in emigration. Yearly over 170,000 migrants were leaving for France, Holland, Belgium, Switzerland, West Germany etc., in search of employment.[47] Thousands of families emigrated not only to escape poverty, but also to protect their sons from a lengthy military service.[48]

A prolonged war was fought at the expense of the nation's social services, development and the depopulation of the country which already had a low natural rate of population growth.

General Spinola, whose book *Portugal and the Future* was published in February 1974, expressed fears that Portuguese dictatorship and its policies propelled the nation towards inevitable disaster.[49]

Conclusions

There are few people in today's Portugal who do not agree that the country was bled white for the sake of colonial interests. The general feeling is that the ruling group failed to redistribute economic gains more equitably and to improve the welfare of the people both in the metropolis and in Africa. In the light of recent events, it is becoming more and more apparent to all, that Portugal's African possessions were not profitable to the nation as a whole.[50] Gains from African territories merely benefited small groups of businessmen and settlers. Ending the wars and granting independence to the colonies became a logical necessity. Even if a complete economic break with the African territories takes place, the long term benefits will outweigh the losses. The diversion of material and human resources from the war effort to the development of domestic economy will now become possible. On the other hand, Angola and Mozambique will undoubtedly avail themselves of international aid from which they were previously excluded.

Portugal's prolonged colonial presence in Africa served merely the fractional interests. The nation itself was a pawn in the hands of the dictatorial regime which identified its own interests with those of the small group of exploiters.

This situation explains Portugal's reluctance to relinquish her African territories. Having never reached the stage of a 'mature colonial power' she was unable to adopt a more sophisticated neo-colonial method of economic and political control over the 'liberated' territories. This anachronistic approach could not have continued indefinitely. The untenable position in which the regime found itself, hastened its demise in April 1974. What may have appeared rational to the ruling elite became obviously irrational in the eyes of the majority of the nation.

NOTES

1. J. Duffy, *Portuguese Africa*, (Cambridge, Massachusetts: Harvard University Press, 1959) pp. 226–234).
2. José de Macedo, *Autonomia de Angola*, 1910; cited by R. J. Hammond in Portugal and Africa 1815–1910, (Stanford, California: Stanford University Press, 1966) p. 296.
3. R. J. Hammond, *op. cit.*, pp. 294–296.
4. A. K. Smith, 'António Salazar and the Reversal of Portuguese Colonial Policy', *Journal of African History*, Vol. XV, 4, 1974, p. 657.
5. Costa, who occupied the posts of governor of Moçambique District in 1896, governor of Benguela in 1903, and governor general of Angola in 1906, submitted a report entitled 'Estudos sobre a administração civil das provincias ultramarina' to the Colonial Congress of 1901. It included the details of the proposed colonial organisation. J. Duffy, *op. cit.*, pp. 235 and 242).
6. A. K. Smith, *loc. cit.*, pp. 658–661.
7. *Ibid.*, p. 666.
8. *Ibid.*, pp. 662–663.
9. James Duffy, *op. cit.*, p. 270.
10. R. J. Hammond, *op. cit.*, p. 202.
11. *Ibid.*, p .185.
12. It is possible that a large segment of the Portuguese society genuinely believed in that 'myth'.
13. James Duffy, *Portugal in Africa* (Harmondsworth, Middlesex: Penguin Books Ltd., 1962) p. 210.
14. R. H. Chilcote, *Portuguese Africa* (Englewood Cliffs, N. J.: Prentice-Hall, Inc., 1967) pp. 17–18.

15. António de Oliveira Salazar, *The Decision to Stay* (Lisbon: Secretariado Nacional da Informacão, 1966).
16. *Ibid.*
17. It is highly questionable whether any dictatorial government would agree to the granting of political freedom to any part of a country under its rule, particularly if that territory was of some economic importance and had a large population. It was recognised that should such independence be granted, the rest of the population would feel that it too had an equal right to similar freedom.
18. W. Minter, *Imperial Network and External Dependency: The Case of Angola*, (Beverly Hills/London: Sage Publications, 1972) p. 21.
19. *World Bank Atlas*, 1972.
20. Professor Kuznets' opinion that the size distribution of income remains more unequal in the less developed than in the more developed countries has been challenged but not convincingly refuted. (See: S Kuznets, *Modern Economic Growth*, London: Yale University Press, 1966, pp. 424–25). Kuznets' hypothesis has been based on overall measures of inequality but a recent analysis of the trends in the income shares of the different deciles seems to put in doubt the evidence provided by overall co-efficients. (See: P. Robert, 'Income Distribution: A Time-Series and a Cross Section Study', *The Economic Journal* 84/335/September 1974, pp. 629–35).
21. For the description and analysis of the mechanisms, active at the informal level, through which the inordinate influence of powerful economic groups was exercised in the Portuguese economy, see: Harry M. Makler's 'The Portuguese Industrial Elite and its Corporate Relations: A Study of Compartmentalization in an Authoritarian Regime' (*Economic Development and Cultural Change*, vol. 24, number 3, April, 1976, pp. 495–52.
22. The overall measures used by Kuznets include a measure of inequality and concentration ratio. (See: S. Kuznets 'Quantitative Aspects of the Economic Growth of Nations': VIII Distribution of Income by Size', *Economic Development and Cultural Change* 11/2/, Part II, 1963).
23. OECD Labour Force Statistics 1961–1972 (Paris, 1974).
24. OECD National Accounts Statistics 1960–1971.
25. W. Winter *op. cit.*, p. 6.
26. J. O'Brien, 'Portugal in Africa: A Dying Imperialism' *Monthly Review*, May 1974, p. 21.
27. The war period data is excluded from the tables as being abnormal.
28. A. K. Smith, *loc. cit.*, p. 666.
29. S. H. Frankel, *Capital Investment in Africa* (London: Oxford University Press, 1938) p. 204.
30. Portugal held only ten per cent of the shares. The Company's charter expired in 1942.
31. M. A. El-Khawas, 'Foreign Economic Involvement in Angola and Mozambique' *Issue* 4(2), Summer 1974, p. 21.
32. J. A. Marcum, *Portugal and Africa: The Politics of Indifference* (Syracuse: Syracuse University, 1972) p. 10.
33. Eduardo de Sousa Ferreira, *Portuguese Colonialism from South Africa to Europe* (Freiburg: Aktion Dritte Welt, 1972) p. 55.
34. J. A. Marcum, *op. cit.*, p. 10–11.
35. *Ibid.*, p. 36–37.

36. The imposition of a tax creates a need for money income which has to be earned.
37. International Labour Office, African Labour Survey (Geneva, 1962) pp. 299–300.
38. Americo Boavida, Angola: *Five Centuries of Portuguese Exploitation,* (Richmond, B.C.: LSM Information Center, 1972) p. 5.
39. ILO, *op. cit.,* p. 300.
40. J. O'Brien, *loc. cit.,* p. 28.
41. ILO, *op. cit.,* p. 312–13.
42. The obligation to supply personal services in the form of labour can be considered as a tax.
43. Sources of information on the size of the white population of Angola are not consistent. The figure varies from 350,000 to 500,000.
44. Colin Legum, *Africa Contemporary Record* (London: Rex Collings, 1973) B480.
45. *Africa South of the Sahara* (London: Europa Publications Ltd., 1974) p. 139.
46. Eduardo de Sousa Ferreira, *op. cit.,* p. 51.
47. J. A. Marcum, *op. cit.,* p. 36.
48. 'Change in Portugal', *The Economist,* May 4, 1974, p. 35.
49. *Ibid.*
50. An analysis based on Portugal's Balance of Payments Statements with the African territories, in recent years, shows that the total surplus of the metropolis ranged between one and three per cent of national income, an insignificant proportion if compared with the magnitude of the metropolitan war expenditure alone.

11

THE FISCAL ROLE OF THE MARKETING BOARDS IN NIGERIAN ECONOMIC DEVELOPMENT, 1947-61*

G. K. Helleiner

Nigeria's Marketing Boards, are statutory monopsonies handling Nigeria's major agricultural exports. They had their origins in wartime arrangements for the orderly marketing of West African produce and the protection of United Kingdom supplies of raw materials. After the war they assumed the responsibility for the stabilisation of producer prices and the development of the producing industries. The interpretation and implementation of the Marketing Boards' responsibility for stabilisation have received a great deal of attention from the economics profession. It is not, however, the most important aspect of Nigerian Marketing Board practices.

Stabilisation, of whatever sort, has never constituted the sole responsibility of the Nigerian Marketing Boards. That it has occupied so much of economists' attention indicates more about the main preoccupations of the economics profession in the immediate post-war years than it does about its importance to the Nigerian economy. Growth should always have carried greater weight in Nigerian policy formation than stability, and there exists no conclusive evidence that the two are correlated. With the recent general revival of professional interest in the more 'classical' problems of economic growth it seems particularly appropriate that the emphasis, as far as discussion of Nigerian (and other) Marketing Boards is concerned, should now be properly placed. The Marketing Boards have been and continue to be an extremely effective (though, of course, far from the only) instrument for the mobilisation of savings for government-sponsored economic development.[2]

*Reprinted by permission from *The Economic Journal*, Vol. 74, No. 3, (1964).

They have had, since their very inception, considerable powers to accumulate and expend funds earned from their trading operations for development purposes. But the Marketing Boards have long since exceeded the limits originally set for their activities in this area. Within the last few years the Regional Governments of the Federation have stated quite explicitly that the Marketing Boards are an important source of revenues for their development budgets.

This paper will discuss the experience of the Nigerian Marketing Boards since their establishment with respect to the accumulation and disposal of the vast trading surpluses.

The Accumulation of the Trading Surpluses

It is widely recognised that the period 1947-54 was one during which Nigeria's Marketing Boards acquired enormous reserves. Table I shows the total accumulations of the four Nigerian Commodity Marketing Boards until their dissolution in 1954.

TABLE I

Total Accumulation by Nigerian Commodity Marketing Boards, 1947–54
(£ thousands)

	Cocoa	Palm oil	Palm kernels	Ground nuts	Cotton	Total
Initial reserves	8,896·6*	11,457·0†		4,487·8†	250·0‡	25,091·0‖
Net trading surplus§	33,797·4	2,269·7	18,790·8	22,483·6	6,968·6	84,310·1
Excess of other income over expenditures‖	3,349·3	2,497·3		3,563·9	1,102·7	10,513·2
	46,043·3	35,014·8		30,535·3	8·321·3	119,914·7

Sources: Annual Reports of Nigerian Marketing Boards.

*Reserves accumulated in respect of Nigerian cocoa by West African Produce Control Board before 1947 and turned over to the Nigeria Cocoa Marketing Board upon its creation in 1947.

†Reserves accumulated in respect of Nigerian produce by West African Produce Control Board in 1947–49 period and turned over to the Nigeria Oil Palm Produce Marketing Board and the Nigeria Groundnut Marketing Board upon their creation in 1949.

‡Grant from U.K. Raw Cotton Commission to the Nigeria Cotton Marketing Board in compensation for previous underpayments to Nigerian cotton producers upon its creation in 1949.

§Cocoa: 1947/48 to 1953/54 inclusive; palm oil and palm kernels: 1949–54 inclusive; groundnuts and cotton: 1949/50 to 1953/54 inclusive. Calculated from the original accounts of the Marketing Boards as follows: sales at f.o.b. prices less export duties, value of purchases, total expenses and decrease in stocks. The resulting figures for trading surpluses sometimes differ from those stated in the accounts.

‖Calculated from the original accounts of the Marketing Boards. Primarily interest on reserves held in U.K. securities. The figure for groundnuts includes trading surpluses earned on other minor commodities under the jurisdiction and control of the Nigeria Groundnut Marketing Board (benniseed, sunflower seed, soya beans, groundnut oil and groundnut cake); that for cotton includes development premium paid by the U.K. Raw Cotton Commission.

By 1954 nearly £120 million had been mobilised by these four Boards, over £100 million (net) of which[3] had been realised as 'trading profits' during this seven-year period alone. (For comparative purposes it may be worth observing that the two principal sources of government tax revenue at this time each earned less over the same seven-year period. Between 1947/48 and 1953/54 import duties accounted for a total of only £93·5 million, whereas export duties totalled only £56·7 million of revenues.)

The largest trading surpluses had been realised by the Cocoa Marketing Board, but all four had piled up substantial reserves. Only palm-oil producers, who received over £6·9 million in subsidies in 1953 and 1954 received any stabilisation benefits, in the form of price supports in lean years, during this period; and even these substantial subsidies could not alter the fact that they had already contributed far larger amounts to the Oil Palm Produce Marketing Board's reserves.

These accumulations were a not inconsiderable share of the total earnings on exported produce which could have been distributed to Nigerian peasant producers or what I have called 'potential producer income.' Nor were they the only levy on this potential producer income. Further amounts were withheld in the form of export duties and, from 1953 on, Regional produce sales taxes, which were levied as specific duties upon each ton of produce sold to a Marketing Board. Table II summarises these government withdrawals from the Marketing Board agricultural sector during this and the subsequent period.

It can be seen that during the 1947/54 period over 42 per cent of potential producer income earned from cotton, 40 per cent of that from groundnuts, over 39 per cent of that from cocoa, over 29 per cent of that from palm kernels and 17 per cent of that from palm oil were withheld by the Government through taxes and Marketing Board trading surpluses. By far the greatest share of this total in each case except that of palm oil, in respect of which, as has been seen, substatial trading losses were incurred in 1953 and 1954, was made up of Marketing Board trading surpluses. In peak years individual Marketing Boards alone withheld over 40, 50, and even 66 per cent of potential incomes of producers of particular crops.

Less well known is the Nigerian Marketing Board experience since 1954. With the constitutional revisions of that year, which involved the devolution of considerable powers to the Regional Governments, there came a reorganisation of Marketing Board structure as well. Henceforth, instead of being organised on a nation-wide commodity basis, they conducted their operations on a Regional cross-commodity basis. Each Regional Marketing Board handled all the relevant exportable produce of its region of jurisdiction. Effectively, this meant that the Eastern Region Marketing Board did the bulk of its business in palm oil and palm kernels, the Northern Region in groundnuts and cotton and the Western Region in cocoa and palm kernels. These were not the only commodities handled by the Marketing Boards, but the remainder were of small relative importance. The Regional Marketing Boards took over the assets of the former Commodity Marketing Boards, their distribution being determined by the Region of origin of the products on which the surpluses had been earned. As can be seen in Table III, this meant that the Eastern Region, dependent upon palm produce, came off very poorly, whereas the cocoa-producing Western Region received close to half the redistributed unspent total of £87 million. This table also shows clearly the pattern of Regional concentration in agricultural export production.

The year 1954, which divides Nigerian Marketing Board history into two separate periods distinguished by different institutional arrangements, also marks the end of a period of export prosperity and the beginning of a period of declining barter terms of trade.

No longer was a large trading surplus to be relied upon year after year simply by the holding of the producer price line as commodity prices followed their standard post-war upward course; for world primary product market conditions had by now changed significantly in character. The usual instability of Nigerian export prices continued as before, but the price fluctuations were now about a steady or even declining trend.

Given that Nigeria's Marketing Boards began the period appa-

TABLE II

Government Withdrawals from Major Components of the Marketing Board Controlled Agricultural Export Sector in Nigeria, 1947-62

	Export duties		Marketing Board Trading Surplus		Produce purchase tax		Total withdrawals, £000's	Potential producer income, £000's	Total withdrawals as a % of potential producer income
	£000's	% of potential producer income	£000's	% of potential producer income	£000's	% of potential producer income			
Cocoa									
1947/48 to 1953/54	27,565	17·6	33,797	21·6	390	0·2	61,752	165,829	39·4
1954/55 to 1961/62	36,917	17·9	12,841	6·2	4,163	2·0	53,920	206,216	26·1
Total	64,481	17·8	46,638	12·8	4,553	1·3	115,672	363,046	31·9
Groundnuts									
1947/48 to 1953/54	11,329	11·5	27,797	28·1	425	0·4	39,549	98,776	40·0
1954/55 to 1960/61	20,825	14·0	-2,053	-1·4	3,574	2·4	22,346	149,660	14·9
Total	32,154	12·9	25,743	10·4	3,998	1·6	61,895	248,436	24·9
Palm Kernels									
1947-54	11,872	9·4	25,096	19·9	—	—	36,968	126,438	29·2
1955-61	15,125	13·1	11,883	10·3	4,327	3·7	31,335	116,558	27·1
Total	26,997	11·1	36,978	15·2	4,327	1·8	68,303	242,996	28·1
Palm Oil									
1947-54	7,356	9·0	6,544	8·0	—	—	13,899	81,608	17·0
1955-61	9,646	13·3	4,305	5·9	4,592	6·3	18,543	72,421	25·6
Total	17,002	11·0	10,849	7·0	4,592	3·0	32,442	154,028	21·0
Cotton									
1949/50 to 1953/54	2,687	11·7	6,969	30·3	70	0·3	9,726	23,014	42·3
1954/55 to 1960/61	5,771	13·5	-1,696	-4·0	722	1·7	4,796	42,753	11·2
Total	8,458	12·9	5,272	8·0	792	1·2	14,522	65,767	22·1

TABLE III

Total Transfer of Assets from Nigerian Commodity Marketing Boards to
Nigerian Regional Marketing Boards*
(£ thousands)

Marketing Board	Eastern Region	Northern Region	Western Region	Total†
Cocoa	176·1	135·5	32,625·1	32,936·7
Oil palm produce	11,248·4	484·5	10,199·0	21,931·9
Groundnut	39·6	24,722·6	—	24,762·2
Cotton	—	7,309·2‡	73·0	7,382·2
	11,464·1	32,651·8	42,897·2	87,013·0

Sources: Annual Reports of the Marketing Boards.

*These transfers were not all made at the same time. The final allocations were not resolved for several years.

†Excluding Southern Cameroons.

‡Including development premia from the liquidation of the U.K. Raw Cotton Commission of £803·1 thousands.

rently still pursuing stablisation as their principal objectives, it is noteworthy that they nevertheless continued, in the aggregate, to accumulate trading surpluses. Admittedly these accumulations were now much smaller in magnitude. Still, between 1954 and year-end of 1961, another £21·8 million was added to the Marketing Boards' resources through their trading activities. Although this amount is less than one-quarter the size of the aggregate trading profits of the previous seven years, it remains a sizeable sum. Earnings on the reserves accumulated earlier produced a net surplus on other operations of another £9·5 million (see Table IV).

Aggregation of Marketing Board data for this period conceals, however, important differences between the experiences of individual Marketing Boards. One of the Marketing Boards, that handling the produce of the Northern Region, actually ran a net deficit on its trading operations. Indeed it ran a net overall deficit as well, in spite of its earnings on assets during this period. From 1954 until 1961 this Marketing Board paid to agricultural producers £3·2 million[5] more than it earned from the sales of their produce. Moreover, these subsidies were paid both in respect of groundnut and cotton production.

The greatest trading surpluses over the 1954–61 period were earned by the Western Region Marketing Board, which, as was noted earlier, was already the wealthiest at the outset of the period. Over £14·3 million were withheld from Western Region producers, £9·7 million of which came from cocoa production. The remaining £4·6 million came from palm-kernel producers, who contributed in the East and West together over £10·7 million to total Marketing Board reserves. The Western Region Marketing Board's wealth also produced net income of another £5·3 million, mainly from interest on the securities held in its investment portfolio.

The proportions of Nigerian export producers' potential income which were withheld during the latter period were, in general, of course, rather smaller than they had been between 1947 and 1954. Palm oil was again the only exception to this rule. The most dramatic reductions in this proportion were those for groundnuts—from 40 to 14·9 per cent, and for cotton—from 42·3 to 11·2 per cent. (These percentages are still positive because of the withholding of export duties and produce sales taxes, which more than offset the Marketing Board trading losses.) These products are produced in the Northern Region, where the Marketing Board had not yet abandoned its policy of attempting to stabilise producer prices, and had therefore, as has been seen, actually incurred trading deficits. There was also a substantial drop in the share of cocoa producers' potential income which was withdrawn—from 39·4 to 26·1 per cent. Export duties, in all cases, now not only removed a larger proportion of potential producer income than previously but also withheld a larger share than did the Marketing Boards in the form of trading surpluses. The higher export duties were the result of the shift from specific to *ad valorem* duties at the end of 1950 and the introduction of a progressive rate, increasing with the world price, together with a higher base rate, a few months later. Produce purchase taxes on groundnuts and cotton obviously also withheld greater shares of potential producer income than did the Marketing Boards (which ran deficits). What is notable is that in the Eastern and Western Regions the governments were able to continue the withdrawal of over 25 per cent of total export producers' income even in a period of stagnant or deteriorating world export markets.

Some of the tax burden upon cocoa farmers was eased by the increasing productivity achieved through the use of insecticides during these years; but producers of palm oil and palm kernels enjoyed no such improvements and, in fact, suffered from steadily declining real incomes from 1954 onwards. While Marketing Board trading surpluses were no longer at this time the most important means of withholding income from export producers, it is with them that this paper remains primarily concerned.

TABLE IV
Total Accumulation by Nigerian Regional Marketing Boards, 1954–61
(£ thousands)

	Eastern Region	Northern Region	Western Region	Total
Transfer from Commodity Marketing Boards	11,464·1	32,651·8	42,897·2	87,013·1
Net Trading Surplus*†	10,736·2‡	− 3,202·7	14,303·9‖	21,837·1
Excess of other income over expenditure*§	1,718·9	2,451·2	5,349·1	9,519·2
Total	23,919·2	31,900·3	62,550·2	118,369·4

Sources: Annual Reports of the Marketing Boards.

*Eastern Region: 1955/61 inclusive; Northern Region: 1954/55 to 1960–61 inclusive; Western Region: 1954/55 to 1960/61 inclusive.

†Calculated in the same way as Table I.

‡Treatment of the produce sales tax has been altered so as to make the Eastern Region's trading results comparable with those of the other Regions.

§Calculated in the same way as Table I. Principally interest earned on reserves. Includes trading results in minor commodities.

‖This figure incorporates corrected trading results for year 1960/61, which were furnished by the Western Region Marketing Board. The originally published accounts were incorrect.

The Evolution of Official Attitudes Towards Trading Surpluses

Why were these trading surpluses earned? Through consideration of policy statements over the entire post-war period one can trace a steady evolution of official attitudes towards the role of the Marketing Boards in development. Prior to Regionalisation the accumulation of large reserves was primarily fortuitous and unpremeditated. It was at that time sincerely intended by the governmental authorities that they should be used for stabilising purposes. From 1954 onwards the earning of trading surpluses became, more and more, a matter of conscious design. The surpluses were now to be used for the intensified development effort. Only in Northern Nigeria has this change of attitude not quite been completed.

Nigerian Marketing Boards have borne a degree of responsibility for the support of research and development ever since their formation. At the time of its inception in 1947 the Nigeria Cocoa Marketing Board was assigned the duty 'to assist in the development by all possible means of the cocoa industry of Nigeria for the benefit and prosperity of the producers.' Similar provisions were included in the ordinances which set up the other three Nigerian Marketing Boards two years later. The funds required for the performance of these duties were clearly to be provided by the Marketing Boards themselves.

Whereas the intention to use reserves accumulated through trading operations for purposes other than stabilisation was thus acknowledged from the outset, these purposes clearly did not constitute at that time a first priority claim upon them:

> The first charge on the [Groundnut Marketing] Board's funds must be for working capital to finance its purchases of groundnuts. . . . Price stabilisation must always constitute the primary claim on the Board's actual and prospective resources after the critical requirements of working capital have been met.[7]

Almost identical statements may be drawn from the early Annual Reports of the Nigeria Cocoa and Oil Palm Produce Marketing Boards.[8] Only after working capital needs and stabilisation reserves had been provided for was significant consideration to be given to research and development allocations. This principle was embodied in a rule which the Groundnut and Oil Palm Produce Marketing Boards (and after 1951, the Cocoa Board as well) adopted to govern the distribution of whatever trading surpluses they might earn. After setting aside the estimated requirements for working capital the remainder was always to be allocated, on a product-by-product basis, in the following proportions: 70 per cent—to be retained for stabilisation purposes; 22½ per cent—to be allocated to development; 7½ per cent—to be expended upon research.

The development allocations were to be turned over in the form of grants to the three Regional Production Development Boards which had been set up at the same time as the Marketing Boards to further 'the development of the producing industries and . . . the economic benefit and prosperity of the producers and the areas of production.'[9] The size of the grant to each Region's Production Development Board was to be determined by the share which the Region in question had contributed to the total sales of the product on which the trading surplus had been earned.

The Nigeria Cotton Marketing Board differed from the others in that it did not adopt the '70–22½–7½' formula and seemed to regard the accumulation of development funds for its programme of doubling the exportable surplus of Nigerian cotton as of equal importance to its stabilisation responsibilities.

> The keynote of the [Cotton Marketing] Board's present policy is the accumulation of funds during the present (1949–50) period of high selling prices. These reserves are the best guarantee of the Board's ability to carry out its main objects of giving maximum price to the producer [sic] and at the same time contributing to the development of the cotton-growing industry and areas.[10]

Even the Cotton Marketing Board, however, was far from giving prime emphasis to development.

There can be little question, then, that the huge trading surpluses earned in the first few years of the Marketing Boards' operations were, with the possible exception of those earned on trading in cotton, not primarily or originally intended to be used for purposes other than stabilisation.

The accumulation of these reserves was, in large part, accidental. There could have been no means of predicting the tremendous commodity price increases of the post-war period or, more particularly, the devaluation of sterling or the outbreak of the Korean War. And, even if there had been, there was considerable question as to whether the raising of producer prices to any higher levels would, in fact, have benefited them or, with the existing inelasticities of food supplies and shipping space for the transport of imports, merely produced price inflation. In any case, there remained in the background the fear of a post-war collapse which had, after all, been nearly universally predicted. The reserves were earned, therefore, from peculiarly favourable world market conditions coupled, perhaps inevitably, with conservative producer price policies.

Since, according to the prescribed formula to which rigid adherence was given, 70 per cent of these accumulating reserves were to be retained for stabilisation purposes, inordinately high stabilisation reserves were soon accumulated. By the year-end of 1954 Nigerian Marketing Boards held upwards of £66 million of investments in the United Kingdom which were specifically allocated to the provision of 'economic security' to the farmers. As Marketing Board reserves mounted, some modifications to the system of distribution of trading surpluses were introduced. In order to enable the Production Development Boards to plan their

H

programmes more effectively the Oil Palm Produce Marketing Board guaranteed them a minimum allocation of £800,000 for each of the years 1950–55, thus abandoning in principle the '70–22½–7½' formula. In order to fulfil this obligation during its two years of trading losses it was necessary actually to reduce reserves which were not originally to be employed for development purposes at all. This may be said to mark a major breach in the idea that the Marketing Board's assets were purely stabilisation reserves. The Groundnut Marketing Board made a similar guarantee of £500,000 per annum for each of the seasons 1950/51 to 1954/55, but at no time was this guaranteed minimum greater than 22½ per cent of that year's trading surplus. More significantly, perhaps, the Marketing Boards undertook to lend to the Central Government 'a sum which they can be reasonably certain they will not require within the next fifteen years'[11]—ultimately placed at £14 million.

Reserves of the size which had been accumulated by 1954 constituted a very great temptation to the Regional Governments, which had been granted vastly increased responsibility for the promotion of economic development following the constitutional revisions of 1954. The World Bank Mission estimated that liquid reserves of £25 million were adequate for the fulfilment of the stablilisation responsibility and recommended that the remaining surplus (or 'second line reserves') be 'loaned on a long-term basis to government for development purposes.'[12] At the same time it recommended that no further stabilisation reserves be accumulated.

The World Bank was taken at its word—and considerably more than its word! But a further recommendation to the effect that the Marketing Boards henceforth confine themselves to the stabilisation of producer prices and the improvement of quality it was found more convenient to ignore. Having seen, semi-accidentally, the enormous potential for the raising of revenues which the price-fixing function of the Marketing Boards offers, first the Western Region, and then the Eastern Region as well, began consciously to take advantage of it for development purposes. Both the Western and the Eastern Region Marketing Boards continued to earn trading surpluses after 1954 which cannot reasonably be regarded as accidental or intended for stabilisation.

The altered views of the Regional Governments with respect to the primary functions of the Marketing Boards can be seen in their planning documents. The Western Region's 1955–60

development plan announced final abandonment of the '70–
$22\frac{1}{2}$–$7\frac{1}{2}$' formula for distribution of the Western Board's trading
surpluses, offered a strong defence of the Marketing Board's right
to contribute to development, and provided for £20 million in
loans and grants to come from the Board for the use of the
Regional Government during the plan. This was about two-thirds
of the total capital funds expected and nearly 20 per cent of the
total capital and current revenues anticipated for the planning
period.[13] The 1960–65 Western Region plan called for a further
contribution of £21 million from the Western Region Marketing
Board over the course of the five-year period;[14] and, with over
£14·5 million already having been granted under the former plan,
another £10 million was called for in the 1962–68 plan. In the
latter it is stated boldly that, 'In the public sector, the Marketing
Board is the main source of savings for the improvement of
agriculture and allied industries and the provision of social
services.'[15] The Marketing Board's contribution is, in fact, 40 per
cent of the total available domestic finance for the capital programme. By this time these savings could no longer refer merely
to the running down of previously acquired assets. It was now
obviously intended to run trading surpluses to finance the
Regional Government's programme. The Western Region Marketing Board had by now become, apart from its other responsibilities, a fiscal arm of the Western Nigerian Government. This
emphasis upon using the Board as a supplier of savings for
development purposes has, incidentally, been very much under-
played by the Annual Reports of the Board itself; this seems to
indicate that the Board is somewhat sensitive to producer com-
plaints on the matter.

The operations of the Eastern Regional Marketing Board were
evolving in much the same manner during this period, although
the amounts which it now accumulated from trading surpluses
were somewhat smaller than those piled up in the West. To be
fair, an allowance should be made for the fact that the Eastern
Region Marketing Board began with by far the lowest reserves;
but it also had the smallest need for them—with respect both
to working capital requirements and to stabilisation reserves.

The Eastern Region's development programme for 1958–62
already showed that the Marketing Board was expected to contribute £5 million towards the construction of the new University
of Nigeria at Nsukka, and a further £500,000 to the Eastern
Region Development Corporation.[16] The current (1962–68) plan
lists not only the Marketing Board reserves but also 'Marketing

Board's earnings in the Plan period'[17] as a source of finance. Altogether, the Marketing Board's contribution to the present plan is to be £13·6 million, a large share of total available domestic resources for the capital programme. Thus, the Eastern Region Government is also employing the Marketing Board as a revenue raiser.

By 1962 even the Northern Region Government was consciously employing the Northern Nigeria Marketing Board as an important source of revenues for its development effort, though in a much modified fashion. That it was the Northern Regional Marketing Board which had formerly taken its stabilisation responsibility most seriously and had consequently been the weakest accumulator of reserves is reflected in its aggregate trading losses and its policy statements. As late as 1958 it was still saying that, 'The main object of establishing Marketing Boards was to ensure stable prices for produce.'[18] Subsequent Annual Reports modified this approach, emphasising that stabilisation constituted only 'one of the principal objects'[19] of the Board. By 1962, however, the Northern Nigerian Government had announced its intention of 'relieving the Board of its liability for subsidising the producer prices of crops in lean years, and fixing producer prices annually at such a level in relation to world prices as to anticipate a surplus on the year's operation to cover operating costs.'[20] All of the Northern Nigeria Marketing Board's reserves above and beyond its needs for working capital (about £6 million) are to be mobilised for the use of its proposed 'Development Bank.' Even with the explicit abandonment of year-to-year stabilisation, the Northern Nigeria Marketing Board remains the only one which has at no time stated its intention of running current trading surpluses for the purpose of contributing to regional economic development. Government attitudes in the Northern Region, in this as in most other matters, have been more conservative than those in the Eastern and Western Regions, where the Marketing Boards had abandoned their role as trustees for the farmers and assumed that of tax collector in the mid-1950s.

The Disposal of the Marketing Board Trading Surpluses

How were the vast reserves accumulated by Nigeria's Marketing Boards ultimately employed? During the period before their Regionalisation, as has been seen, the Marketing Boards held the bulk of them as stabilisation reserves in the form of United

Kingdom and Commonwealth securities. Some of their profits, however, were spent upon or reserved for research and economic development. As has been seen, this was in keeping with announced policy.

By year-end of 1954 (see Table V) over £23 million had been granted to the Regional Production Development Boards. With the final allocation of the dissolved Commodity Marketing Boards' assets, their total contribution to the Production Development Boards reached £24,666,700. The latter Boards were not able to spend these amounts as quickly as they were received, and there-fore accumulated substantial reserves of United Kingdom securities themselves. The amounts which were spent or lent until the mid-1950s were concentrated in agricultural development projects (including government-owned plantations in the Eastern and Western Regions), small-scale processing of agricultural produce both for home consumption and for export, and roads.

TABLE V

Disposal of Funds of Nigerian Commodity Marketing Boards: Cumulative Grants, Investments and Loans Outstanding, 1947–54*

(£thousands)

	Cocoa (Sept. 30, 1954)	Oil-palm produce (Dec. 31, 1954)	Groundnut (Oct. 31, 1954)	Cotton (Oct. 31, 1954)	Total (Sept. 30–Dec. 31, 1954)
Cumulative grants to Production Development Boards†	8,851·4	8,357·7	6,178·3	271·0	23,658·4
Cumulative research and development expenditure†	2,051·8	2,469·0	86·0	1,328·4	5,935·2
Loans outstanding to Government of Nigeria	2,494·0	—	—	—	2,494·0
United Kingdom Securities	24,119·1	23,775·1	13,570·0	4,920·8	66,385·0

Sources: Annual Reports of the Marketing Boards.

*This is not a complete listing. Current assets and current liabilities are excluded.

†Further allocations were made from Commodity Marketing Board funds after this table's 1954 cut-off date, in the extended period during which their affairs were finally wound up.

In addition to these allocations, the Commodity Marketing Boards also spent nearly £6 million on their own research and development schemes. The largest items of this type were the support of the West African Institute for Oil Palm Research and the West Africa Cocoa Research Institute, grants in support of the Faculty of Agriculture at the University College, Ibadan, and expenditures on roads, distribution of improved seed, stores, etc., in connection with the development of cotton production in the Northern Region. Smaller sums were spent upon other research institutes, surveys, experiments and investigations, co-operative marketing schemes and so forth.

A further commitment had been entered into by the Marketing Boards to lend £14 million to the Federal Government. By 1954 only £2·5 million had been lent (by the Cocoa Marketing Board), and the remaining obligations were assumed by the successor Regional Marketing Boards.

A completely different pattern of disposition of Marketing Board funds emerged following their Regionalisation. Led by the Western Region Marketing Board, the Boards began to supply funds in the form of grants and loans to the Regional Governments, directly to purchase equity in and offer loans to private companies, and to purchase Nigerian Government securities. At the same time expenditures for research and development were continued and expanded in amount. Grants to the successors of the Regional Production Development Boards, now renamed Development Corporations, and to the similarly organised Regional Finance Corporations, on the other hand, were sharply curtailed. These Corporations sharply accelerated their own development expenditures, however, by running down their unspent reserves accumulated from earlier years' Marketing Board grants. By 1962, as a result of these new investments and expenditures, Nigerian Marketing Board holdings of United Kingdom securities had been all but eliminated (see Table VI). Nor was there much left in any other reasonably liquid form of investment which might be employed for stabilisation. By 1961 even working capital requirements for one of the Boards were being supplied through the banking system rather than from the Marketing Boards' own reserves.

By far the greatest beneficiaries of this reserve disposal programme were the Regional Governments. Grants totalling over £33 million had been made by 1961, and loans of a further £16·8 million were outstanding at year-end. Some of these (grants of £1·4 million, loans of £6·4 million) may be considered merely as continuations of the Marketing Boards' allocation of funds to the Development Corporations, since, particularly in the Western Region, where grants from the Marketing Board to the Development Corporation ceased as a matter of policy in 1955, the Regional Governments now became key sources of the Development Corporations' finance. Of the remainder, much was allocated to specific projects: notably the building of the University of Nigeria in the Eastern Region and the University of Ife in the Western Region, and a road-construction programme in the Western Region. But the bulk was turned over or lent to the Regional Governments for general use in the accelerated development effort.

Grants and loans to the Regional Development and Finance Corporations, even allowing for those which were made through the medium of the Regional Governments, were much reduced in the post-1954 period, totalling about £17·2 million.[21] These institutions, however, were much more active during the latter period; by 1962 they had totally exhausted their 1955 reserves of £13 million. In the second half of the 1950s a large proportion of their funds went into loans to and equity in modern manufacturing enterprises, construction and real-estate firms, and indigenous banks, as well as into the government plantations and other schemes which had been begun earlier.

Other grants and expenditures totalling £9·1 million were in continuation of the 'own account' research and development activities begun in the earlier period. The Western Region spent the greatest amount in this way, the bulk of it (nearly £5 million) going for support of cocoa research and extension by the Regional Department of Agriculture; a further £591,000 was employed to subsidise the sale of chemicals used for spraying cocoa trees against capsid and black pod. The Northern Region spent over £1·6 million on the development of an agricultural research station (at Samaru, now a part of the new Sir Ahmadu Bello University) and a further £1·2 million on the continued development of cotton production, as well as further amounts upon a variety of experimental schemes and investigations in river transport, textile production, groundnut decortication, and cocoa and palm produce production. The Marketing Boards also continued to support such research institutes as the West African Institute for Oil Palm Research (which received the largest share of the Eastern Region Marketing Board's other grants and expenditures) and the West African Stored Produce Research Unit.

104   AN ECONOMIC HISTORY OF AFRICA

TABLE VI

*Disposal of Nigerian Regional Marketing Board Funds: Cumulative Grants,
Investments and Loans Outstanding, 1955–61* (£thousands)*

	Eastern Region (Dec. 31, 1961)	Northern Region (Oct. 31, 1961)	Western Region (Sept. 31, 1961)	Total (Sept. 30– Dec. 31, 1961)
Cumulative Grants to Regional Government	7,500·0	—	25,589·1	33,089·1
Cumulative Grants to regional development and finance corporations	2,800·0	1,883·2	—	4,683·2
Other Cumulative Grants and expenditures	212·1	3,226·7	5,717·4	9,156·2
Loans outstanding to Federal Government	1,816·9	3,323·6	—	5,140·5
Loans outstanding to Regional Government	—	6,811·2	10,000·0	16,811·2
Loans outstanding to Regional Development and finance corporations	500·0	—	4,200·0	4,700·0
Equity investment in Nigerian private companies	3,545·0	276·0	3,080·0	6,901·0
Loans outstanding to Nigerian private companies	—	800·0	6,288·2	7,088·2
United Kingdom Securities	3,202·2	6,578·0	1,721·6	11,501·8
Federation of Nigeria Securities	—	3,025·1	—	3,025·1

Sources: Annual Reports of the Marketing Boards.

*This is not a complete listing. Current assets and current liabilities are
excluded.

A major innovation in the 1955–62 period was the increasing
use of Marketing Board funds for the purposes of loans to and
purchases of equity in Nigerian private companies. This occurred
at the same time as the Regional and Federal Governments and
the Development and Finance Corporations (using funds previously acquired from the Marketing Boards) were also embarking
on this course. It is this area in which the greatest possibilities
for misuse of funds have been located.

These funds were concentrated in a very few indigenous financial institutions, a real estate concern and two successful industrial
enterprises—a cement plant and a textile factory. Of the three
Boards, the Western Regional Marketing Board channelled the
largest amounts into private enterprise, quite exclusive of those
grants to the Development and Finance Corporations which, as

has been seen, were actually indirect investments in private enterprises.

The bulk of these went to a bank and a real-estate concern, the affairs of which were closely bound up with those of the political party then in power in the Western Region and its leading members. While it is in any case worth questioning the wisdom on development grounds of devoting £6·7 million for the purpose of 'preventing the complete domination of expatriate firms and individuals in the field of real property,'[22] and a further £3·1 million 'to assist the growth of well established indigenous banking institutions so that they might be able, if placed in a strong financial position, to assist in the private sector of the country's industrial and commercial activities,'[23] there can be no doubt as to the impropriety of these investments.[24]

The propriety of the largest investment in a private concern by the Eastern Region Marketing Board is also subject to question. This was an investment of £3 million in a bank with a record of connections with the former leader of the political party in control of the Region. As in the West, the Development Corporation of the Eastern Region was also beginning to invest in private enterprises of questionable worth at this time. From a development point of view it is less a matter for concern that ethical standards were not maintained in these instances than that these funds might have been allocated more rationally.

There were, however, more worthwhile undertakings in the area of Marketing Board support of private ventures, notably the taking up of shares in two of the most successful manufacturing enterprises to have been set up in Nigeria, the Nigerian Cement Company at Nkalagu (Eastern Region) and Maduna Textiles (Northern Region); but the amounts involved in these totalled only £2·2 million.

The recent practices of Nigeria's Marketing Boards with respect to the making of loans and investments in private companies illustrate both the opportunities and the dangers of activities of this sort. On the one hand, government loans to, and investment in, the desired type of private concern is a useful means of achieving expansion and diversification of the economy while maintaining indigenous participation and the commitment to private initiative in a situation where the supply of domestic capital and entrepreneurship is limited. On the other hand, the probability that there will arise from such activities conflicts between public and private or political interests, with the possibility of resulting investment misallocations, is great; particularly is this so where, as in Nigeria, the standards to be expected from those in public life are less than clear and where the number of persons sufficiently wealthy and sophisticated to be engaged in activities of the type which it is intended to encourage is very small.

It would be difficult to summarise the wisdom or foolishness of Marketing Board allocations in a phrase or two, particularly in view of the fact that much was merely passed on to other decision-making authorities. On the face of it, however, the Marketing Boards performed reasonably well. The allocations the wisdom of which it is necessary seriously to question were not, after all, large relative to the total development loans and expenditures made. Disappointment over the misuse or misallocation of some of the funds accumulated should not therefore be permitted to destroy one's perspective on their overall performance as contributors to the development effort.[25]

NOTES

1. This study is part of a broader analysis of the structure and growth of the Nigerian economy which is being prepared under the auspices of the Economic Growth Center at Yale University. Most of the research underlying this paper was undertaken while I enjoyed an Associate Research Fellowship at the Nigerian Institute of Social and Economic Research in Ibadan. I am grateful to Mr. M. O. Kayode for statistical assistance, to the officers of the three Nigerian Marketing Boards for their co-operation, and to Professors Donald Mead, Hugh Patrick and Donald Snodgrass of Yale University, who offered comments on an earlier draft.
2. Stabilisation and mobilisation of savings are not the only possible aims of Marketing Board policies. In a discussion of the Ghanaian experience with Marketing Boards Reginald Green also lists the establishment of confidence in the future of the industry, the pursuit of general fiscal and price policies for the entire economy, income redistribution and the pursuit of international price stabilisation. Reginald Green, 'Ghana Cocoa Marketing Policy, 1938–1960,' *Nigerian Institute of Social and Economic Research, Conference Proceedings*, December 1960, pp. 132–160. One might also add the improvement of marketing facilities and quality of produce.
3. Including the accumulations in respect of Nigerian oil palm produce and groundnuts by the West African Produce Control Board during the 1947–49 period before the creation of the Nigerian Marketing Boards for these products.
4. 'Potential producer income' is defined here as actual producer income plus export duties, Marketing Board trading surplus and produce sales tax. Strictly speaking, the potential for producer incomes is actually higher than this if, as is likely, there exists positive price-elasticity of supply and greater than unit elasticity of world demand for Nigerian produce.
5. Only groundnut and cotton trading are included in this figure. Rough

calculations suggest that a further large deficit was encountered in ground-nut trading during the 1961/62 season, but there are as yet no figures to confirm them.

6. Nigeria Cocoa Marketing Ordinance of 1947, Section 16.

7. *First Annual Report of the Nigeria Groundnut Marketing Board*, p. 16.

8. Although not, as will be seen, from those of the Nigeria Cotton Marketing Board.

9. The Cocoa Marketing Board spent its own development allocations until 1951, but thereafter it, too, turned them over to the Production Development Boards. The Cotton Marketing Board never did transfer any development funds to the latter Boards, retaining its authority to spend them itself because of 'the facts that the present main area of cotton production is a confined one, and that the industry is still relatively small and requires separate and special fostering care' (*Second Annual Report of the Nigeria Cotton Marketing Board*, p. 16).

10. *First Annual Report of the Nigeria Cotton Marketing Board*, p. 21.

11. *House of Representatives Debates*, First Session, 1952, Vol. I, p. 46.

12. International Bank for Reconstruction and Development, *The Economic Development of Nigeria* (1955), p. 88.

13. Western Region of Nigeria, *Development of the Western Region of Nigeria, 1955–1960 (Sessional Paper No. 4 of 1955)*, p. 15.

14. Government of Western Nigeria, *Western Region Development Plan 1960–1965 (Sessional Paper No. 17 of 1959)*.

15. Government of Western Nigeria, *Western Nigeria Development Plan 1962–68 (Sessional Paper No. 8 of 1962)*, p. 12.

16. Eastern Region, Nigeria, *Development Programme, 1958–62 (Eastern Region Official Document No. 2 of 1959)*.

17. *Eastern Nigeria Development Plan, 1962–68 (Official Document No. 8 of 1962)*, p. 17.

18. *Fourth Annual Report of the Northern Regional Marketing Board*, p. 8.

19. *Fifth Annual Report of the Northern Regional Marketing Board*, p. 7.

20. Government of Northern Nigeria, Ministry of Economic Planning, *Development Plan, 1962–68*, p. 44.

21. Some of this amount, moreover, was immediately on-lent to private companies. In this case the Development Corporations were little more than intermediaries.

22. Federation of Nigeria, *Report of Coker Commission of Inquiry into the Affairs of Certain Statutory Corporations in Western Nigeria, 1962*, Vol. 1, p. 65.

23. *Ibid.*, p. 26.

24. Nor was this the whole story. The activities of the Western Nigeria Development Corporation also involved gross improprieties and careless-ness, the whole of which are documented in the Coker Report cited above.

25. One further minor point concerning the expenditure of these funds should be made in passing. This concerns the losses incurred through the delay between the dates at which the bulk of the trading surpluses were earned and the dates at which they were expended. These losses took two forms. As a result of the timing pattern of the Nigerian investments in and sales of United Kingdom securities, considerable capital losses were

suffered. At the same time, increases in the prices of Nigerian imports probably diminished the real value of the proceeds of the securities' sales. Neither of these losses were large enough, however, to alter the conclusions which can be reached on other grounds concerning the success of Nigerian Marketing Board experience; and neither relate to the more general issues discussed below.

PART THREE

Land, Agriculture, and Trade

12

ECONOMIC MAN IN AFRICA*

William O. Jones

Few propositions are as crucial to orthodox economic analysis as those relating supply and demand for commodities and services to price. The notion that producers and consumers change their behaviour when prices change, and in a predictable direction, is basic to most economic analysis. In almost all modern societies, whether they be relatively free from state control or rigorously socialistic, prices are used to guide the economy into optimum, or supposed optimum, utilisation of scarce resources. It should, therefore, be a matter of serious concern to economists engaged in studying or advising the underdeveloped countries to know whether the inhabitants of these countries do respond to price and income incentives in the expected fashion, whether they are indifferent to price, or whether they respond perversely.

Economists who have studied the societies of tropical Africa may find it particularly easy to attribute economic backwardness to the absence of economic motivation—of a desire for material things—in a people apparently as different from Europeans and Americans as the African. Just as some nineteenth century Americans denied the Negro a soul in an attempt to justify slavery, so have some twentieth century Europeans denied the African Negro an economic spirit in an attempt to justify colonial rule.

Popular ideas about the economic reactions of Africans are what they are partly because of our sources of information about them:

(1) Anthropologists who wish to counteract what they believe to be an over-riding economic determinism and who frequently fail to realise that the economist's analysis is concerned with

*Reprinted by permission of Stanford University, Food Research Institute Studies, (1960).

111

aggregates, not individuals, and with only one part, not the whole, of human aspirations.

(2) Traders who are apt to find perverse any behaviour of clients or customers that reduces trading profits.

(3) Employers who in every land have a pronounced tendency to deplore the disinclination of employees to identify employers' interests with their own, and

(4) Government administrators who may attribute resistance to their recommendations and requirements to anti-social and therefore perverse motives.

In general it is asserted that Africans respond to price changes in an unpredictable fashion, that they either tend not to respond at all, or that they do so in what seems to be a perverse fashion, i.e., when prices rise, less is produced, when wages rise, fewer hours are worked.

If these allegations are true, they of course make impossible the efficient functioning of a free market economy. They also destroy the effectiveness of price manipulation in achieving the goals of a planned economy. If they are true, the only road to economic advancement in Africa, and that a dubious one, is through direct controls on employment, output, and consumption, through the completely authoritarian state in which every economic decision, no matter how detailed, is made and implemented by the planning bureaucracy.

Unorthodox Behaviour Explained

The various kinds of unorthodox economic behaviour attributed to African producers and consumers have had for economists the usual fascination of the bizarre, and whether true or not have been explained as deriving from a variety of alleged characteristics of African society and the African personality. Some of the explanations offered for the African's uneconomic behaviour as regards prices, savings, investment, and innovation are summarised briefly in this section.

The simplest explanation offered for unorthodox price response is that Africans are not interested in having any goods and services other than those they now have. If this is so, a rise in the price of farm products, for example, or an increase in output per acre or per man hour, would lead the farmer to reduce inputs until his total net return was no greater than it had been before; elasticity of supply would then be equal to unity, but negative. A slightly more sophisticated statement, that level of living tends to approach the standard of living, causes elasticity of supply to be negative but not necessarily equal to unity. A variant of the same theme asserts that Africans are not unwilling to consume more goods and services, but that they value leisure more, or at any rate so highly as to make their response to price incentives extremely weak.

Another explanation of the supposed failure of supply and demand to respond to price depends on the conservatism of Africans—'the dominion of custom'—that causes them to cling stubbornly to customary usages. The strictures of custom are reinforced by the communal character of African life and by the heavy obligations of each individual to his lineage.

Sometimes irrationality is also given as part of the explanation: not the economist's meaning of irrationality that accepts the ends but questions the means, but the reformer's meaning which questions the ends themselves as irrational—e.g., owning more cattle instead of eating more meat, preferring to consume a combination of foods that do not constitute a 'balanced' diet, preferring ceremonials to productive investment, or indeed any pattern of tastes differing sharply from the European.

Finally, the failure of prices to perform their expected function is attributed to the African's unfamiliarity with economic exchange in general and with markets and money in particular. Ignorance of exchange in turn is often attributed to the fact that Africans live in self-sufficient economies, or did until very recently, in which the household was able to supply all of its own needs. It is argued that because Africans are ignorant of exchange, prices do not react to changing conditions of demand and supply and buyers and sellers stubbornly adhere to traditional prices long after they have ceased to be appropriate. One consequence of the unfamiliarity of Africans with markets is the phenomenon known as target demand, a demand for money 'largely derived from a demand for specific things for which there is a felt need' (9), in a society in which the necessities of life can be obtained without money.

It is apparent from the foregoing that most explanations of unorthodox economic response in tropical Africa rest upon notions about personality—individual economic aspirations and rationality—and about the structure of African societies—the extent of tribal ties and of economic ties. Economic aspirations are said, on the one hand, to be so low as to be satisfied with minimum effort, on the other hand, to be so high as to cause all income to go into current consumption. Irrationality manifests

I

itself in exaggerated time preference and in erratic, impulsive consumption. The strong bonds between the individual and the tribe are believed to result in loss of self-reliance, inventiveness, and ambition. And in the self-sufficiency of small economic groups is found both a cause and a consequence of the African's unfamiliarity with the workings of economic markets.

These explanations seem plausible; whether they are correct and whether the phenomena they purport to explain are real is another matter. The following pages present a number of accounts of the behaviour of Africans in actual market situations, accounts demonstrating that economic man is no stranger to tropical Africa and strongly suggesting that, given full opportunity to pursue his personal objectives, he can be relied on as a powerful agent to move African economies to greater productivity and wealth.

Reactions to Price Changes

In Kampala, Uganda, studies of expenditures by African labourers over a period of years show shifts in consumption patterns in 1953 that appear to be strongly related to price (Chart 1). The market for foodstuffs in 1953 was marked by great increases in prices of bananas, sweet potatoes, and manioc, and by the stability of the price of corn. The general price rise was caused by poor crops in late 1952, resulting from inadequate rainfall; if government had not intervened, corn prices might have risen in the same way as did prices of the other staples even though corn stocks were fairly large. Through government control of distribution and supplies, however, the price of corn meal was kept fairly steady at between 27 cents and 30 cents per pound. In other years this would have been considered a high price for corn meal, but in 1953 it made it the cheapest of all the starchy staple foodstuffs in terms of calories. Government's efforts to hold down the price of corn meal in Uganda markets were greatly assisted by the response of corn growers to the high prices that had prevailed in 1952 when the crop had been short and prices uncontrolled. The administration guaranteed a price of 15 cents per pound to growers, with the consequence that in Buganda the area of the spring crop was at an all-time high of 236,000 acres, or 90,000 acres more than the largest previous crop (15). Supplies steadily improved as this crop was harvested.

The reaction of purchasers to the general rise in prices and to the relative cheapness of corn varied with the tribe. Traditional food patterns differed sharply, the Baganda relying very heavily on bananas (matoke), and the Batoro and Banyankole consuming large amounts of manioc with bananas somewhat less important.

The Banyankole, who previously had consumed little corn meal, increased their expenditure on this foodstuff about fivefold, and reduced expenditures on bananas and manioc accordingly. Data are not available for years immediately after 1953, but a study conducted in 1957 showed corn meal to have largely displaced manioc in the Banyankole diet, whereas expenditures on bananas had returned to the 1952 level. It could be that the relatively low prices of corn in 1953 provoked a change in the diet that persisted after prices returned to more normal relationships. Lack of information about Banyankole expenditures before 1952, however, makes this sort of generalisation precarious.

Batoro expenditure patterns show similar changes in 1953— decline in consumption of manioc and bananas, great increase in consumption of corn. In 1957 Batoro expenditures on corn were much less than in 1953, although greater than in 1949–52, and expenditures for manioc were about the same as in 1953. Expenditures for bananas, on the other hand, were higher than had been reported by any of the earlier surveys. The price distortion in 1953 clearly seems to have affected expenditures in that year, but changes appear not to have been permanent, except as they may have accelerated a declining trend in expenditure on manioc.

The Baganda, who customarily spent as much as 25 per cent of all expenditures on bananas, compensated for high prices in 1953 by increasing their consumption of corn and of sweet potatoes. Probably the shift from bananas to sweet potatoes should be regarded as an income effect rather than a price effect. Sweet potatoes in 1953 were much more expensive than manioc or corn but may have been more acceptable to the Baganda because they can be prepared in much the same way as bananas. When the very high prices paid for bananas began to press on income, the Baganda, who were the wealthiest of the three groups, shifted to another preferred food, even though its cost too was abnormally high.

The data obtained by the Kampala expenditure studies are entirely consistent with orthodox notions of economic response. They also suggest strongly that even the most firmly rooted consumption habits can be upset by a sharp change in relative prices.

Reference has already been made to the way in which food farmers increased their output of corn when faced with an unusually attractive price. This is but one of many instances in which

CHART 1.

Kampala, Uganda: Expenditures on Starchy Staples by African
Labourers by Tribes, and Average Market Prices, 1949–57*

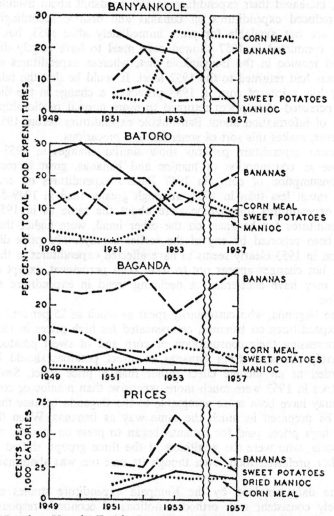

*Based on Uganda, E. Afr. Stat. Dept., *The Pattern of Income, Expenditure, and Consumption of African Labourers in Kampala: September 1950* (May 1951); Uganda, E. Afr. Stat. Dept., *The Pattern of Income, Expenditure and Consumption of African Unskilled Labourers in Kampala: September 1951* (January 1952); *ibid.*, September 1952 (May 1953); *ibid.*, September 1953 (January 1954); and *ibid.*, February 1957 (June 1957).

output of an agricultural commodity in tropical Africa has responded positively to the stimulus of prices. Sometimes this has produced results contrary to those desired by colonial administrators, as when Tanganyika farmers have found it more profitable to grow cotton and purchase food rather than try to grow all of their own food requirements, or when West African farmers have devoted most of their efforts to the remunerative business of producing cocoa, with consequent curtailment of food farming. To most economists these would appear to be proper decisions leading to economic efficiency, but to those administrators who customarily think in terms of local self-sufficiency they have been most distressing.

In Tanganyika Territory attempts were made over a period of years to achieve territorial, provincial, even district self-sufficiency in foodstuffs, and the African farmers were required by law to grow specified areas of certain staple foodstuffs, even though it was recognised that these crops were economically unattractive. In 1950, for example, the Department of Agriculture report on the Southern Province states (10):

> This has been a disappointing year for being self-sufficient within the Province. . . . There were also many local food shortages although most of these were alleviated by internal distribution. Some of the local shortages were accountable to climatic conditions, e.g., floods on the Ruvuma and the erratic incidence of rainfall.
> The fact remains, however, that there could have been no such shortages if the rules of cassava plantings had been fully implemented. In a good grain year little cassava is needed, but within the economic range it is a marketable commodity for export. The price is, however, low and compares unfavourably with other crops, e.g., sunflower, cashew nuts and tobacco. It is not, therefore, popular as an economic crop. Unfortunate as it is to have to instigate innumerable prosecutions, it is essential to enforce the rules for minimum plots of cassava as an insurance against food shortage.

Further on, the report complains that 'Over recent years the peasant has become increasingly money conscious and has been developing the idea that if you have money you cannot be short of food.'

Two years later, however, the departmental report expressed concern over the large crop of manioc harvested in the Newala District of the Southern Province in response to attractive prices, a crop sufficient to provide exports amounting to 17,000 tons of dried roots. It was recommended that 'when other districts are growing sufficient for their own needs it would be best to discourage production in the Newala District to some extent . . .'(11).

The impression is clearly given by the official reports that far from being handicapped by the absence of economic man in Tanganyika, the agricultural authorities were embarrassed by his presence. In 1954 they were still placing stress '. . . on the need to plant up adequate acreages of cassava in all Provinces . . .' despite the fact that the Southern provinces continued to export dried roots overseas (12), and despite the fact that in many parts of Tanganyika manioc grows poorly, if it all. By 1956, however, as African farmers in areas where manioc was an economic crop continued to expand output in response to good prices, the Department began to alter its rigid devotion to self-sufficiency, and to apply its rule for compulsory planting more selectively '. . . more reliance being placed on the greater production of crops for sale where cassava does not crop well' (13).

In the Belgian Congo, too, economic man has sometimes thwarted administrators' plans. In 1951 the Belgian authorities were distressed because African farmers found higher returns in the production of cotton and peanuts than in growing food crops. The area planted to manioc in Leopoldville had declined eight per cent, and similar declines had occurred in Equateur, Orientale, and Katanga Provinces. In Kasai and Kivu Provinces, although plantings had increased, much of the crop was left in the field because the price was too low to cover the cost of harvesting. The actions taken by the authorities to increase the supply available in Kasai was not, as one might have expected, to raise the price, but rather to forbid shipment out of the Province, in effect lowering the price (1). Similarly in the region of Feshi, where manioc is the principal crop, its sale outside the district is forbidden in order to protect the local food supply (7). As a result, a crop that might be sold in order to purchase badly needed higher quality foods is only partly harvested.

Economic African man not only finds himself in conflict with bureaucratic European man in the persons of colonial administrators; his behaviour also seems strange and sometimes perverse to agricultural officers who are ruled more by technological than by economic considerations. In the Western Region of Nigeria, the principal cash crop, cocoa, is extremely liable to attack by Black Pod (*Phytophthora palmivora*) which destroys pods and reduces leaf growth (2, p. 22). Damage by Black Pod can be much reduced if the cocoa is harvested frequently and infected pods removed. The Department of Agriculture, however, has had only limited success in persuading farmers to pick pods frequently in order to control the disease. Failure of farmers to heed the admonitions of agricultural officers may sometimes be due to ignorance, indifference, or hostility, but the most effective obstacle to general adoption of the recommended methods is their cost. According to Galletti, Baldwin, and Dina, who conducted an intensive study of Nigerian cocoa farming in 1951–52 (2, pp. 216–17.),

> . . . about 60 per cent of the cocoa acreage belongs to 20 per cent of the farmers and the farmers holding this acreage have 5 acres or more each in one village. To control Black Pod effectively these farmers would need permanent labourers throughout the year. But most labourers are migrants and few wish to take up permanent work on cocoa farms, especially as wages are not always paid regularly and punctually. Other farmers show little interest . . . because their holdings are so small that the extra income to be gained is not enough to make the effort required seem worthwhile . . . The distance of cocoa plots from the farmers' residence is often great, and to walk 5 miles or so each way every three weeks to remove black pods on half an acre of cocoa does not seem to the Yoruba farmer to be time well spent.

Clearly the reason why the control scheme has not been well carried out is because the marginal cost it entails is greater than the marginal revenue it brings in.

Somewhat similar difficulties were encountered in the Kasai when producers' co-operatives sponsored by the Congo administration acquired small flour mills for transforming dried manioc roots into flour. Technically the mills were satisfactory, producing a clean white flour at lower cost and with less effort than the customary product of mortar and pestle. Nevertheless, deliveries of dried roots to the mills were small, much less than would justify their purchase and maintenance. The explanation was not far to seek. Manioc farmers did not object to the mills themselves, they were not indifferent to their labour-saving advantages, and they were not hostile toward the co-operative itself, at least as far as could be determined. The difficulty was purely economic. Flour produced in the co-operative mills was sold through 'modern' trade channels to merchants supplying the cities or to European employers. When sold in this fashion manioc commanded no more than the official minimum price of 1·10 francs per kilo—a minimum become a maximum when offered by large buyers. But manioc sold on local traditional markets to African traders and consumers brought as much as 4·50 francs per kilo (5, p. 266). It is not at all remarkable that local farmers preferred to mill their own flour in order to be able to sell it on the local market.

In some parts of tropical Africa, particularly in West Africa, manioc farmers present another sort of riddle to the uninformed observer. In their study of food farms in the cocoa belt of western Nigeria, Galletti and his associates commented on the large amount of manioc that was left in the field unharvested. Harvests yielded only about 45 per cent as much manioc per acre as might have been expected on the basis of crop harvesting experiments undertaken in the Nigerian Agricultural Census of 1950/51, whereas harvests of yams were 80 per cent of expected values, harvests of corn 85 per cent. Similar figures are reported from an agricultural survey in southeastern Ghana in 1952–53 where annual output of manioc averaged only 0·6 tons per acre although yields of 3 to 9 tons were to be expected. In the Ivory Coast, too, an agricultural survey of the Bouaké revealed manioc production to be only a small fraction of what it would have been if all the crop had been harvested.

It might be thought that the apparently wasteful practices suggested by these reports from Nigeria, Ghana, and the Ivory Coast were occasioned by peculiar circumstances at the time of the surveys, and in fact governmental propaganda to grow more food and relatively high prices at time of planting may have been contributory causes. Other information, however, makes it clear that in most years manioc, and taro too, are only partially harvested in many parts of tropical Africa. The general explanation is again economic, and derives from the distribution of the costs of producing these two roots crops. It costs little to plant a field of manioc or taro, and the crop can be grown to maturity with a minimum of care. For manioc even land cost is trivial when the crop is grown, as it often is, in fields, that would otherwise be abandoned to bush. By far the largest cost of producing manioc and taro is that assumed in lifting the mature roots from the field and transporting them to market. Many African farmers grow manioc as a speculation, to be marketed if the price is high enough when the crop is mature to yield a return greater than cost of harvest, to be abandoned if it is not.[1]

The effect of price on cocoa production in Nigeria and Ghana was long recognised by colonial officers, and it is only in recent years, partly as an apology for activities of the Marketing Boards, that it has been brought in question. Galletti's study of Nigerian cocoa farmers confirms the analyses of West African agricultural officers going back to World War I.[2] Reports of conditions in 1918 and 1919 are particularly interesting because they show that not only does output rise when prices go up, it also declines when prices fall. The following excerpt from the Gold Coast *Report on the Agricultural Department for the Year 1918* describes the consequences of low prices (3):

> In the remoter districts all over the country where there was no local market and the cost of transport to the nearest buying centre was more than the produce would have realised, the cocoa crop was left ungathered and the majority of the farms entirely abandoned, some of the owners even leaving the districts in search of employment. This resulted in a deplorable condition of the farms, diseased and squirrel eaten pods of two seasons crop were hanging on the trees together with the fresh young pods, branches attacked by Loranthus parasite, numerous dead and decaying branches covered with white-thread fungus, and occasional dead trees killed by root diseases, all supplemented by a perfect forest of young cocoa seedlings springing up all around, as well as a superabundance of untended sucker growths.

It should be pointed out that Department of Agriculture officials were not entirely pleased with the consequences of African farmers' economic aspirations. The same report speaks of 'the mistaken belief that the larger the area [in cocoa] the bigger the profit' (3). Apparently the authorities were disturbed by farmers' pursuit of the good returns that could be obtained from cocoa groves.

With the re-opening of trade channels after the Armistice cocoa production began to increase, although immediate recovery from neglect during periods of low prices was, of course, not possible. But the report for 1919 states that (4):

> Throughout the cocoa area the revival of the market resulted in a reawakened interest in farms which had been temporarily abandoned during the dormant condition of the industry. The 'cultivation' accorded consisted merely of clearing the trees of bush growth in young farms, cutlassing under growth to permit collection of crops, and occasionally a minimum of rough pruning. Young farms have been observed to be the greater sufferers from war-time abandonment, and in spite of the signs of recovery it is probable that some time must elapse before even pre-war conditions can be generally reported.

During the war farmers had turned their attention from cocoa for export to food for domestic production, but with the return of good prices for cocoa the production of foodstuffs declined. When this shift of inputs became apparent to the Agricultural Department officers their earlier concern over the decline in production of unprofitable cocoa now became a concern over the decline in production of less profitable food crops, and they urged that 'departmental effort should be increasingly concentrated on food production' (4).

The Africans involved in the economic transactions described in this section do not appear to have been much different from men everywhere in their response to changing conditions of demand and supply and in their ingenuity in devising satisfactory solutions to new problems. Certainly they show every evidence of wanting to increase their command over goods and services and of going about the business of doing so in a rational way, even when they find their desires to be in conflict with those of the dominant European administration. It seems clear that a great many Africans are well familiar with the workings of markets and know how to participate in them to their own advantage.

Economic Man and Social Goals

Against the illustrations offered here of shrewd adjustment to changing market conditions, can be brought forth many other illustrations of the sort most often advanced to prove the African's childish lack of understanding of economic affairs. In the United States, too, it would be possible to compile an impressive collection of anecdotes in which the irrational economic behaviour of American consumers, even of American businessmen of some prominence, was the theme. But it is not intended to argue that economic motivation is as dominant in the societies of Africa as in those of the western world. All that can be said is that the economic drive is present in a great many Africans who are well able to order their affairs to serve it. And for the purpose of economic analysis this is enough.

Sylvia Leith-Ross, writing over 25 years ago of the Ibo women, found their preoccupation with material things, and above all with money and prosperity, frightening and disheartening (8). Long before that, however, the pioneer economists of France and England perceived how, in a properly ordered economy, the self-seeking of individual members of society could be directed to serve the objectives of all. More than this, in all western civilisation as we now know it, economic drive has proved to be perhaps the most powerful force that the state can mobilise to its ends, whether these ends be economic growth, fostering of favoured sectors of activity, the preservation of its sovereignty, or world domination.

The question of economic motivation in Africa is of fundamental importance because no other motivation can be substituted for it without great loss in effectiveness. If it is present in a significant degree, even though it may be lacking or muffled by custom in many members of society, conventional analysis will show how it can be fostered and used to serve the objects of society. If the society is one of economic freedom and economic equality, the efficient producers and efficient traders will displace the inefficient and total productivity will increase. If all members of the society are assured equal access to markets, to resources, and to knowledge, the society increasingly will realise the potentialities of its citizenry and its natural endowment. Or if the society is not economically free but state directed, the planning authorities can utilise economic drive wherever it is present in much the same ways.

It is not the absence of economic man that has put tropical Africa so far behind the great societies of Europe, Asia, and America. He lives in Africa today, as he has for millennia, and will eagerly serve African society as he has other societies when his presence is recognised and his tremendous energies are freed to work for the common good.

NOTES

1. The practice is closely parallel to that followed in the Salinas Valley in California, one of the most highly commercialised farming districts in the world. There farmers plant lettuce on speculation, only to plough it under when mature if prices are too low to cover harvesting costs.
2. Cf. also the report on cocoa prepared by the Food and Agriculture

REFERENCES

Organisation of the United Nations in 1955 (16).
(1) Belgium, Min. Col., *La Situation économique du Congo Belge en 1951* (1952), pp. 25–36.
(2) R. Galletti, K. D. S. Baldwin, and I. O. Dina, *Nigerian Cocoa Farmers* ... (Nigeria Cocoa Mkt. Bd., London, 1956).
(3) Gold Coast, Dept. Agr., *Report* . . . *for the Year 1918* (1920), pp. 11–12.

124 AN ECONOMIC HISTORY OF AFRICA

(4) ——, *Report . . . for the Year 1919* (1921), pp. 11, 14.
(5) ——, *Manioc in Africa* (Food Research Institute Studies in Tropical Development, Stanford, Calif., 1960).
(6) F. H. Knight, 'Exchange,' in *Encyclopaedia of the Social Sciences* (New York, 1931), Vol. V, p. 666.
(7) A. Lambrechts, K. Holemans, and O. Rots, *Étude sur l'alimentation indigène dans le territoire de Feshi* (Memoires Acad. Roy. des Sci. Col., Brussels, 1956). Vol. IV, p. 22.
(8) Sylvia Leith-Ross, *African Women: A Study of the Ibo of Nigeria* (London, 1939).
(9) S. D. Neumark, 'Economic Development and Economic Incentives, *South African J. of Econ.* (Johannesburg), March 1958, p. 62.
(10) Tanganyika, Dept. Agri., *Annual Report: 1950* (1952), pp. 154–55.
(11) ——, *Annual Report: 1952*, Pt. I (1953), pp. 16–17.
(12) ——, *Annual Report . . . 1954*, Pt. I (1955), pp. 11–12.
(13) ——, *Annual Report . . . 1956*, Pt. I (1957), p. 13.
(14) Jean Tricart, 'Le Café en Côte d'Ivoire,' *Les Cahiers d'Outre-Mer* (Bordeaux), July-Sept. 1957.
(15) Uganda, Dept. Agr., *Annual Report . . . for the Year Ended 31st December, 1953* (1954), p. 10.
(16) Food and Agriculture Organisation of the United Nations (FAO), *Cacao: A Review of Current Trends in Production, Price, and Consumption* (Commodity Series, Bull. No. 27, Rome, November 1955).

13

GHANAIAN CAPITALIST COCOA-FARMERS*

Polly Hill

It is one of the misfortunes of contemporary Africa that the business of farming is usually referred to so slightingly and contemptuously, especially by economists. Many present-day writers take for granted that the so-called 'small peasants' who produce the food and export crops are invariably, in certain broad and important senses, 'inefficient'. There is much too much of a tendency to consider yield per acre as the measure of efficiency, irrespective of whether land is plentiful. The farmers are often considered to be people who would choose to take up other economic occupations were they better educated or more intelligent. I think it is time that opinions such as these were openly challenged and in order to stimulate further controversy and to emphasise that this 'business of farming' is a business, I have given this chapter a somewhat provocative title. In my opinion the migrant cocoa-farmers of Southern Ghana, with whom I am here concerned, were real economic innovators: people who bent their energy and intelligence to the business of cocoa-farming with supreme success. But, because of the load of condescension showered on farmers as a class, it did not occur to anyone that this might be so and it is only now, with the aid of the Department of Agriculture's maps, compiled for swollen-shoot disease control purposes, that the real account of what happened is being revealed.

The social organisation of cocoa-farming in Ghana as a whole is very heterogeneous indeed and the type of farmer with whom I am concerned is only one of many. There is much variation

*Here reprinted, with slight revision, from the *Ghanaian Bulletin of Agricultural Economics*, 11, No. 1 (March 1962), this brief article appeared before the publication, in 1963, of my book *The Migrant Cocoa-Farmers of Southern Ghana: A Study in Rural Capitalism*.

as between different districts, this reflecting differences in population density, customary conditions of land tenure, accessibility of land and so forth. In some districts 'native farmers' (i.e. farmers who were born in the district in question) predominate and some of these farmers may, if one wishes, be referred to as 'peasants'—though, for myself, I prefer to avoid the use of this word with all its emotional overtones, and to refer to 'sedentary' or 'non-migrant' farmers. In certain areas the farms owned by these sedentary farmers are, most of them, of the traditional size of about one to three acres, this perhaps corresponding (it is a matter which should be investigated by agricultural economists) to the area which could be conveniently cleared and planted by one man in a single season. This type of farmer was described by W. H. Beckett in his famous book *Akokoaso*, which was based on work done while he was a member of the staff of the Department of Agriculture in the 1930s. While in various parts of Ghana, including south-eastern Ashanti, there are many thousands of such farmers (nearly half of whom are women farmers in their own right), they have always accounted for rather a small proportion of Ghana's total cocoa exports, and were certainly not the pioneers responsible for the original development of cocoa growing, as has always been supposed.

In this short chapter I shall not attempt to classify Ghana's cocoa-farmers further. Apart from the sedentary, small-scale farmer and the farmer with which this chapter is concerned, there are many other types, of whom the most important at present are the Ashanti and Brong-Ahafo farmers who have been responsible for the vast expansion of production that has occurred in Ahafo and elsewhere in the west. Unfortunately we know very little, as yet, about the social organisation of production in these newer cocoa-growing areas, and there are no Department of Agriculture farm-maps to come to our aid, but I would like to hazard the guess that in West African conditions very rapid expansion of production, such as has occurred in the last thirty years in Ahafo (and which occurred between about 1890 and 1930 in southern Ghana), always involves the large-scale migration of farmers into uninhabited forests. True forest dwellers, residing in their small towns, such as Akokoaso or Asafo-Akim, are not of the stuff of which pioneering farmers are made. The migrant farmer's homelands lie south of the deep forest: they were the farmers behind the spectacular increase in Ghana's cocoa exports from nil in 1890 to about 40,000 tons in 1911—since when Ghana has always been the world's largest cocoa producer. These farmers own most of the cocoa land in Southern Akim Abuakwa south of Kibi, except in the immediate neighbourhood of the old towns such as Apapam, Apedwa, Asafo, Tafo, Kukurantumi and Asamankese. The Department of Agriculture's maps showing farm boundaries, which can be referred to at the various Area Offices, show that this is so.

In this chapter I shall briefly list some of the reasons why it seems justifiable to regard the migrant cocoa-farmers of southern Ghana as 'capitalists'—a term which I am, of course, employing in a rather general sense. Although my enquiries are based on present-day oral interview in the field, yet my approach is essentially historical so that I often speak of the farmers in the past tense. Nevertheless, I must make it quite clear that most of my findings apply, in general, to the present day, though the situation has been much obscured by swollen shoot disease which destroyed most of the cocoa trees owned by the migrants in southern Ghana. Although since about 1929 the farmers have usually travelled part of the way to their new lands by lorry (in the first twenty years of the migration, before the opening of Pakro railway station in 1911, they always travelled by foot), the migration has continued on traditional lines to the present day and will continue indefinitely, the farmers being committed to this way of life. Contrary to widespread (almost insistent) belief, the poverty resulting from swollen shoot put a brake on the migration: the migration slowed down because the farmers lacked the cash to travel to their new lands.

(1) The most obvious reason for regarding the migrant farmers as capitalists is that they bought their land for the particular purpose of growing cocoa on it. When the migration first began, in the early 1890s,[1] the land that the travelling farmers bought was situated in western and north-western Akwapim, especially in the Adawso area. (At that time virtually all the migrant farmers were Akwapim, from Aburi, Mampong, Mamfe, Larteh, Akropong and elsewhere.) In about 1897 the westward migration over the river Densu into Akim country began—see map. The forests of southern Akim Abuakwa enclosed within the arc of the river Densu were scarcely inhabited, as contemporary maps show, and the chiefs who 'owned' the land, Apapam, Asafo and the rest, were only too glad to sell portions to the stranger-farmers, all of whom lived in areas of south-eastern Ghana where cocoa would not grow or where, as on the Akwapim ridge, there was insufficient land. (The Akwapim migrants were soon joined by Shai, Krobo, Ga and others, including the Anum/Boso who did

not start buying land until about 1907.) The main source of money for land-purchase was the oil palm, which was grown extensively in Akwapim and Krobo countries, oil and kernels being exported to the value of over £200,000 in 1890. The cultivation of one economic crop therefore led directly to the development of another. The Akwapim had a number of other sources of income, including rubber trading, Gold Coast rubber exports having risen from £55,000 in 1889 to £231,000 in 1890; this business also involved travelling, much of the rubber, which was all of natural origin, being collected in distant parts of Akim country and Ashanti. Then there were the travelling craftsmen of Akwapim, such as carpenters, who journeyed widely in West Africa, often returning home to invest their savings in land for cocoa.

(2) The migrant farmers themselves have always regarded cocoa growing as a business, though they have not boasted about this. It cannot be too strongly emphasised that, with the Akwapim at any rate, this business was not an extension of their general farming activities, for it was women who were responsible for producing, as well as selling, most of the food crops in the homeland, other than yam and the oil palm, while it was the men who, accompanied by their womenfolk, migrated to grow cocoa. Many of the men were literally unemployed (it should be noted that exports of palm produce did not fall significantly until cocoa growing had been established for some twenty years) and were looking for a worthwhile occupation. They were not concerned, as are so many traders and taxi drivers, to 'get rich quick' and then go out of business; all the time they were interested in expansion. From the earliest times it has been conventional for a large part of the profits from growing cocoa on one land (I shall define a land at (4) below), to be invested in the purchase of another. As time went by, nearly all migrant farmers owned several lands acquired at intervals as the cash became available—my enquiries in Akwapim have shown that the typical Akwapim farmer, except in a few of the smaller towns such as Tutu, owns three or four lands, acquired by his forebears and himself. Exceptional migrant farmers, and I have interviewed many of them, acquired long sequences of a dozen lands or more.

With regard to the quite spurious anxieties that are often expressed about an imminent land shortage, it should be noted that when a farmer, or a family, owns more than a small number of lands, it is usual for some of them to lie unplanted for

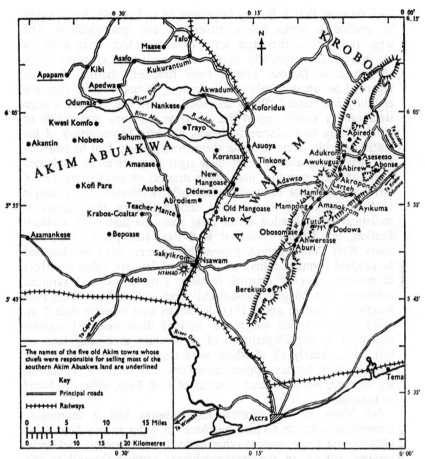

The historic cocoa-growing area, in relation to the Akwapim Ridge.
This map appeared previously in Hill, *The Migrant Cocoa-Farmers
of Southern Ghana*, Cambridge, 1963

decades: thus, much land that was acquired in the 1930s has
never yet been planted, although suitable for cocoa.

(3) For an activity to count as business, it must be conducted
on a reasonably large scale, otherwise it more resembles a hobby.
Here again, the migrant farmers qualify as businessmen, in terms
both of the number of separate lands acquired and their area.
This is not to say that all the farms are or were large, and
indeed, statistical generalisation about farm size is fraught with

K

such dangers that it is very important to understand the structure in qualitative terms before attempting any quantification. The large tracts of a thousand acres or more which were acquired by individuals, especially in the very earliest days when many of the most famous estates were founded, should often be regarded as areas within which farming is undertaken; they are certainly not 'farms'. When an Aburi farmer bought such a large tract (and I would regard the Aburi as the most remarkable of all the early cocoa-farmers), it was not long before many of his matrilineal kin came to settle there, both to help him to establish his own farms and to exert their right to portions of unplanted land for their personal use, and a mosaic, or cellular pattern of farm-ownership or occupation gradually developed. The example of Kofi Pare, an Aburi farmer, should indicate the dangers of statistical generalisation about farm size—the first need is classi-fication, not figures. Thus, at Kofi Pare (the place which now bears Kofi Pare's name), present-day farmers may be classified as original farmers, inheritors of original farmers, other members of matrilineages of original farmers, sons of original farmers, outsiders who bought 'secondhand' land and so forth. Kofi Pare bought the land in about 1911; it had an area of more than 2 sq. miles, part of which was resold; in 1959 there were 137 farmers registered by the Department of Agriculture as owning land on this estate, nearly all of whom were close relatives of Kofi Pare himself or of his six original associates—the latter, it is interest-ing to note, were all close relatives of Kofi Pare, either by blood or marriage.

(4) Many of the farmers have always had a thoroughly commercial attitude to land-purchase. In order to buy land more cheaply and for numerous other agricultural, economic and social reasons, certain of the land-purchasers formed themselves into groups or clubs, known as companies, for the purpose of acquir-ing blocks of land which were then divided into strips from a base line, each farmer being allocated a strip of a width pro-portionate to his cash contribution. (Such a strip, whether planted or not, I refer to as 'a land'—but lands are not necessarily bought through companies.) These companies, which were unimportant until after 1900, were characteristically composed of groups of friends, not relatives, each man being concerned to buy land for his own use. In the early days companies proper were formed only by farmers who belonged to patrilineal societies, such as Larteh and Mamfe, where sons inherit the property of their fathers. Nowadays, farmers from matrilineal societies, such as

Aburi, form and join companies—though family lands, with their farms presenting a mosaic pattern, as at Kofi Pare, then develop within the strips. Where strip-farms are shown on the Area Office maps (for the maps to be comprehensible for research purposes, it is desirable for them to be redrawn on a much smaller scale than that used by the Department, which is 40 inches to the mile), it means that the land was originally acquired by a company. There are many districts of southern Akim Abuakwa, such as the Nankese area, where all the land was sold over half a century ago, most of it to companies: in that particular area a typical company land has an area of between about 300 and 1,000 acres. (5) Contrary to popular belief, the enterprising individual farmer did not find himself unreasonably hampered by the demands made on him by the members of his 'wider family' or lineage. It is very interesting to note that, without doing violence to the traditional structure of society in the various home towns, it was possible for an individual to be accorded full scope to invest 'family money' in the acquisition of cocoa lands which, for some time at any rate, were likely to be regarded as his individual property. The older and less active members of an Aburi *abusua* (matrilineage) were usually clever enough to realise where their interests lay: they urged the younger men on, realising that only through individual initiative could the wealth of the *abusua* as a whole be increased. On the other hand, the fact that individual property is always in process of conversion to family property has provided individuals with a great incentive to acquire additional lands for their own use.

(6) If an individual is to count as a capitalist, he must operate either on borrowed money or with his own savings. The migrant farmers did both. The original 'pump-priming' savings were those derived from the sale of palm produce, etc., but such sums were far from sufficient. Little progress would have been made had the farmers not ploughed back the proceeds from growing cocoa on one land in the purchase of another land—to the extent that many farmers regarded land as the only reliable 'savings bank'. Then, the land sellers had been willing, from the earliest times, to accept payment for land in instalments—thus enabling those with very small savings to buy land and sometimes to pay for it, in part, from the cocoa grown on it. (I think this idea of paying in instalments has been an important, though theoretically unrecognised, feature of West African economic life for a very long time.) Sometimes, though not for philanthropic reasons, a rich farmer would be prepared to help a poor farmer by reselling

him land, from lots acquired earlier, on 'easy terms'. The farm labourers, too, were originally attracted to this work by the prospect of future income from plucking cocoa from the farms which they were helping to establish. And, while on the subject of farm labourers, it must be noted as a most important point of principle (though, again, one that has gone unnoticed) that farmers never 'wasted' their savings on farm labour employment: they never employed labourers until, with the help of their families, they had established sufficient bearing-cocoa to reward their labourers with a share of the cocoa income. (This is why lump sum compensation received for swollen shoot was so seldom used for the finance of labourers.)

(7) The idea of 'branch' businesses is familiar to many capitalists and also to the migrant farmers. The migrant farmer, like the owner of a chain of retail stores or cinemas, both works himself and co-ordinates and directs the activities of others. Although successive Directors of Agriculture, especially around 1914, failed to realise this, it is a fact that earlier-acquired lands (which had proved fruitful) were never abandoned when a new land was acquired. Whether or not labourers were employed (and Akwapim farmers, incidentally, are much more inclined to employ labourers than are Krobo), it was usual for a relative to be installed on each land and for the farmer, while perhaps working primarily at one place, to spend much time travelling about supervising the work on all the lands. I think it is very hard on the farmers that ignorant town-dwellers should so often accuse them of being 'absentees': indeed, I think that the emotive word 'absenteeism', with its suggestion that the farmer is too lazy to perform his proper duty, should be dropped from our vocabulary in this context.

(8) If the word 'capitalist' is to be employed in a respectable sense, and not just as a term of abuse, then I think its creative aspect should be emphasised, and this usually involves the capitalists in taking a long view. Certainly, the farmers have always been very long-term in their attitude. There is evidence that between the wars, before the swollen shoot destroyed so much of their cocoa, the farmers responded to a higher world cocoa price by buying more land and *vice versa*. Here again, we note, they did not just sit back enjoying their profits. But, like smaller businessmen the world over, they were rather disinclined to invest the profits from one kind of enterprise (cocoa) in establishing another (say, wholesale trading)—though it seems that many of the earliest lorry-owners were migrant cocoa-farmers.

(9) Business is apt to be all-demanding and the farmers' whole way of life was altered by the 'cocoa business'. Although many present-day migrants are of the third generation, their fathers as well as themselves having been born away from home, yet they still insist on regarding themselves as strangers in the farming area, people who are temporarily resident for business purposes in their cottages ('villages') in the forest or in stranger-towns, of which the most notable is Suhum. Ties with the home town are maintained in many ways: the profits from cocoa growing were partially devoted to building houses in the home town and many children are sent back to school there.

(10) The farmers, as businessmen, were unimpressed by the colonial administration and undertook their own development expenditure to provide better links between the cocoa forests and their homeland: before 1914 the Akwapim farmers had hired contractors to build three bridges over the river Densu (being businessmen they recouped their expenses by charging tolls) and a little later they invested at least £50,000 in the building of motorable access roads to Akwapim.

If it be accepted that these migrant cocoa-farmers of Southern Ghana are businessmen (or capitalists), not small 'peasants' who by an unplanned process of trial-and-error happened to create the world's largest cocoa-growing industry, then it is obvious that many stereotyped notions about cocoa-farmers as a group are really misleading. We must study the farmer, not patronise him: we must assume that he knows his business better than we do, until there is evidence to the contrary (here again, I emphasise the word 'business', for this is not to say that the farmer will be unappreciative of skilled technical advice and help); and at all costs we must avoid generalisation about different types of farmer, who are as different as chalk from cheese. To illustrate this last point, I will take a practical example. Agricultural economists are often criticised for their failure to agree on the matter of the cost of producing cocoa. But how can they agree when 'it all depends'? With the migrant farmers of southern Ghana an important determinant of costs is the speed with which the farm was established. If two farmers own farms of 25 acres, one of which was fully planted in three years with the help of gangs of daily-paid labourers, the other in 25 years, with the aid of youthful members of the family, then the costs of production, however computed, are likely to work out much higher in the former than in the latter case. This is not an unrealistic example. The migrant

farmers were secure within their boundaries, which were
established at the time of the purchase of the land, and they
did not have to clear and plant their land to assert their rights.
Many company farmers had not completed the planting of their
strip-farms, acquired perhaps 35 years earlier, when the swollen
shoot became serious.

I shall conclude with a further reference to this highly complex
question of farm size and scale of production. As most migrant
farmers not only own several farms in different areas but are
also apt to stand, as it were, in varying relations to these
farms (according as to whether they were inherited, self-acquired,
usufructuary grants, etc.), the notion of scale of production is
fraught with difficulties, such as require rather formal language
for their proper expression. While there is usually some
tendency for farms to get smaller as time goes by, the process
of sub-division tends to peter out in the long run—thus, with
patrilineal peoples a son's inherited farms are seldom sub-divided
on his death among his sons, the grandsons of the original
farmer. With matrilineal migrants the opposite process of consolidation on death (as when the property of three brothers, who,
each had his own farm, passes to one inheritor), sometimes
operates so powerfully as to counteract the sub-division tendency.
From the angle of the efficiency of farming, the principal problem
may be not 'fragmentation' (and it should be remembered that
many of the small farms shown on the maps are no more than
kitchen gardens owned by women relatives and others who happen
to reside in the farming area), but the fact that, especially with
Aburi farmers, too much responsibility is apt to fall on the
inheritor, who inherits all the lands formerly owned by his
maternal uncle or elder brother. This problem often seems much
worse on paper than in fact, owing to the willingness of many
inheritors to depute full responsibility to him who happens to be
resident on any land even to the extent of raising no objection
to his name being registered with the Department as the true
owner. The Aburi-style family land (such as Kofi Pare), and a
strip-farm acquired through a company, are such different types
of organisation that the practical agriculturists who work in the
field should lose no opportunity of contrasting and comparing
them.

NOTES

1. See Marion Johnson's two remarkable articles 'Migrants' Progress' (5)
for the earlier history of land-purchasing.

REFERENCES

Beckett, W. H., *Akokoaso: A Survey of a Gold Coast Village*, London School of Economics, Monographs on Social Anthropology, No. 10, 1944.

Brokensha, D. W., *Social Change at Lareth*, Ghana, Oxford, 1966.

Hill, Polly, *The Migrant Cocoa-Farmers of Southern Ghana*, Cambridge, 1963.

Hill, Polly, 'The Types of Southern Ghanaian Cocoa-Farmers,' in *African Agrarian Systems*, ed. D. Biebuyck, Oxford, 1963.

Johnson, Marion, 'Migrants' Progress' Parts I and II, *The Bulletin of the Ghana Geographical Association*, X, Nos. 1 and 2, 1964, 1965.

Green, R. H. and Hymer, S. H., 'Cocoa in the Gold Coast: a study in the relations between African farmers and agricultural experts', *The Journal of Economic History*, XXVI, No. 3, September 1966.

14

SOME SOCIAL AND ECONOMIC IMPLICATIONS OF PATERNALISM IN UGANDA*

Cyril Ehrlich

It is a commonplace that British government in Uganda was, from its inception, essentially one of benevolent paternalism— just rule by kindly parents. It is also evident that, particularly in the final decade before independence, the dilemma of this policy lay in its conflict with a growing realisation that the children would soon come of age. The political aspects of this dilemma are familiar.[1] Its social and economic implications are perhaps less clear.

For nearly sixty years the basis of Uganda's economy has been one of peasant, as opposed to plantation, production. The debate over the comparative advantages of these systems has been lengthy and still continues.[2] Despite new evidence we have probably still not advanced much beyond the position of the late 1930's when Hancock wrily remarked that 'What has so far been proved is simply the fact that colonial idealists do not all think alike'.[3] There is one aspect of this discussion, however, which has received less attention than it deserves. It has generally been assumed that the peasant method, though possibly less efficient in the production of export crops, at least in times of prosperity, enjoys the overwhelming advantage of creating an *integrated* economy and society. Plantations, in contrast, are regarded as the imposition of an alien structure upon the indigenous society:

'A plantation system is not a society', said Sir Hugh Clifford, Governor of the Gold Coast. 'It is an economic agglomeration created for the pursuit of profit. It substitutes itself for those primitive societies which in sickness and in health sustain their members'. And David Apter expresses a widely held view when

*Reprinted by permission of Cambridge University Press from *Journal of African History*, VI, 2, 1963.

he acclaims this statement as 'probably a classic of sophisticated awareness of the problem of economic and social change'.[4]

The purpose of this essay is not to defend plantation methods, though some defence is possible, as Wickizer, among others, has made clear. It is rather to examine, in the light of Uganda's economic history, the assumption that peasant production automatically leads to a society which is something more than a mere 'agglomeration'. This assumption is sometimes made explicit, as for example, by Sir Hector Duff:

'Whenever it is adequately guided, instructed, and encouraged, [peasant production] will effect more in the long run—it will open up a country more widely, thoroughly, and economically— than would be possible in any other way.'[5] The writer of a standard book on this subject, quoting Duff with approval, even credits the system with 'making the natives into producers and traders on their own account'.[6]

Judged against the experience of Uganda these statements are very much open to question. Sixty years of peasant production have not opened up the country widely and thoroughly, and have certainly not made the natives into producers and traders on their own account. Uganda is not an integrated economy society, but essentially an agglomeration; a mixture, not a compound. If this is so, why is it so? Surely not because of any lack of adequate guidance, encouragement and instruction. Perhaps the answer lies rather in the nature of the demands which successful peasant production of world crops has made upon the administering authority and the pattern of the latter's response to those demands. This is the pattern of economic paternalism.

The general nature of these demands and their *raison d'être* are familiar:

An indigenous economy has never been converted to exchange production without some degree of instruction or assistance from the foreign Government; wherever a native community is making any change in its system of production there will be found officials and ordinances.[7]

The new crops have to be produced by men who are, at least during the early years, not always convinced of their advantages, particularly if they are not food crops.[8] Moreover they have to be produced to a consistent standard of quality acceptable in world markets. The conversion from subsistence to exchange production also involves the establishment of local markets

which not only absorb the new products, but also offer a range
of consumer goods which will in turn encourage peasants to desire
cash and thus to continue to produce the new cash crop. Hence
the role of the trader becomes central to the process of development. To say that these are some of the demands made upon
colonial governments, at least in the early stages of development,
is merely to assert the obvious. Even the trading function can
become a concern of the government, for if indigenous traders
of the right type and in sufficient numbers do not appear, as
in Uganda, then it has either to assume this function or to encourage alien traders to enter the country.

But it is also arguable that, having of necessity assumed considerable powers of economic control in the early years, the
government later finds it difficult to relinquish such powers.
Officials and ordinances continue to proliferate, quality standards
acquire a life of their own, even losing touch with market realities,
and the Government, which began as an initiator of economic
change, tends increasingly to be restrictive in its influence.

A great deal depends here upon what meaning we attach to the
term 'economic development'. If by this we merely mean an increase in the wealth of society and in the incomes of its members,
then probably a generally favourable view can be taken of the
economic progress of Uganda in the twentieth century and of the
official policy which has been largely responsible for that progress.
But some economists are not content with so narrow a definition.
They define economic development as 'the widening of people's
access to alternatives'[9] or, as Professor Lewis puts it: 'The
advantage of economic growth is not that wealth increases
happiness, but that it increases the range of human choice'.[10]

If we accept the latter view, then, if a government persistently
restricts people's range of choice, it thereby tends to inhibit
economic development. Moreover, the bland use of the word
'development' for policies which ignore this fact, merely confuses
our understanding of the developmental process. The main burden
of this essay is that in Uganda official policies, because of their
restrictive nature, have been increasingly ineffective in stimulating
true economic development, and, more fundamentally, in establishing a society capable of future autonomous development.

Perhaps the most striking deficiency in Uganda's economy and
society is the paucity of economic sense and enterprise among its
people. Several observers have commented upon this. In 1934
Dr Mair described people's 'failure to make a very simple calculation of economic advantages'.[11] In 1952 a visiting American

economist wrote a provocative and essentially accurate account of the lack of economic sense among East Africans.[12] More recently an experienced administrative officer has written of the Iteso:

> Though money is nowadays the medium of exchange, barter is by no means a custom of the past . . . cattle are regularly obtained by traders in exchange for bicycles. Though an owner is often unwilling to part with a beast for six hundred shillings, he is usually prepared to accept a bicycle valued at 300/–.[13]

Similarly evidence is available of a widespread lack of entrepreneurial skills. In 1954 this was officially recognised by the appointment of a committee to make recommendations for the advancement of Africans in trade and commerce.[14] Throughout the cotton industry there is not a single African entrepreneur of any standing. Producers have little sense of the market value of their product and little ability to drive a hard bargain. The Lukiiko Forest Officer, for example, reported in October 1958, that farmers in Buganda were selling trees worth 100/– to sawmills for 10/–; one man sold two square miles of forest for 600/–, which works out at about 25 cents a tree.

Such generalised accusations of economic illiteracy are, of course, open to criticism. 'There can be little doubt', writes Bauer, generalising from West African experience, 'that, like other human beings, the African, once having entered the market economy, will tend to concentrate his activities on those products which are relatively more profitable'.[15]

There are several answers to this. In the first place there are fundamental differences in historical experience between West and East Africa. As early as the 1850s West African traders shipped palm oil direct to England and even chartered a vessel for this purpose.[16] In contemporary West Africa there are native traders with annual turnovers amounting to several hundred thousand pounds. The contrast with Uganda is depressingly self-evident. Secondly the question of responsiveness to market stimuli is surely a matter of degree, and it is possible to exaggerate the implications of African reactions to price changes. One did not need to be a William Lever to realise that coffee was more profitable than cotton in Buganda in the early 1950s and therefore to shift away from the latter crop. Thirdly we might well accept Bauer's statement if we take literally the phrase 'entered the market economy'. The problem in Uganda is that the overwhelming majority of the people have still not entered the market economy in any permanent or thorough going sense, but merely dwell on its periphery. 'Most farmers are still essentially subsistence peasantry with cash crops as a subsidiary activity.'[17] Moreover nearly 80 per cent of total money incomes is concentrated in Buganda and the Eastern Province.

We shall, perhaps, approach a better understanding of this problem if we attempt to list those desirable entrepreneurial skills which we consider to be lacking among Uganda Africans. They are, first, the ability to recognise market opportunities and the alternative possibilities of action which those opportunities present; secondly, the ability to make rational decisions based on the foregoing knowledge; thirdly, to take action. This last is the most important of all: the entrepreneur is essentially the man who 'gets things done', even when his actions are not entirely based upon rationalised knowledge . . . when he has to act upon a 'hunch'.

'In short the entrepreneur must be willing to behave in an independent manner, overcome resistance to change, and assume personal responsibility for the outcome of his actions.'[18]

In any society there will probably be obstacles to such activity, but in Uganda these obstacles have tended to occur in an acute form. First there is the prevalent unwillingness among the people themselves to devote personal abilities and energies to business. This initial apathy is enhanced by several factors: the restrictive effects of tribal custom, extended family obligations, a lack of social mobility, a narrow horizon of expectations (the inability to think long term), and the high risks of enterprise. But it could be argued that the attitude of the central authority is of greater importance than any of these. A wise government would not merely, or even primarily, attempt to increase business ability through direct action (the 'promotion of Africans in trade' and such-like curious activities), but would rather try to make the social environment congenial for economic activity. This can be done broadly in two complementary ways. First by refusing to discourage indigenous business activity, even at the humblest levels such as hawking, where experience can be gained, despite its administrative untidiness and its occasional impingement upon vested interests and non-commercial shibboleths. 'Established' traders do not like hawkers, whether in London's Oxford Street or in a Uganda township. Public health authorities do not like the dirt that comes with commerce. But in a poor society it is not authority's primary task to support established interests, and dirty development might sometimes be preferable to moribund purity.[19] Secondly, a wise government would refuse to gear social and particularly educational policy to the production of a non-commercial élite which, being highly paid and highly regarded, naturally attracts the most talented members of society away from the commercial sector.

Many aspects of Uganda government policy can be shown to be in direct conflict with this 'ideal'. But before turning to some of these it will be as well to examine two alternative hypotheses. It could be argued in the first place that African economic ignorance is due not to paternalistic influence but to inherent inability. This must be rejected as a racialist myth. Essentially it is a revival of Bucher's outmoded and discredited thesis that primitive man has no sense of economic values. Most social scientists would nowadays accept Firth's statement that 'Primitive economic systems differ only in degree and not in kind from our own'. But, to quote Firth again, 'These differences mean a lot when the member of a primitive society is trying to adapt himself to Western economic patterns.... The difficulty is that one cannot secure the material benefits of civilisation and retain the work habits of a primitive economy'.[20] The essential failure of paternalism in Uganda has been its inability to assist Africans to adapt and develop these primitive economic attitudes. In some cases it has even buttressed them against the impact of the market economy.

A second and superficially more attractive hypothesis, popular among Europeans in Uganda and among Africans themselves, is that African economic education has been hindered by the constant stream of Indian immigration. Obviously this argument contains a germ of truth, for the traditional Indian family business and the language barrier which it erects offer little scope for African 'apprentices' to learn much of business. Moreover it is strengthened by the definition we have adopted of economic development: in terms of increasing national income the contribution of Indian immigrants to Uganda's economic development has been prodigious, but in terms of widening opportunities for Africans their role has been more open to question. Yet it must be remembered that this role has been acted out against the backcloth of paternal authority. Protection against the supposed depredations of Indian traders has encouraged among Africans a woeful inadequacy in market haggling. Protection against indebtedness has hindered access to capital. The question is a complex one, but it is unlikely that a check to Indian

immigration would, in itself, have made much difference to the
pattern that has emerged. But in the absence of any serious work
on this subject, the impact of Indians upon East African societies
remains a field of guesses and inadequately based generalisations.

NOTES

1. Cf. *inter alia*, D. A. Low and R. C. Pratt, *Buganda and British
Overrule, 1900–55* (London, 1960), and D. E. Apter, *The Political Kingdom
in Uganda* (Princeton, 1961).
2. Two important recent contributions, by V. D. Wickizer, are 'The
Plantation System in the Development of Tropical Economies', *Journal of
Farm Economics* (Feb. 1958), and 'The Smallholder in Tropical Export
Crop Production', *Food Research Studies* (Feb. 1960).
3. W. K. Hancock, *Survey of British Commonwealth Affairs* (London,
1940), 11, Part 2, P. 176.
4. David E. Apter, *The Gold Coast in Transition* (Princeton, 1955), p. 51.
5. Sir Hector Duff, 'Cotton Growing in Nigeria', quoted by I. C. Greaves,
Modern Production among Backward Peoples (London, 1935), p. 212.
6. Greaves, p. 212.
7. Greaves, p. 195.
8. 'Originally the object in growing cotton was simply to get money to
pay taxes', Apter, *Uganda*, p. 187.
9. P. Bauer and B. Yamey, *The Economics of Under-developed Countries*
(London, 1957), p. 152.
10. W. A. Lewis, *The Theory of Economic Growth* (London, 1955), p. 420.
11. L. P. Mair, *An African People in the Twentieth Century* (London,
1934), pp. 151–2.
12. E. Hoyt, 'Economic Sense and the African', *Africa*, XXII (1952).
13. J. C. D. Lawrance, *The Iteso* (London, 1957), p. 148.
14. Cf. Uganda Protectorate, *The Advancement of Africans in Trade*
(Entebbe, 1955).
15. P. Bauer, *West African Trade* (Cambridge, 1954), p. 426.
16. K. Dike, *Trade and Politics in the Niger Delta* (London, 1956), p. 122.
17. I.B.R.D., *The Economic Development of Uganda* (1962), p. 17.
18. Meier and Baldwin, *Economic Development—Theory, History, Policy*
(New York, 1957), p. 358.
19. Cf. Hunter's criticism of 'The police in East Africa harrying the
vegetable sellers, usually women, on a periodic round-up of unauthorised
markets in an urban estate', G. Hunter, *The New Societies of Tropical
Africa* (London, 1962), p. 26.
20. Raymond Firth in *The Institutions of Primitive Society*, ed. E. E.
Evans-Pritchard (Oxford, 1954), p. 23.

15

SHARES OF RACIAL GROUPS AND OF FIRMS IN THE IMPORT TRADE OF NIGERIA AND THE GOLD COAST*

P. T. Bauer

Shares of Racial Groups in Direct Importing

In West Africa the first stage in the import trade, that is, direct importing, is largely in non-African hands. From information extracted by the Department of Statistics in Nigeria from customs records it appears that in 1949 about 85 per cent of the import trade of that country was handled by European firms, about 10 per cent by Levantine and Indian firms, and about 5 per cent by African firms. Since then the African share has probably increased slightly, partly as a result of preferential treatment in the allocation of import licences in the commodities affected by specific licensing.

The information available for the Gold Coast is less comprehensive than for Nigeria, but as will be suggested subsequently in this chapter it is sufficient to show that the general pattern of the participation of different groups in the import trade is similar to that in Nigeria. The share of African traders is probably somewhat larger as a result of more marked discrimination in their favour in the administration of import licensing. But as in recent years (especially in 1949 and 1950) specific licensing covered only a comparatively small part of all imports it did not affect the general picture greatly. It is probable that if the statistics for the Gold Coast were available in the same detail as for Nigeria they would show a somewhat larger proportion of importing in Indian and Levantine hands.

*Reprinted by permission of Routledge & Kegan Paul Ltd. from **P. T. Bauer**, *West African Trade*, (1963).

Problems of Presentation of the Shares of Firms in the Trade in Imported Merchandise

Africans frequently maintain that their small participation in direct importing proves that the import trade is in the nature of a monopoly. This is misleading, since a trade can be highly competitive even if all the traders are members of the same expatriate community. In the West African import trade there is in fact a substantial measure of concentration,[1] a large share of the trade being handled by a small number of firms. In view of the political and social importance of this question it seems worth while to investigate the degree of concentration quantitatively in some detail. Some points of presentation need to be clarified before summarising the results.

In computing the share of a firm in the import trade, all financially linked and associated firms have been included with the parent firm. This is the proper course in an examination of the degree of concentration in the import trade.

A special problem arises in the presentation of the shares of the merchant firms in the distribution of petroleum products and cigarettes. With few exceptions petroleum products are imported by the oil companies but are released by them through the merchant firms. Broadly the same applies to a substantial part of the supplies of imported cigarettes for which the leading manufacturer acts as an importer but releases supplies through the merchant firms. In assessing the shares of the merchant firms in the trade in imported merchandise their shares in the sale of these products need to be added to their shares in mercantile imports.

Somewhat similar complications arise for a few other commodities manufactured locally, partly from imported materials, by expatriate enterprises. These are not sufficiently important to justify adjustments in the calculations.

Except for a few commodities it would make little difference whether the shares of individual firms were calculated on the basis of c.i.f. values of imports or of duty-paid[2] landed cost of imports. The principal exceptions are petroleum products, cigarettes and spirits. These products attract duty at heavy rates and their distribution does not conform to the general pattern, as the share of the largest firms is appreciably greater than it is in the general range of merchandise. Where necessary the differences between the participation of the firms in the import trade calculated on the basis of c.i.f. values or on the basis of landed costs will be indicated in the text.

There is another matter of presentation, or rather of terminology, which needs to be mentioned. With few exceptions the leading European merchant firms are members of the Association of West African Merchants (AWAM), a trade association of West African merchant firms which have their offices in Europe. During the war this Association included various temporary or *ad hoc* members. But it is only some of the permanent members who, collectively, are generally referred to in West Africa as the AWAM group. At various times some of these firms have acted in concert in the import trade, though when they did so they were not strictly speaking acting as members of AWAM. These firms were members of the Staple Lines Agreement and the Merchandise Agreement, market-sharing arrangements in operation before and during the war; and they are parties to various agreements with suppliers. Although these firms are colloquially generally referred to as the AWAM group, they are more properly termed the Merchandise Agreement group, as these were the participants in that agreement. This will be the term generally used in this study. It is in no way intended as a term of abuse or criticism, but simply as a convenient collective noun for a distinct group of old-established European firms. Except where the contrary is specifically indicated it does not even imply the existence of concerted action by the group of firms.

The composition of this group of firms is well known.[3] In Nigeria it comprises the following: The United Africa Comapny Ltd. and all subsidiaries, including G. B. Ollivant Ltd. and G. Goytschalk and Co. Ltd.; John Holt and Co. (Liverpool) Ltd.; Compagnie Française de L'Afrique Occidentale; Société Commerciale de L'Ouest Africain; Paterson, Zochonis and Co. Ltd.; and the Union Trading Company Ltd.[4] In the Gold Coast it comprises the same firms with the addition of the Commonwealth Trust Ltd., a special trust which in its trading activities operates as any other concern.[5]

Shares of Individual Firms in the Import Trade in Nigeria

The information to be presented on the shares of firms in the import trade is derived partly from official and partly from private sources or calculated from data so obtained. This section discusses the information available on the import trade of Nigeria.

For Nigeria much of the material was provided by the information on the shares of particular firms in the importation of dif-

L

146 AN ECONOMIC HISTORY OF AFRICA

ferent commodities assembled from customs records by the Departments of Statistics and of Commerce and Industry. This has been supplemented by information supplied by private sources. Information on the releases of petroleum products and cigarettes was obtained partly from the Department of Commerce and Industry and partly from private sources. For most of the data the information was made available both from official and from private sources, and in every instance the figures provided independently by these sources agreed very closely, which confirms the reliability of those data derived from one type of source only.

The information from official sources was largely collected for this inquiry by the departments concerned; it was not available previously. The absence of any official information on this subject before this present inquiry has one important implication. From about 1940 to 1947 the extensive official import control system was administered on the basis of importers' shares in imports in certain pre-war years; this was popularly known as the system of past performance. Yet with negligible exceptions none of the appropriate government departments possessed independently compiled information about the past performance of the importing firms.

The distribution of the import trade in Nigeria among the direct importers is shown in Table 1. The firms A to F⁶ are the members of the Merchandise Agreement group. The residual item Z includes all firms importing individually less than one per cent of all merchandise. It also includes imports of petroleum

TABLE 1

*Shares of principal importers in commercial
merchandise imports into Nigeria, 1949*

Firm	Percentage of value
A	34
B	8
C	7
D	4
E	3
F	2
H	3
I	2
Z (aggregate of all other importers)	37

A–F total: 58

and tobacco products by those importers who are not merchant firms. If these imports are divided among the merchant firms on the basis of commercial releases made to them, the shares of the largest firms in the sale of imported merchandise are raised quite considerably. The share of A becomes about 40 per cent, and that of the Merchandise Agreement group as a whole is raised from 58 to about 66 per cent.

The data presented in Table 1 and the figures just quoted refer to the shares of firms in all commercial merchandise imports. This total includes many items such as mining equipment and supplies, marine and river vessels, ships' and aircraft stores and so forth which are not trade goods in the usual sense of the term. Mining equipment and supplies are imported largely by the mining companies themselves, and ships, boats, stores and supplies by the shipping lines and by the British Overseas Airways Corporation. If these items are excluded, the share of the Merchandise Agreement group of firms in the sales of imported trade goods in Nigeria in 1949 becomes about 70 per cent or slightly more.[7]

In short, in 1949 in Nigeria members of this group imported just under three-fifths of total commercial imports; they handled about two-thirds of the first sales of all imported merchandise, and between two-thirds and three-quarters of the first sales of imported trade goods. The largest single firm and its associates imported about one-third of all commercial merchandise imports, handled about two-fifths or slightly more of the total sales of all commercial imports and a slightly larger fraction of the sales of all imported trade goods.

The shares of firms in the aggregate imports of all commercial merchandise is information which is of limited meaning only. Not only do such figures include imports which are not trade goods and which are not handled by merchant firms at all; but they also obscure the wide differences in the shares of firms and in the degree of concentration in the import of different commodities.[8] For these reasons quantitative information on the proportionate shares of the firms in individual commodities is in some ways of greater significance and interest than their shares in total imports. Table 2 presents this information for Nigeria for twenty-three commodities or commodity groups; in recent years these commodities have represented about three-fifths of the value of all merchandise imports.

As will be clear from Table 2, there are wide differences in the degree of concentration in different commodities which are of some practical interest.

In the absence of licensing the degree of concentration tends to be specially high in standardised bulk staple lines, such as flour, cement, salt, cabin bread and the other items in columns 2–9 in Table 2. This result is as expected, since the economies of large-scale purchasing and bulk handling, transport and storage in these commodities are marked; moreover, they offer few opportunities for the judicious gauging of the requirements of the consumer and the other advantages which flow from close contact with suppliers and with customers.

Flour and sugar imports in 1949 were subject to specific licensing, and this also applied to corrugated iron sheets from certain sources. For reasons of policy, preferential treatment was granted to African importers in the allocation of import licences. It is certain that without this the share of the small firms (included in Z in the tables) would have been appreciably smaller. As direct importing requires considerable capital and skill, this particular type of assistance to African merchants is apt to be costly in real terms, particularly when applied in a sphere of trading where small-scale operations tend to be inappropriate.[9]

The tendency for the degree of concentration to be higher in standardised lower-grade merchandise emerges quite strikingly in the trade in textiles. The share of the largest firm is greatest in the import of bleached and unbleached textiles and becomes progressively smaller for those categories in which variety, design and colour are of greater importance, such as for printed cotton piece goods and rayon piece goods.

The table also provides quantitative information on another proposition which seems plausible on general grounds. A large measure of concentration among overseas suppliers conduces to concentration among importers. This is an instance of the general tendency of a high degree of concentration at one stage of production or distribution leading to similar conditions at subsequent stages. The influence towards concentration in distribution is especially strong where a product is standardised and the overseas supply is largely concentrated. In the West African merchandise trade petroleum products, cigarettes, salt and sewing thread provide obvious examples.[10]

There is also a comparatively high degree of concentration in the import trade in complex durable goods, especially technical goods. The handling of these requires considerable capital and skill, often engineering skill which may also be necessary for post-sales services. Partly for these reasons, the sole agencies frequently granted to distributors of these commodities are also

TABLE 2

Shares of merchant firms in the import or distribution of certain commodities or commodity groups in Nigeria, 1949 (percentages of values)

Firms	1. All commercial imports	2. Cabin bread	3. Cement	4. Corrugated iron sheets	5. Dried fish	6. Matches	7. Salt	8. Sugar	9. Wheat flour	10. All cotton piece goods	11. White bleached cotton piece goods	12. Unbleached cotton piece goods	13. Dyed cotton piece goods	14. Coloured cotton piece goods	15. Printed cotton piece goods	16. Mixed rayon piece goods	17. Pure rayon piece goods	18. Sewing thread	19. Motor vehicles	20. Bicycles	21. Cigarettes	22. Petrol	23. Kerosene
A	34	52	48	39	52	44	58	43	46	33	41	32	33	32	30	30	16	31	28	43	74	58	59
B	8	16	11	18	4	11	6	10	16	8	11	9	11	5	7	5	2	14	12	7	1	12	14
C	7	17	16	12	9	12	20	11	9	7	11	10	4	3	5	3	..	13	..	11	13	12	14
D	4	3	3	2	3	7	4	2	5	5	7	4	7	3	6	2	..	8	20	4	3	5	6
E	3	9	2	2	5	7	3	3	5	5	..	7	4	3	5	..	2	13	..	2	..	6	3
F	2	..	3	3	..	..	..	1	3	1	..	2	1	1	..	2	..	3	12	..	1	1	2
	58	97	83	76	73	81	91	70	84	59	73	64	60	46	54	42	20	82	72	67	92	94	98
H	3	..	2	3	..	12	..	2	5	6	..	7	2	9	7	4	5	..	2	1	..	3	1
I	2	..	1	..	..	..	..	2	4	4	1	2	2	12	2	1	2	..	..	..	..	..	..
Z (all others)	37	3	14	21	27	7	9	26	7	31	23	27	36	33	37	53	73	18	26	32	8	3	1
	100	100	100	100	100	100	100	100	100	100	100	100	100	100	100	100	100	100	100	100	100	100	100

Notes. 1. The symbol .. is used to indicate shares of less than 1%.

2. Columns 1 to 20 refer to percentage shares of imports effected directly by the listed firms.

3. For cigarettes (column 21) the figures refer to the shares of the merchant firms in the sales of all cigarettes; the figures in this particular column include a very small element of estimate.

4. In columns 22 and 23 the figures refer to the shares of the distributors in the trade of petroleum products released by the oil companies from their bulk installations. About one-half to three-fifths of the total supply is handled by one oil company, approximately one-third about equally by two companies, and the balance by the smallest supplier.

largely concentrated in the hands of the leading firms, though not necessarily in the hands of the largest firm. The sole agent often undertakes not to handle other types or brands of the same commodity, and this necessarily leads to a certain spreading of these agencies among the larger firms. The operation of these forces can be seen in the comparatively high degree of concentration in the import trade in motor vehicles and bicycles shown in Table 2. This runs counter to the general proposition that the degree of concentration tends to be highest in standardised staples. However, for the reasons just mentioned the comparatively high degree of concentration in these lines also accords with expectations.

Shares of Individual Firms in the Import Trade in the Gold Coast

The information on the structure of the import trade in the Gold Coast is not available in quite such a comprehensive and convenient form as it is in Nigeria. The material is presented in Tables 3 and 4.

Table 3 refers to 1949 and is based partly on the records of the Director of Supplies and partly on information derived from private sources. The information is not quite comprehensive because in some cases the records of the Director of Supplies covered only those imports which were subject to specific licensing, which applied to imports from certain sources only.

Table 4 is based largely on the records of the Customs Department. It shows the shares of firms in the imports of certain commodities into the Gold Coast for the nine months May–August 1950 and January–May 1951, i.e. nine months out of the thirteen months May 1950– May 1951.

The incomplete coverage of these two tables affects the figures to a small extent. The figures in Table 3 seem somewhat to understate the combined share of B–F in the import of cotton manufactures, while Table 4 certainly overstates both the share of A and the combined shares of A–G in the import of this commodity. The residual groups include one or two firms whose share in total imports may exceed one per cent. Again, the fact that Table 4 does not refer to twelve consecutive months also affects to some extent the shares of the different groups in the imports of sugar and flour. It is almost certain that for various technical reasons connected with the issue and expiry of licences and with the trading methods of African importers, Table 4 somewhat overstates the share of the residual group (Z) in the imports of

TABLE 3

Shares of merchant firms in the import or distribution of certain commodities or commodity groups in the Gold Coast, 1949 (percentage of values)

Firms	Sugar	Flour	Cotton manufactures	Cigarettes
A	31	40	40	57
B				
C				
D				
E	36	20	18	32
F				
G[a]				
H	12	8	10	3
Z (all others)	21	32	32	7

[a] G refers to a member of the Merchandise Agreement group not established in Nigeria.

Note. The figures in the last column differ slightly from those presented in *Economica*, November 1953. The figures in the article referred to the distribution of cigarettes imported in the first instance by the British-American Tobacco Company (over 90 per cent of the total). Those shown here also include cigarettes imported direct by some merchant firms.

TABLE 4

Shares of merchant firms in the import of certain commodities into the Gold Coast, May–August 1950 and January–May 1951 (9 months) (percentage of values)

Firms	Cement	Corrugated iron sheets	Sugar	Wheat flour	Cotton manufactures	Cycles and tricycles	Canned fish	Unmanufactured tobacco
A	49	28	12	30	45	43	36	39
B	7	7	3	5	9	4	15	12
C	5	2	2	3	3	12	8	—
D	4	16	3	5	6	—	5	14
E	1	6	1	1	3	1	4	7
F	2	11	2	4	5	—	6	8
G	—	8	2	2	1	11	6	7
	68	78	25	50	72	71	80	87
H	4	8	4	5	6	1	3	3
Z (all others)	28	14	71	45	22	28	17	10
	100	100	100	100	100	100	100	100

Note. For cement and corrugated iron sheets Z may include a few local authorities and certain government departments; for the remaining items it refers to commercial imports only.

sugar and flour. If statistics were available for twelve consecutive months, it is probable that the share of Z in the import of sugar in 1951 would be about 60–65 per cent and of flour about 40 per cent, instead of 71 and 45 per cent as shown in the table.

But in spite of these imperfections in the data, they show that the broad pattern of participation of the firms in the import trade in the Gold Coast is very similar to that shown for Nigeria in Tables 1 and 2. African participation is larger in the Gold Coast than in Nigeria in the staples subject to specific licensing; and the share of Levantines and of Indians in the imports of certain commodities, especially textiles, is probably larger in the Gold Coast than in Nigeria; lastly, there are considerable differences in the relative positions of firms B–F in the external trade of the two colonies. But these differences do not affect substantially the general picture of the participation of the large firms in the merchandise trade of the two colonies.[11]

The large share of Z in the imports of sugar and flour reflects the strong discrimination in favour of Africans in the administration of specific licensing which applied to these commodities. This discrimination became much more marked in 1950 and 1951, as is obvious from a comparison of their shares in the imports of these commodities as shown in Tables 3 and 4, the former of which refers to 1949 and the latter to 1950–1. In the absence of this discrimination the African share in the direct importation of these commodities would be small; this is evident from the small share of the residual importers (Z) in those staple imports in Nigeria which are not subject to specific licensing.

Regional Trading Representation

The participation of the firms in the import trade of a territory does not measure the degree of concentration in merchandise trade in different parts of that territory. The measure of overall concentration does not necessarily indicate the number of alternative sources of supply open to the population of a particular region. This needs to be discussed in terms of the district or regional trading representation, that is, in terms of the number of firms operating in areas or regions rather than in a particular country or territory. However, this question is less important than in the past, in view of the slow but steady improvement of communications in Nigeria and the Gold Coast, which is likely to continue.

In general, it would appear that throughout most of Nigeria and the Gold Coast consumers have reasonable access to the stores, or at least to the wholesale customers, of at least three or four different importers. This is suggested by information from various sources.

In both Nigeria and the Gold Coast reliable information is available on the number of produce-buying firms (whether acting as agents of the marketing boards or as independent shippers) in different districts. This suggests that the great bulk of producers of export crops have access to four or more buyers of their produce. Generally speaking the consumers of merchandise have access to more alternatives than the sellers of produce. There are more selling points of imported merchandise than buying points of export produce, and merchandise is generally easier to transport than the bulky export produce.[12]

These are large numbers of itinerant traders as well as agents and runners of African traders selling imported merchandise. They are in the aggregate an important channel of distribution in the retail and petty retail trade. Through them the merchandise stores of the importing firms exert influence outside the places in which they are established.

NOTES

1. Which, however, does not necessarily indicate or measure monopoly power.
2. Including excise duty on locally produced manufactures.
3. Its composition was discussed in the Sachs Report published in the Gold Coast in 1948; for this report see Chapter 6, § 4, below.
4. For certain purposes some importers of motor-cars and accessories are also full members of A.W.A.M. In the trade in export produce there are certain substantial non-importing firms who are also members of the Association.
5. Certain German missionary societies financed themselves before 1914 by taking part in trade. At the outbreak of war in 1914 their trading interests in West Africa were taken over by the Custodian of Enemy Property. Eventually they were placed in charge of a special trust, which functions to this day. It conducts an extensive and profitable trading business, and the profits are largely reserved for educational and religious purposes.
6. The code letters are used consistently throughout the book to denote the same firms; for code letter G see Table 3, below.
7. This estimate also allows broadly for the higher rates of duty on cigarettes, petroleum products and spirits. The share of this group in the distribution of these products is much greater than in merchandise imports as a whole; as the share of these firms is larger in those commodities which are liable to heavy duty, their share in the sale of all imported merchandise at market prices is necessarily somewhat higher than their share in imports which are valued at c.i.f.; the difference is of the general order of around 2–3 per cent. Cigarettes manufactured locally

by the Nigerian Tobacco Company are included with imports in these calculations.

8. Information on the degree of concentration in the import trade of different commodities needs also to be presented for another reason. A high degree of concentration in the trade in individual commodities would be compatible with a much lower degree of concentration in the import trade as a whole, if the leading firms in different branches of the trade were not the same. To obtain a reasonably complete and meaningful picture it is necessary to show the degree of concentration in the import trade as a whole, as well as separately for at least some of the major branches of the trade.

9. This tendency has been carried much further in the Gold Coast than in Nigeria (cf. Table 4 below).

10. Most of the imports of sewing thread are derived from the United Kingdom, where one producer holds a dominant position both in the home and the export trade.

11. This broad similarity of the shares of the firms in the import trade of the two colonies is confirmed by other evidence. The records and the Report of the Sachs Commission (a commission of inquiry in the Gold Coast in 1947–8) estimate that the share of the Merchandise Agreement group in the import trade of the Gold Coast was then about two-thirds, which was practically the same as in Nigeria. The structure of the export trade also offers indirect confirmation of this similarity.

12. Information relating to the distribution of merchandise during the war with details of the trading points maintained by the largest firms confirms this general picture.

PART FOUR

Labour: Problems of Supply and Social Aspects

16

THE DEVELOPMENT OF A LABOUR FORCE IN SUB-SAHARAN AFRICA*

Elliot J. Berg

Economic development in any area brings on manpower problems of two general kinds: the securing of unskilled and semi-skilled labour to meet the needs of new farms, factories, and mines, and the training of technical, managerial, and administrative manpower required by a modernising society. In contemporary Africa it is the latter problem which has become of overriding importance. But the development of an unskilled labour force was historically the major concern of governments and employers in Africa, and there still persist important problems related to the use of unskilled labour. It is with the problem of the unskilled and semi-skilled labour force that this paper is concerned.

For the most part, Africa has not passed through any industrial revolution. Probably a greater proportion of land and labour resources are devoted to subsistence production in Africa than anywhere else in the world. Such market-oriented activity as exists is largely agricultural and extractive. Industrialisation, narrowly defined, is only beginning.

This does not mean that Africa has had no problem of labour force recruitment. To the contrary, the problem arose there in almost pure form. Though in much current discussion the 'labour recruitment problem' tends to be seen as a problem of securing an industrial labour force, it has no necessary connection with 'industrialisation' narrowly defined. Its essence is the transfer of labour resources out of subsistence agriculture into paid employment. This is the truly revolutionary change in early economic

*Reprinted by permission from *Economic Development & Cultural Change*, Vol. XIII, No. 4, Part I, July (1965).

development everywhere: inducing men to work for others in return for payment rather than remaining in their traditional, subsistence production-oriented villages. The problem of securing an industrial labour force is mainly an *allocation* problem, though it does have unique features arising from the special discipline requirements of industrial employment and the necessity at some stage to commit the labour force permanently to industrial life. The 'recruitment problem' is the more general, more fundamental problem of getting the raw manpower, the 'bodies,' out of the villages into paid employment for others.

The recruitment problem in this latter sense has largely disappeared in contemporary Africa, completed before industrialisation has made large strides forward. Seventy years ago there were perhaps several hundred thousand Africans with experience of the employment relationship. Today relatively few Africans over 20 years of age have not at some time in their lives worked in paid employment. A labour force has come into existence, eager to take up industrial employment as it becomes available. It is not a skilled labour force. Nor is it, by and large, a labour force fully committed to paid employment; to an important degree it remains 'migratory,' shuttling periodically back and forth from village to town or mine. But it is a labour force—mobile physically and in an economic sense, sensitive to job opportunities, and disposed in growing measure to undertake final commitment to paid employment when it is possible and worthwhile for it to do so.

It is with the process by which this labour force was brought into existence that the present paper is concerned. The geographical scope of discussion is sub-Saharan Africa. In time, the focus is mainly on the years before World War II, in particular the years when the recruitment problem was at its peak of intensity—from the beginnings of modern development in 1880 or 1890 to about 1930.

The Sources of the Recruitment Problem

The labour recruitment problem as we have defined it—the transfer of labour resources out of the villages of the subsistence sector into paid employment—arose in most of Africa with unusual intensity during the first half century of modern African economic development—roughly from 1880 to 1930. Everywhere on the continent the scarcity of labour shaped the pattern of development of the economy. In some areas it set limits to the pace at which economic expansion could take place. The rapidity and urgency with which the demand for labour arose, sparse and badly distributed populations, the natural resistance of villagers to the wage-earning life—these are the elements which led to difficulties in recruiting a work force.

The Speed of Development

Only at the end of the nineteenth century and the beginning of the twentieth did the question of finding labour for local use arise in Africa. Along the west coast of the continent there had long been small groups of African clerks, craftsmen, and labourers at work for European commercial companies, and some too at the southern tip of the continent where Europeans had been installed since the seventeenth century. But contact between European and African until the 1880's was mainly a trading relationship.

The rapidity with which the continent was occupied and its exploitation undertaken was itself a cause of labour difficulties. Because of the very limited economic contact between the continent and the outside world before 1880, and because the indigenous economies were largely self-sufficient agricultural communities, there were no roads and few ports, buildings, or cleared lands. Africa lacked all that stock of accumulated physical capital which Europe had slowly built up before its industrial development began and which, however small, provides a vital first step on the path to rapid economic growth. This was all the more unfortunate because the vastness of the continent and an ungracious nature made the development of transportation and communication facilities an absolute prerequisite to development. Good natural ports were few, and the systems of internal waterways allowing unbroken access to the interior were fewer still. Everything, then, had to be started practically from the beginning, and at once. The demand for labour was highly 'bunched' in time.

The Urgency of the Demand for Unskilled Labour

Not only was there much to be done quickly, but the technical conditions of production of the industries which developed first were such that they demanded relatively heavy usage of unskilled labour. The most conspicuous and important example was transportation. Until the late 1920s or early 1930s, head porterage was the common method of transport for relatively vast quantities of goods. The use of animal transport was not possible in many areas because of the presence of the tse-tse fly, and bad roads made worse by violent rains ruled out the use of carts and wagons except in Southern Africa. Water transport was available in some areas: the Senegal, Gambia, and Niger Rivers provided some in West Africa for part of the year, and the great lakes of East Africa offered easy access to some parts of that area; the Congo River gave the Belgian Congo considerable, though discontinuous, stretches of usable waterway, and the Zambezi in Southern Africa allowed some water transport. With the possible exception of the Congo River, however, nowhere in Africa were there to be found the kind of unbroken all-year water highways that aided in the development of Europe, Russia, North America, and parts of Asia. Railways of course were quickly laid down; by 1910 in most areas they provided the skeleton of a modern transport network. But since African economic development centered on the export of minerals and other raw materials, rail lines ran from ports to specific producing areas, and even after railways had joined the coast with key interior points, head transport remained the only way to carry goods to and from points off the line of rail.

Until the spread of road transport in the 1920s and 1930s therefore, head porterage was often the only way to transport goods in many parts of Africa. To the extent that this was so, the technical coefficients, so to speak, in transportation were fixed and highly unskilled-labour-intensive. Where porterage alone was available as a means of transport, there were no practicable alternative combinations of factor inputs.

In agricultural and especially plantation production, similarly, possibilities of altering factor combinations were limited by the nature of the activity. There is no known way to pick palm nuts mechanically, nor can the use of labour be much economised in cocoa, coffee, and banana production. Even the clearing of ground for the establishment of new farms and plantations was largely labour-intensive work.

In some of the early activities there was a greater range of choice. Tractors could have been used for some agricultural activities. In mining and in construction of railways, roads, ports, and buildings, there are clearly alternative methods of achieving given results. But even where this was so, the economic and cultural context within which development began was such that employers and governments invariably chose methods involving least use of capital and skilled labour and most use of unskilled workers.

In the first place, relative factor costs were such that the use of capital-intensive methods was discouraged. In the pre-1880 period of contact between European and African wage rates for unskilled labour were extremely low. This was due on the one hand to the limited demand for labour, and on the other hand to the low supply price of that quantity of labour which was required, explainable mainly by the fact that wage earning was a definitely subsidiary activity for all but a very few Africans. The urgent demand for labour in many parts of the continent after 1880 set in motion upward tendencies in wage rates, but by liberal application of force and other measures governments and private employers sought to restrain these tendencies.

Equally important in accounting for the choice of labour-intensive methods by most employers was the fact that all factors other than unskilled labour were extremely expensive. Aside from the high costs of purchasing and transporting machinery to Africa, and the rapid depreciation of such machinery under African conditions, utilisation of machine methods necessarily involved the use of skilled labour. And skilled labour cost a great deal; in most cases it had to be imported from Europe at prices which reflected not only conditions in the labour market for skilled workers in metropolitan countries, but a high premium for the dangers and inconveniences of African life. Even rich and thriving enterprises, therefore, would have tended to economise on skilled labour and capital-using methods where they could do so. Individual settlers and governments, most of whom were far from rich and thriving, simply had to forego capital-using methods and use local labour abundantly, for they did not ordinarily have access to the investment funds needed to finance capital-intensive methods.

The Inadequacy of Labour Supply

The rapidity with which the demand for African labour arose, and the tendency to rely on unskilled labour even when other methods of production were possible, meant that there emerged, in the space of a few years, a relatively heavy demand for African labour in many areas. For a number of reasons this demand was not easily satisfied.

1. SPARSE POPULATION

The first reason is a simple one: there were not many people

M

in Africa. Very little is known about early demographic trends in Africa. In pre-colonial times, and for some decades after European establishment on the continent, it does appear, however, that African population growth exhibited a certain sluggishness; numbers of people do not seem to have expanded to a level justified by the availability of land. Just why this should have been so is not very clear. The slave trade was surely a factor. Between the seventeenth and nineteenth centuries as many as forty or fifty million Africans may have been carried off to the New World; and the tribal wars and social disruption which were largely a consequence of the slave trade had equally important demographic effects. But whatever the reasons, most of sub-Saharan Africa was sparsely peopled when colonial rule began and remains relatively underpopulated today. Some areas of dense population did exist: Basutoland, Ruanda-Urundi, parts of the savanna belt in West Africa, parts of Nigeria, some places in East Africa. But these were the exceptions.

Low population densities did not usually mean that, in absolute terms, there were too few men to meet the labour needs created by the coming of the European. Even today there are, as noted earlier, only about eight million Africans in paid employment out of a total sub-Saharan population of perhaps 180 million. What low population densities do imply, however, is that cultivable land was relatively abundant in the subsistence sector, so that population pressures or rural overcrowding could not readily be counted on to push men out of the villages into employment outside. Pressure of people on the land, which in other parts of the world often acted as the main stimulus pushing men into non-village employments, would not contribute greatly to the creation of a labour force in most of Africa.

2. MALDISTRIBUTION OF POPULATION

Even if the relatively scarce African populations had been found living in areas close to where they were needed, it would have been difficult to attract them into wage employment. But it so happens that natural resources useful in the modern world and the people required to exploit them have rarely been found in the same place in Africa. In West Africa, population is relatively dense in the Sudanese belt, the savanna regions of the interior, while the demand for labour arose near the coast where minerals and cocoa- and coffee-growing proved possible. The Copperbelt-Katanga region in Northern Rhodesia and the Belgian Congo, which became the greatest mining and industrial area in

Central Africa, was very nearly unpopulated in 1900.

The difficulties of travelling the long distances often required was not the only obstacle to voluntary movement of villagers to non-village employment. More important was the fact that the climate of the regions where mines and industries were located was often radically different from the climate of the manpower-rich regions. In West Africa workers had to be drawn from the dry savanna zones of the north into the hot, humid forest regions near the coast. The residents of tropical regions in Central Africa had to move to the more temperate (colder) regions in South Africa. Inhabitants of mountainous areas were needed frequently in lowlands. To move from one climatic zone to another involved a certain number of minor discomforts. In the matter of food, for example, the savanna people every-where in Africa are grain-eaters, accustomed to a diet based on sorghums (millet) and maize, whereas the forest people among whom they frequently worked used root crops (cassava, for example) as their staple. But these were minor matters. The real difficulty raised by large-scale movement of people from one climatic zone to another was the apparent inability of many African groups to stand up under the brutal change in natural conditions between their homelands and the new workplaces. This not only limited voluntary migration, but restricted employers in their search for recruited labour—recruited in the formal sense of being contracted for work by a recruiting agent or organisation. Until the 1920s, death and sickness rates in mines, railway sites, and urban centres were high, sometimes appallingly high. Pneumonia, miner's pthisis, tuberculosis, influenza—these and other diseases struck down African wage earners by the thousands. Invariably it was the African from a different climate who was hardest hit.[1]

The Release of Labour from the Villages; Process and Policies

Put in its simplest terms, the recruitment problem in Africa arose from the tenacity of social systems. Well-knit, integrated social systems yield stubbornly to change, and this is particularly true of tradition-oriented pre-industrial societies facing the onslaughts of economic change. It is universally observable that people in pre-industrial agricultural societies do not ordinarily relinquish, even temporarily, the security and certainty of their traditional way of life unless they are compelled to, or unless certain changes occur within the society. In most cases people in these societies have to be pushed from the land; rural life must be made untenable for them. Enclosures and rising population accomplished this in eighteenth century England;[2] in India and other parts of over-populated Asia it was made easy by a generalised rural misery.[3] In Africa it was particularly difficult because of abundant land and limited needs in the villages.

The Role of Expanding Wants and Voluntary Entry into the Labour Market

Some occasional individuals in subsistence agricultural societies do respond quickly when alternatives to village life present themselves; these are men ready for a change, either because they want for personal reasons to escape from their society, since they belong to subordinate groups (serfs, slaves, etc.), or from other causes. Also, occasional mass movements into non-village employment may occur when disaster strikes—crop failure, for example—and migration outside is the only alternative to starvation. But general and persistent movement into outside employment rarely occurs until one or both of two things happen: (1) new wants are developed by significant numbers of villagers, wants that can only be satisfied, or can be satisfied much more easily, by taking employment outside the village; (2) old needs are translated into money terms, so that earning of money becomes, if not essential, then highly desirable. The use of money to purchase cattle or to make bridal payments or to commute obligations to village chiefs are African examples of this phenomenon. These changes involved new demand for money income and created a general propensity to engage in income-earning activity.

The factors determining the speed with which new wants were accepted and old needs transformed in Africa are complex; little is known about them as yet. A number of tentative general statements can nonetheless be made, for certain recurring patterns appear in the different parts of the continent. First, the absorption of new wants and the propensity to earn money seems to have occurred most rapidly in societies which had pre-colonial traditions of markets and money and which had the most intensive trading contact with the outside world. The reactions of West African peoples, for example, were by and large quicker and more widespread than were those of most peoples elsewhere on the continent.

These and other goods which could be fitted into traditional patterns of production and consumption were everywhere the early object of African money-earning activity. One commodity, however, deserves to be singled out for special mention: textiles. The possibility of buying European cloth and, especially in Southern Africa, blankets seems to have been the single greatest incentive to money earning in the early years in most parts of Africa. Before the coming of the European, cloth was, in most places, a rare and expensive commodity. In some places its ownership and use was restricted to chiefs and members of the nobility; among the Ganda only members of the court could wear white cotton cloth, and a commoner could be executed for owning any kind of cloth.[4] Among the Ashanti of the Gold Coast, none except chiefs could wear cloths above the shoulder. Even where tribal custom did not limit the possession of cloth to the upper classes, economic factors worked to do so; cloths were woven in limited numbers by village handicrafters, and their price was beyond reach of the ordinary man.

It was therefore natural that European textiles had immediate and enormous appeal to Africans. They were comfortable and durable and so had great utilitarian value. And because of their traditional association with the rich and the powerful, they were prestigious goods. Most important, they were cheap, far cheaper than the local product; any man could earn enough money to dress himself and his wife. It is no wonder that the possibility of earning money for cloth was one of the most powerful motives for voluntary emigration.

The attractions of imported goods and the conversion of customary obligations into money payments did create a demand for money incomes in the villages and hence stimulated the voluntary migration of men into employment outside. But changes of this sort do not happen quickly, and the numbers who chose to earn money by wage earning were during the early years hopelessly inadequate to meet the demand for labour in most places. In time—and, all things considered, not very much time—voluntary migration did provide the major source of labour almost everywhere; by 1930 migratory flows of labour induced by largely voluntary desires for money income provided most of the labour force in all countries in Africa. But from the beginnings of European production in Africa, until about 1930, European employers and governments in Africa did not wait for expansion of wants to incite Africans to leave the villages for work. They pursued an aggressive policy of labour recruitment by 'artificially' creating needs for money income and by the use of force.

The 'Artificial' Creation of Needs for Money: The Role of the Trader and the Tax Gatherer

THE ROLE OF THE TRADER

If the African could not see quickly enough that greater consumption was the only path to the good life, there were other ways to make the earning of money a necessity for him. One way, widely followed in Southern Africa, was for a trader to urge on the villager whatever goods struck his fancy and thereby entangle him in debts he could not pay off except by working for a time outside the village. This was good business for the trader, who usually was also a labour recruiter; it was the essence of the 'advances system' which was of prime importance in the recruitment process all over Southern Africa.

The advances system lent itself to abuse. Traders could push commodities on Africans who were not keen to have them, and since no money changed hands, prices were scarcely considered. In years of bad village harvests the African would often sign agreements with traders to the effect that the family would be provided with goods which would be paid for later; the African could then vanish, perhaps never to return.[5] Colonial administration throughout Southern and East Africa tried to regulate the system by imposing legal limits on the amount of advances that could be given villagers. But the legal limitations had little effect. As late as 1918 European farmers in Northern Rhodesia were saying that labourers could only be got by taking Africans indebted to storekeepers in the rural areas.[6]

TAXATION AND LABOUR SUPPLY

The advances system was of basic significance mainly in those areas in which small European traders had penetrated the countryside. In West Africa, the Congo, French Equatorial Africa, and— less clearly—East Africa, this was not the case. Other means of stimulating African needs for money income had to be used in these areas. The obvious method by which to do so was the imposition of direct money taxes on villagers, and this was done not only in areas where the advances system did not take root, but everywhere in Africa except in the Gold Coast.[7]

While in some instances the aim of taxing Africans was to raise revenues, more commonly direct taxes were levied primarily to force them out of the village into wage employment. Parents were responsible for the tax; the theory was that they would press their sons into accepting employment outside the village. The tax,

however, proved inoperative, both because Africans resisted it
and enforcement was difficult. It was abandoned in 1905.[8] Similar
taxes were nonetheless levied in Southern and East Africa. The
governor of Kenya Colony said in 1908: 'Taxation is the only
possible method of compelling the native to leave his reserve for
purposes of seeking work. . . .'[9] A poll tax was duly introduced in
1908 (a hut tax had existed since 1899). The tax provided that
Africans employed by Europeans would pay only half the tax
required of those who did not work for Europeans.[10] Similar
legislation had been passed in Nyasaland in 1901.

Taxation brought the money economy into every village by
creating a fixed money obligation. It contributed to the beginning
of a flow of 'voluntary' labour from the villages. Its influence
can, however, be exaggerated. There were severe limitations to
its effectiveness as a recruitment device. The level of taxes, in the
first place, could not be fixed too high. If the tax burden was too
heavy, villagers might simply refuse to pay, as is suggested by
high rates of defaulting in bad years.[11] In the early days, further-
more, there were political risks in setting the tax level too high;
unrest or even rebellion might ensue. Finally, in British areas the
level of taxes was limited by official sentiment, strong in some
quarters, that relatively high taxes on Africans smacked of compulsory labour; any colonial administration that sought to raise
its tax rates would therefore have to override the objections of
the governors, in some cases, and of the Colonial Office almost
always. In this they were rarely successful.

If all villagers earned their tax money by migrating for wage
employment, the total quantity of labour made available through
taxation would have been substantial. But many of them had
alternatives to wage earning for Europeans. In some areas they
could grow export crops. In others, they could work for other
Africans who grew export crops. And where these alternatives
were closed, there was often the possibility of increasing output of
local foods or other crops, such as cotton and tobacco, which could
be marketed locally.

It is true that there were usually severe obstacles to expanding
the village output of marketable crops. New tools might be
required—ploughs instead of hoes, for example—and few Africans could afford them.[13] More important, roads and railways did
not service the majority of rural areas, and so transport costs
especially of local foods which are heavy in weight per unit of
value, were prohibitive. In addition, economic policies such as the
compulsory growing of crops (as in French and Belgian Africa)

and the granting of purchase rights to monopolies depressed the prices of local foods and made it more difficult for Africans to earn tax money without migrating outside. In the Congo a discriminatory price policy worked in the same direction.[14] European firms were aware that by purchasing African-produced foodstuffs they were curtailing their own labour supply, and occasionally attempts were made to curtail such purchases, in Northern Rhodesia, for example, European enterprises before World War I bought foodstuffs from distant parts of the country, even though it was more expensive, in order to reduce local African possibilities for income earning through expansion of agricultural production.[15]

But despite the obstacles, hundreds of thousands of Africans earned tax money either by growing export crops, by growing food or other crops for sale, or by working for Africans who grew cash crops. In West Africa, Uganda, and parts of Tanganyika, where peasant production of export crops developed, men could grow crops themselves or work for those who did. Even where there was little opportunity in this direction, the food and crop growing alternative was often possible. It may have required great effort to transport produce to market, and the African may have had to content himself with an abnormally low price for his produce, but it was still an alternative to leaving the village, and many Africans preferred it. And whatever policies were designed to prevent it, it often was the case that increasing agricultural output for sale was the economically attractive alternative for raising tax money.

All these considerations militated against the effectiveness of taxation in driving men out of the villages. And there was an additional disadvantage; the tax-induced labour flow was imperfectly distributed over time, the demand for labour tending to be greatest for European farms at harvest time, precisely the time that most Africans are needed in their villages. Men who migrated for tax money usually did so during the slack season in the village, at the times when demands for labour were at seasonal minimums. In some parts of Africa this problem did not arise. In West Africa, for example, migrants come from northern savanna regions to forest regions, where coffee, cocoa, and bananas are grown; here the seasonal inactivity in the north occurs at the time of the harvest in the forest regions.

Taxation of Africans, then, was helpful but hardly sufficient to recruit a labour force. From the points of view of the European enterprises, taxation presented one general inconvenience: though it led to an increase in the quantity of effort villagers would devote to income earning, it left to the African the choice of how and when to allocate this increased effort. When there were alternatives to wage earning for Europeans either in the villages or outside, taxation did not necessarily result in a flow of labour into European enterprises. Even when there was no alternative, and the total yield of labour from taxes was greater, it tended to be badly distributed over the year.

THE ROLE OF FORCE

The growth of African demand for money items, arising either 'naturally' by expansion of wants or 'artificially' through advances and the imposition of direct money taxation, was a considerable factor in the release of a labour force; by the early 1930s it was probably the main stimulus to the flow of labour from the villages. But in the two or three decades following European establishment in Africa the keystone of recruitment policy was force—the squeezing of Africans out of the villages by a battery of measures involving, to one degree or another, the use of compulsion.

The forms of compulsion were manifold; they varied from territory to territory and over time within each territory. Traditionally the forms of force used in Africa are classified in two categories, 'direct' and 'indirect,' though the lines between them were often unclear. The major forms of direct compulsion were the use of communal labour for local public works; labour drafts for major public works and for porterage; labour drafts for private employers; labour taxes; convict labour; and labour battalions. Into the category of indirect or veiled compulsion falls a wide range of measures: some tax policies; economic policies designed to discourage non-wage-earning alternatives to money making; land policies restricting Africans to certain areas—that is, the 'native reserves' policy followed in white settler Africa; and finally, most types of formal labour recruiting.

Direct or Open Force

The forced labour arrangements practised in various parts of the continent have been surveyed by many writers;[16] it is necessary only to mention them here. Communal labour for public works was used everywhere in the continent. It did not generally involve a serious degree of compulsion, nor did it have a significant effect on the labour market, except—as in French Africa and Uganda

170 AN ECONOMIC HISTORY OF AFRICA

—when it was used for non-local work. Traditional obligations of villagers to the chief for local purposes gave a customary sanction to this kind of labour recruitment, and it was also of patent utility to the villagers involved. Labour battalions, on the other hand, were never used outside of French and Belgian Africa, and there they were not widespread. Convict labour was widely used in all areas; governments generally allowed local construction projects. All governments used labour drafts for porterage purposes and for large public works projects as well, whenever necessary. Direct labour drafts for private employers, on the other hand, were rare in the territories under British control; indirect methods were more in fashion there. Labour taxes were a feature only of the early years in the Belgian and French Congo. At the time these taxes were imposed, there were few European enterprises demanding wage labour; economic activity centered on the *cueillette*—the gathering of produce such as rubber, ivory, and palm nuts. The labour taxes were designed to assure European concessionary companies a certain collection of this produce.

Direct force was widely used in the first stages of African economic development—until about the end of World War I. It thereafter became a minor element in most African labour markets. If it was true that conscript labour was used in Nigeria and other British territories in the 1920s, its use was hedged with greater and greater restrictions.[17] In French West Africa and the Belgian Congo, direct government drafting of men for private employers became increasingly rare.[18] Even in Portuguese Africa the laws regulating labour were amended so as to make unlawful the drafting of men for private employers.[19]

One reason for the declining presence of overt compulsion in the labour market after 1920 was the fact that the use of open force was repugnant to many Europeans; it ran counter to accepted canons of civilised behaviour. It was not hard for Europeans in Africa to work out consoling moral justifications for the use of force, but this was not so for Europeans at home. Domestic opinion within all of the metropolitan countries was unwilling to countenance the use of open force in securing labour for colonial enterprises. This opinion was most aggressive and articulate in England, but it existed in France and Belgium as well. There was also a growing world opinion on the management of colonial labour, an opinion quickly aroused to protest. After World War I this current of thinking found concrete expression in the Anti-Slavery Committee of the League of Nations, in ILO Conferences, and ultimately in the ILO Forced Labour Convention of 1930.

In addition to domestic and world opinion, there is a third and much more important reason for less resort to open force in dealing with colonial labour; it was not really necessary, since there were better, more refined methods of securing labour, most of them involving indirect or veiled compulsion. Except during the first few years of European rule in Africa, indirect force had in fact always been the dominant recruitment method. The decline of open force after 1920 did not therefore mean that compulsion itself was being swept out of the labour market. During the 1930s, as before, indirect methods involving the use of force remained in full sway.

Indirect or Veiled Force

Many policies can be described as involving indirect force; direct taxation of Africans, curtailment of African land rights through 'native reserves' policies (as in Kenya, the Rhodesias, and South Africa); economic policies designed to prevent the expansion of African agricultural production; and others. But by far the most fundamental was the kind of veiled force that was everywhere inherent in the system of formal and informal recruiting that developed throughout the continent. The system had three players: recruiters or 'labour agents,' European administrative officers, and African chiefs. Together this powerful trinity did more than any other force to provide the labour sought by European enterprises in Africa.

Whatever his form, the labour recruiter's function was everywhere the same: the rounding up of African manpower by any available means. In the early days it was not unusual for a recruiting agent—or more often his African helpers (known as 'messengers' in Southern Africa and *capitas* in the Belgian Congo) —to simply come into villages and by violence or threats of violence carry off a certain number of men.

By the 1920s most governments in Africa had introduced legislation to control the abuses of recruiting; they required licensing of recruiters and outlawed fraud and violence. These regulations, coupled with a tendency for the rough-and-ready recruiter of the early years to be replaced by a more respectable professional, made recruiting a more orderly business. But neither wise laws nor gentlemanly recruiters could eliminate the essential nature of the recruiter's job: to get men out of the village by pressure and promise. It was only the development of more voluntary migration that shifted the recruiter's role; instead of man-gathering he became a forwarding agent.

The recruiter's role cannot be appreciated apart from the activity of his two allies, his auxiliaries, as it were, in the struggle to find labour; the local European administrative officer and the village chief or headman. Without their help the recruiter was often disarmed and doomed to failure, though in later years, when his role became more that of organising an essentially voluntary flow of labour, this was not so. From the point of view of understanding the actual mechanism by which most organised recruitment took place, therefore, it is more important to consider the administrator and the chief than the recruiting agent himself.

THE ROLE OF THE ADMINISTRATOR

The arm of colonial government in the African countryside was the European administrative officer—the District Commissioner or Native Commissioner in English-speaking Africa, the *Commandant de Cercle* in French Africa, the *Agent Territorial* in Belgian Africa. In most places the administrative officer was the sole European in steady contact with the African tribesmen. He collected taxes, made census counts, built roads and bridges, and regulated disputes between tribal groups and within them. He was a formidable gentleman with enormous authority. Behind him, Africans knew, was all the power of the European state.

From the beginning of European occupation the question of the administrator's role with respect to labour recruiting was continually in dispute. The opposing forces were clearly aligned: employers wanted administrators to give more help to recruiters; mainly on the grounds that the government had a responsibility for the economic development of the territory, development required labour, and labour would not be forthcoming in sufficient quantity without the administrator's assistance to recruiters. Metropolitan governments, on the other hand, tended to be wary of allowing such assistance to be given by colonial administrators, fearing that forced labour would be involved. Local colonial administrations either shared the employer view or were torn between the two. The policy compromise worked out in most areas was that the administration's representatives in rural areas were to 'encourage' but not compel Africans to sign on with recruiters.

THE ROLE OF CHIEFS

Many observers of labour problems in Africa have assigned to the African chief a subordinate role, emphasizing the fact that he was a passive and unwilling player, the instrument through which recruiters and administrators worked.

While it was true that the chiefs acted in many instances unwillingly, and only in response to the wishes of the administrative officer in his area, it would be a mistake to ignore the more independent part played by some chiefs in all areas.[20] For the fact is that there were plenty of carrots made available to co-operative chiefs by recruiting agents, and the administrator's stick was not always required. Chiefs who proved amenable with recruiting agents could always count on rich rewards; the giving of gifts— sometimes substantial ones—was a major part of the recruiter's stock-in-trade.[21] In many cases chiefs received a per capita bonus for men supplied and in some instances were granted payments according to the length of service of recruits from their villages.[22]

The Decline of Forced Labour and the Flow of Volunteers

The depression of the 1930s brought to an end a decade of exceptional economic growth in most of Africa. With respect to the recruitment problem, it ushered in a new phase; after 1930 resort to forced labour of either the direct or indirect type came to play a role of steadily declining significance. It by no means disappeared. But the trend was clearly toward increasing freedom in the labour market, at least with respect to the villager's decision to work or not to work outside. During World War II this trend received a sharp setback; compulsory labour was introduced, reintroduced, or intensified in much of the continent. Since 1945, however, compulsion has declined almost to vanishing point. Except in Portuguese Africa and Liberia, the fundamental decision, the choice between staying in the village and going out to work for wages, has for almost 20 years been made by the Africans themselves, without the benefit of non-economic pressures exerted from outside the villages.

The disappearance of force as a major instrument of labour policy in Africa is due partly to political and ideological factors. Political change in most parts of the continent since World War II made it risky, impossible, or even inconceivable that colonial powers continue to exert pressures on Africans to hire themselves out to European enterprises. And the change in the climate of world opinion with regard to colonial policies in general and labour policies in particular worked to the same end. But most important, in the years since 1930, there has been a steadily diminishing need for forcing men to work (except for special reasons, such as during World War II). Sufficient numbers of Africans have in most cases come voluntarily out of the villages.

The depression of the early 1930s marked the turning point. It radically changed conditions in the labour market; with the prices of primary products sinking to new lows, the volume of wage employment contracted sharply. Perhaps for the first time in most African countries, there were more men offering themselves for wage employment than there were jobs to be had. In some territories the recovery was relatively quick, and by the mid-1930s new highs were reached in the volume of wage employment. But for some of the territories where labour supply difficulties had been most persistent and troublesome—Kenya and the Congo, for example—the demand for labour in the 1930s never attained the heights of the late 1920s. This meant that the period of the 'thirties was for many territories a decade of relative repose; it gave the process of want-creation another decade to percolate, as it were, throughout the countryside and allowed time for penetration and consolidation of the habit of labour migration in every village. The effects did not show until after World War II, when in response to increasing demands for labour, floods of Africans poured voluntarily out of the villages.

NOTES

1. Cf. R. L. Buell, *The Native Problem in Africa* (New York, 1928), Vol. I, pp. 31–32, 355, 570, 602, 827–28; Vol. II, pp. 324, 560, 571, 576., reprinted by Frank Cass, 1965.
2. Cf. P. Mantoux, *The Industrial Revolution of the Eighteenth Century*, rev. ed. (New York, 1947), pp. 429–36; J. D. Chambers, 'Enclosure and Labour Supply in the Industrial Revolution,' *Economic History Review*, second series, v, No. 3 (1953), 338 ff.
3. Charles Myers, 'India,' in W. Galenson, ed., *Labor and Economic Development*, (New York, 1959), p. 27.
4. C. C. Long, *Central Africa* London, 1876(), pp. 104, 113; and J. H. Speke, *Journal of the Discovery of the Source of the Nile* (Edinburgh, 1863), p. 345. See Hilda Kuper. *The Uniform of Colour* (Johannesburg, 1947), p. 130, for the role of cloth among the Swazi; L. H. Gann, *The Birth of a Plural Society* (Manchester, 1958), p. 156, and Audrey Richards, *Land, Labour and Diet in Northern Rhodesia* (London, 1939), for Rhodesian tribes. For Uganda see P. G. Powesland, *Economic Policy and Labour* (Kampala, 1957), pp. 2–7. On the West Coast of Africa it was the custom, until the mid-nineteenth century, to pay wages in cloth, which served as a widespread medium of exchange. See *Report from*

the Select Committee on the West Coast of Africa (1842), pp. 12–13, Appendix II.

5. D. M. Goodfrellow, *A Modern Economic History of South Africa* (London, 1931), p. 146.

6. L. H. Gann, *The Birth of a Plural Society* (Manchester, 1958), pp. 155–56.

7. It is not a question here of labour taxes of the kind levied in the Congo Free State and French Equatorial Africa, which were aimed at forcing villagers to gather and transport wild produce such as rubber and ivory; these fall in the category of pure force and are discussed later.

8. L .C. A. Knowles, *The Economic Development of the British Overseas Empire*, 2nd ed., Vol. I (London, 1928), p. 177; Vol. III (1936), pp. 321–23.

9. Norman Leys, *Kenya* (London, 1924), p. 186, reprinted by Frank Cass, 1973.

10. Marjorie Ruth Dilley, *British Policy in Kenya Colony* (New York, 1937), p. 240; and Gann, *op. cit.*, p. 80., reprinted by Frank Cass, 1966.

11. Cf. Hailey, *op. cit.*, 1938 ed., Ch. 10, for references to the numbers of tax defaulters in the various territories during the 1930's.

12. See for example, the results of attempts to increase the taxes in Southern Rhodesia, as described by Phillip Mason, *Birth of a Dilemma* (London, 1958), pp. 218, 227. See also the view of the governor of Tanganyika toward taxes in the Governor's Covering Dispatch, G. St. J. Orde-Browne, *Report Upon Labour in the Tanganyika Territory, 1925* (London, 1926), p. 10.

13. Sheila T. Van der Horst, *Native Labour in South Africa* (London, 1942), pp. 104–7, reprinted by Frank Cass, 1971.

14. It was common practice in the Congo, for example, to buy crops (grown under compulsion in the first place) at lower prices if they were of African origin than if grown by European farmers or agricultural enterprises. See *Le Problème de la Main-d'oeuvre au Congo Belge, Rapport de la Commission de la main-d'oeuvre indigène 1930–1931, Province Orientale*, M. le Colonel Bertrand, rapporteur (Bruxelles, 1931), pp. 12, 41, 84, 104.

15. Gann, *op. cit.*, p. 124.

16. Hailey, *op. cit.*, 1938 ed., pp. 608–7; ILO, *Forced Labour Report, op. cit.;*—, *Recruiting of Labour in Colonies . . .* , *op. cit.;* and Buell, *op. cit.*, Vols. I and II discuss forced labour arrangements in many African countries in the mid-1920's.

17. Cf. *Compulsory Labour for Government Purposes in Kenya* (London, 1925); Hailey, *op. cit.*, 1938 ed., p. 623.

18. *Loc: cit.*

19. ILO, *Forced Labour Report, op. cit.*, pp. 206 ff.

20. An ILO survey or recruiting practices in the 1930's said: 'In the early days of opening up a territory the chief may be the most effective authority in the land. Not infrequently this situation has brought recruiters into such close relations with chiefs as to make the latter direct purveyors of labour . . .' *Recruiting of Labour in Colonies. . . . ,op cit.*, p. 129.

21. Cf. *ibid.*, p. 142–46.

22. Cf. *ibid.*, pp. 226–27; and Buell, *op cit.*, Vol. II, p. 834.

17

BACKWARD-SLOPING LABOUR-SUPPLY FUNCTIONS AND AFRICAN ECONOMIC BEHAVIOUR*

M. P. Miracle and B. Fetter

It was long held that economic man was not found among the indigenous populations of Africa. In the early years of colonisation, statements to this effect were common. A French governor of the Ivory Coast complained in 1911 that 'the indigenous populations are excessively lazy and will never devote themselves to regular work.' A mission sent to Africa by the Belgians in 1915 and 1916 to study problems of developing their colony concluded, after a visit to a number of African colonies in addition to the Belgian Congo, that Africans generally and the Congolese in particular had been in a state of indolence for centuries and that economic development was impossible without coercion to 'educate' them to appreciate the value of work.[2]

The validity of these beliefs about African economic behaviour did not arouse much interest among scholars until well after World War II. Most of the literature on the subject dates from the late 1950s and has been increasingly critical of the accuracy of the early views as descriptions of current behaviour. But although there is mounting evidence that the economic response of Africans is not now peculiar, it is still commonly argued that this is a recent development—that at the beginning of colonial rule and for at least two or three decades thereafter Africans did not respond to economic stimuli as one would expect from economic theory.

Yudelman takes the position that in Rhodesia, at least, economic man has become an increasingly larger proportion of the tribal or traditional sector. However, he says, one still finds

*Reprinted by permission from *Economic Development and Cultural Change*, Vol. 18, No. 2, Jan. 1970.

examples of earlier economic behaviour patterns displayed by
'traditional man in transition toward becoming economic man,'[4]
who co-exists with fully evolved Africans who have become
economic man. Rivkin has argued that, generally, in Africa a
majority of Africans have been responding to economic incentives
since the latter part of the colonial period and particularly since
World War II, but that in some of the more isolated areas the
earlier behaviour patterns still prevail.[5]

More specific views about the behaviour of labourers are to
be found in arguments that the elasticity of the labour supply
has increased and that the bend in the labour supply curve has
flattened over time. Berg argues in a 1961 article that the response
of those already in wage employment is now altered so that
'the sharply backward-bending "time in employment function" of
early years has become a more gently backward-turning curve,'[6]
and this coupled with the effect on the curve of new entrants to
the wage labour force at higher wages has made 'the aggregate
supply curve for labour for the exchange economy as a whole
(the relation between the general level of wages and the total
quantity of labour available in the exchange sector) . . . positively
sloped through most of its length.'[7]

The purpose of this paper is to argue that even if changes of
this sort in the shape of the labour supply have occurred—and
this needs careful testing[8]—they do not necessarily imply changes
in the economic behaviour of African wage labourers. Stated
another way, it is our contention that a better explanation is
that it was a change in economic conditions within which African
labourers acted which produced the reported changes in labour
response rather than a change in behaviour patterns.[9] An examination of the nature of the process of moulding tribal economies
into larger and structurally different regional and colonial economies strongly suggests that in the early years of colonial rule a
sharply backward-bending labour-supply curve would have been
just as consistent with maximisation of individual worker welfare as a more gently backward-bending or positively sloped
curve was at later periods.

We have so far investigated only one region—the copper belt
of Congo (Kinshasa) and Zambia, one of the principal areas in
Africa employing migrant labour—but the evidence[10] suggests
that, until the nature of the economic conditions and changes
during the colonial phase is known in some detail for that
region, we should at least reserve judgment on other areas of
Africa.

N

Misinterpretation of Target Income

The data from which the backward-bending supply curve was usually generated consist primarily of casual observations that Africans working for non-Africans would work less when their wages were increased. Given the general belief that there is very little or no specialisation and exchange in the tribal economies, it was easy to explain such behaviour as that of individuals earning wages only for items that could not be obtained through their non-wage activities (and particularly for some non-African item or items which would be unavailable in the tribal economies). Thus, wage earning would be oriented toward saving a fixed sum or target from wages, and, assuming items purchased with such earnings were sufficiently few and gave satisfaction for a considerable length of time after purchased, such individuals might be expected not to work regularly for wages and to reduce the length of periods in wage employment whenever changes in wage rates permitted.

Such behaviour would be consistent with a backward-bending supply curve. Over time—and writers such as Rivkin and Yudelman suggest three, four, or more decades are required—Africans are viewed as finally learning to enjoy more non-African consumption goods, or buying items that give satisfaction for a shorter period after the act of consumption begins, until their targets were sufficiently large and flexible that they could be met only by longer and longer periods in the wage-labour force, assuming non-wage opportunities to earn money did not grow as fast as the desire for non-African consumption goods. Thus this view of Africans as workers and consumers suggests that there was a long period involving decade and generations before they reached the position that characterises Western economies, where individual demand for items produced by others is greater than the means for obtaining such items.

In the copper belt and its hinterland, at least, the evidence strongly suggests that indeed there was a desire in the first years of colonial rule to shorten the period spent working for white employers, but that the target demand consisted much more of taxes imposed by the new rules than lack of wants for purchased consumption goods.

A variety of consumer goods from Europe had been available in the tribal economies for decades when the first European administrators arrived; and in many areas imported goods became increasingly plentiful with the influx of European and

African traders that accompanied creation of the new colonies and new economic activities which were initiated. Such traders toured the countryside buying such things as ivory and rubber which had an international market, and sometimes also foodstuffs and livestock needed to feed the developing cities, railroad gangs, and mines.

For the last thirty years before colonial rule, if not earlier, European cloth, hoes, knives, guns, gunpowder, salt, distilled drinks, bracelets, and beads were made widely available in central Africa through caravan trade, and all of these items except guns and gunpowder were by no means unfamiliar to Africans, having been produced locally and often entering into commerce as far back as we have any record.[11] The imported goods were generally of considerably higher quality than locally made items with which they competed, but their usefulness was fully appreciated by Africans, and all accounts suggest there was a keen demand for them.

Nor is there, in fact, empirical evidence to show that Africans did not appreciate many, if any, useful imported items that were introduced after colonial rule, such as bicycles. As early as 1912, six years after mining was started in the copper belt[12] and two years after the Belgian Congo became a colony, one-fourth of the bicycles in Elisabethville, the principal city of the area, were owned by Africans.[13] Thus the assumption of target income resulting from limited appreciation of imported goods is suspect. Rural Africans were already accustomed to consuming most of the goods available in urban areas, and the advantages of working there must be reckoned largely in the terms of the level of income that could be earned and in the fact that such work was paid in the currency required for taxes[14] rather than in the currencies of precolonial trade (such things as hoes, salt, coweries, cloth, bracelets, or copper crosses).

If there are difficulties with the limited-wants hypothesis, the reluctance of labourers to migrate must be explained by wage levels in urban employment relative to rural income opportunities, or costs associated with working for whites.

Very little information is available on money wages during this period[15] and almost nothing is known or can be determined about the level of income from rural opportunities, but the costs associated with working for European employers clearly were much larger than heretofore assumed.

At the very beginning of the colonial period, in fact, so great were the costs of leaving the tribal economies to work in the developing urban areas that it is difficult to imagine a wage that would have both allowed employers a profit and still made urban employment attractive. Had it not been for imposition of taxes payable only in the currency of the new rulers, there is little basis for supposing rational labourers would have made themselves available in the first years of colonial rule.

Probably the most important component of total costs as perceived by labourers was the risk of illness or death. In 1911, one year after the beginning of Belgian rule, the head of Katanga's medical service estimated the annual death rate among Africans in Elisabethville to be 24 per cent per year because of outbreaks of typhoid fever, influenza, tick fever, pneumonia, and so forth. Thus, if tropical Africa then had the reputation in the Western world of being the white man's grave, at least some of its urban centres deserved the same reputation among Africans,[16] and the fact that administrators often attributed recruiting difficulties to epidemics[17] suggests that rural Africans were conscious of disease problems in the urban areas.

Fear of disease alone may well have sufficed to prevent most African labourers from offering themselves for work periods longer than the minimum required to pay taxes.[18] Many preferred to run the risk of defaulting on taxes and not getting caught; most of those who did work, whether by coercion or otherwise, reportedly shortened their urban sojourn whenever an increase in wage rates allowed.[19]

Other aspects of urban life, plus being away from home, worked similarly, but probably less strongly, as deterrents. Most, if not all, white employers regarded African labourers as inferiors if only because they lacked needed skills and had unfamiliar languages and customs. The practice of flogging labourers was not uncommon in the early days and was still used by some employers as late as 1959. Labourers could not bring families with them in the early years of colonial rule, and not only were there few unattached African women in urban areas but migrants often returned home to find their wives had been taken by another man in their absence.[20]

African labourers were often unaccustomed to, and disliked, the staple foods available in urban areas. European employers in the city gave rations of maize, then of little importance in the diets of most peoples of the copper belt hinterland, and made it available as meal that was processed in what the African consumers considered an inferior way. Maize rations were ground in steam-powered mills which produced a much coarser product than the hand-ground manioc, millet, or sorghum flour to which they had been accustomed. Instead of fish they received meat, instead of palm oil, peanuts.[21]

Prices were high, and storekeepers often managed to cheat their customers. Perhaps a general fear of the unfamiliar was also of some importance in the first few years. Urban centres ruled by whites were unlike anything in the histories of these peoples, and reports of curfews and other restrictions placed on Africans only aggravated doubts and fears.[22]

There was also a considerable cost in getting to urban areas. In the early portion of the colonial period, transportation was not available and most workers had to walk for several days through the territories of previously hostile tribes to reach urban centres.

Changes over Time

By 1960 the nontribal portions of the national economies of central Africa were still highly dependent on migrant labour. All evidence, however, suggests the reluctance to migrate had been greatly reduced although not primarily because of consumption motives. Goods taken back to the tribal economies by migrants were much the same as half a century earlier. Cloth or clothing, tools, bicycles, and ornaments were the major items during both periods. By 1960 there had been some addition of such things as construction materials—particularly sheet metal for roofs— and in some areas ploughs and grain-grinding mills were added to tools purchased. But neither the changes in the number of kinds of imported goods or quantity of import each in demand appears sufficient to explain disappearance of backward-bending supply curve in terms of changes in consumption habits. On the other hand, there were striking changes on the cost side.

By 1918 the death rate among Africans in Elisabethville had already fallen to an estimated 10 per cent per annum compared with 24 per cent per year seven years earlier.[23] There was a gradual relaxation of the prohibition against bringing African wives and children into the urban areas, and wives per 100 workers increased from eighteen in 1925 to eighty-three in 1955.[24] Extension of the railway and development of roads[25] greatly reduced the effort required of migrants in reaching employment centres[26] and made it easier for rural kinsmen to send them shipments of familiar food-stuffs to supplement the less desired and more expensive food-stuffs available in urban areas.[27]

Summary

It has been commonly assumed that African economic behaviour tended, during the colonial period, toward the development of response to economic incentives from the unorthodox to the orthodox. This paper presents evidence which suggests that if there has been a disappearance of the backward-bending supply curve of labour in recent years, as is widely assumed, a change in the nature or strength of the response of Africans to economic incentives did not necessarily take place. It may merely reflect changes in economic conditions rather than change in the response of individuals to the economic conditions they face.

Recent research in the copper belt of central Africa and its hinterland both casts doubt on the heretofore common explanation of changes in the shape of the supply curve for labour and suggests a plausible alternative.

The usual explanation of the apparent disappearance of the backward-bending supply curve over time in Africa is expansion of hypothesised target incomes because of assumed greater familiarity with goods available only through working for non-African employers. For most Africans in the copper belt's hinterland, the availablity of goods that were procurable only by earning wages from non-African employers changed relatively little during the colonial period; many more items were obtained by exchange before colonial rule than has usually been assumed. On the other hand, there were dramatic changes in the death rate of Africans living in urban areas and among conditions which initially were strong deterrents to sojourns in urban areas.

This, and similar evidence reported for Upper Volta, suggests that we should suspend judgment on whether the economic behaviour of African migrant labourers has changed significantly over time and should begin to test the hypothesis that it has not. It also suggests that research on the economic conditions which Africans face may be more fruitful for understanding the requirements for rapid economic growth than has usually been assumed.

NOTES

1. Gabriel Louis Angoulvant, *Guide du Commerce et de la Colonisation à la Côte d'Ivoire* (Paris: Office colonial, 1911), p. 167.
2. E. Leplae, 'Histoire et développement des cultures obligatoires de coton et de riz au Congo Belge de 1917 à 1933,' *Congo* 1, no. 5 (May 1933): 667.

3. See Elliott J. Berg, 'Backward-sloping Labour Supply Functions in Dual Economies—the Africa Case,' *Quarterly Journal of Economics* 75 (August 1961): 468–92; E. S. Clayton, *Economic Planning in Peasant Agriculture* (London: London University, Wye College Publications, 1963), pp. 55–59; E. Dean, 'Economic Analysis and African Response to Price,' *Journal of Farm Economics* 47, no. 2 (May 1945): 402–10; Mark Karp, *The Economics of Trusteeship in Somalia* (Boston: Boston University Press, 1960), pp. 52–70; William O. Jones, 'Economic Man in Africa,' *Food Research Institute Studies* 1 (May 1960): 107–35; Marvin P. Miracle, 'Response to Economic Incentives in Central Africa,' *Proceedings of the Western Economic Association* (1962), pp. 28–32; and *Maize in Tropical Africa* (Madison: University of Wisconsin Press, 1966), pp. 253–59; S. D. Neumark, 'Economic Development and Economic Incentives,' *South African Journal of Economy* 26 no. 1 (March 1958): 55–63; Robert M. Stern, 'The Determinants of Cocoa Supply in West Africa,' in *African Primary Products and International Trade*, ed. I. G. Stewart and J. W. Ord (Edinburgh: Edinburgh University Press, 1965), pp. 65–82; Arnold Rivkin, 'Economic Incentives in African Life,' *Journal of African Administration* 12, no. 4 (October 1960): 224–27; Delane E. Welsch, 'Response to Economic Incentive by Abakliki Rice Farmers in Eastern Nigeria,' *Journal of Farm Economics* 47, no. 4 (November 1965): 900–915; and Montague Yudelman, *Africans on the Land* (Cambridge, Mass.: Harvard University Press, 1964), pp. 85–103, 174–78.

4. Yudelman, p. 95.

5. Rivkin, p. 225.

6. Berg, p. 487.

7. *Ibid.*

8. That there was generally a backward-bending supply curve for labour in the copper belt is suggested by early observers such as John Bensley Thornhill who commented: 'It was unwise to raise native wages from 3s. a month (six yards of calico) to 5s. 10d. (over eleven yards), for this increased the cost of transport and development work by nearly £10,000 a year. This increase of cost, due to humanitarian motives, had the effect, in a few months, of enormously reducing our supply of voluntary labour, for the natives got too much calico and would not do any more work.' (*Adventures in Africa* [London: John Murray, 1915], p. 160). However, there may have been considerable variation in the shape of the labour-supply curve from one tribal economy to another. Although a backward-bending supply curve is generally suggested for the copper belt at the beginning of colonial rule, the Luapula tribe of Northern Rhodesia, then one of the three major sources of labour, appears to have displayed a positively sloped curve, and the major concern of British administrators was that these migrants would become permanent mine workers unless agreements for their return were negotiated with the Belgian administration controlling the copper belt (see L. P. Beaufort to Alfred Sharpe [draft], November 25, 1909, and H. Marshall Hole to D. E. Brodie, January 8, 1910, both in Zambia National Archives, ZA 3/3/2, no. 9).

9. For another argument that reported backward-bending supply curves in underdeveloped countries may reflect economic conditions rather than unorthodox response to economic incentives, see Benjamin Higgins, 'The Dualistic Theory of Underdeveloped Areas,' *Economic Development and Cultural Change* 4 (January 1956): 99–112.

10. For evidence suggesting that our hypothesis concerning labourers' behaviour is reasonable for Upper Volta as well as the copper belt, see Elliott Skinner, 'Labor Migration among the Mossi of the Upper Volta,' in *Urbanization and Migration in West Africa*, ed. H. Kuper (Berkeley: University of California Press, 1965), p. 65.

11. See Marvin P. Miracle, 'Plateau Tonga Entrepreneurs in Historical Inter-regional Trade,' *Rhodes-Livingstone Journal*, no. 26 (December 1959), pp. 34–50; idem, 'African Markets and Trade in the Copperbelt,' in *Markets in Africa*, eds. Paul Bohannan and George Dalton (Evanston, Ill.: Northwestern University Press, 1962), pp. 700–704; idem, 'Aboriginal Trade among the Senga and Nsenga of Northern Rhodesia,' *Ethnology* 1, no. 2 (April 1962): 212–22; idem, 'Trade and Economic Change in Katanga, 1850–1959,' in *African History*, ed. Jeffrey Butler, Boston University Papers on Africa, vol. 3 (in press).

12. In 1904 modern mining began in the copper belt with opening of the gold mines at Ruwe. In 1905 tin was also mined, 5·5 metric tons being smelted in crude clay foundaries, and Tanganyika Concessions Limited was employing some 3,000 workers. The first serious efforts to develop copper mining were in May 1905, when an ox-drawn caravan loaded with mining equipment left Benguela, Angola, for Katanga, but little copper was mined until the railway from the Rhodesias reached the copper belt. On October 1, 1910 the first train steamed into Elisabeth-ville and the mining boom was on. About 1,000 metric tons of copper were mined in 1911, and total mineral production totaled 2,492 metric tons in 1912. The European population of Elisabethville grew from sixty in 1910 to 1,200 in 1912. By 1914 total mineral production had reached 10,722 metric tons and 2,400 African labourers were employed by Union Minière. (See Anonymous, 'Angola-Katanga,' *The African World* [October 1934], p. 70; Comité Spécial du Katanga, *Comité du Katanga 1900–1950* [Brussels: Cuypers, 1950], pp. 30, 134; A. de Bauw, *Le Katanga* [Brussels: Cuypers, 1920], p. 13; and Union Minière du Haut Katanga, *Union Minière du Haut Katanga 1906–1956* [Brussels: Cuypers, 1956], pp. 214–16.)

13. *Journal du Katanga*, August 13, 1912.

14. Sale of foodstuffs to whites was a possible alternative for obtaining the money in the required currency needed for taxes in some areas, but there is no evidence to suggest that this was commonly done, and there is good reason to think Africans would have hesitated to make such sales. The colonial administration condoned, if not encouraged, village raids for procurement of foodstuffs needed by developing urban centres. Because of such raids, cattle herds were eliminated entirely from Katanga, and a number of instances of villages being reduced to famine conditions for at least a season are reported (J. Vandermissen, 'Essais d'introduction de matériel de culture de l'élevage à traction animale dans la région de Sandoa,' *Bulletin Agricole du Congo Belge* 35 [December 1944]: 202–12; and Vice Governor-General Malfeyt's Ordonnance no. 139 of April 1, 1912). Not only were the areas near the copper belt ones of poorer than average soils and rainfall, and therefore probably with relatively little agricultural surpluses, but transport was difficult and arduous because of lack of beasts of burden (A. Hock, *L'agriculture au Katanga* [Brussels: Misch & Thron, 1912]). Moreover, by bringing surpluses that might be available to administrative centres, Africans ran the risk of singling out

their home area as one worth raiding. The only year for which data on both taxes and commodity prices are available in 1916, but data for that year suggest that not more than 23–24 per cent of African taxpayers at most could have paid their taxes by sale of staple foodstuffs to urban areas. Some 685 'tons' (probably metric tons) of grain, mostly maize, were reportedly bought by the mining areas at an average of twenty francs per sack in 1916. Assuming sacks were 100 kilograms (220·46 pounds)—grain shipped to Katanga from Northern Rhodesia was shipped in bags of 200 pounds as early as 1921—a ton of grain would have paid the tax of, at most, 66·4 workers (if only workers from districts with annual taxes of six francs per adult male sold grain), but more probably only 33·2 workers since the districts nearest to urban areas had a tax of twelve francs per adult male that year (see n. 15 below). This gives a range of 22,472–44,944, at the maximum, as the number of taxpayers that could have paid taxes through sale of the major starchy staples then being purchased. If one divides total tax receipts by the average of tax rates levied, 102,952 males paid taxes in 1916. Both the price of staple foodstuffs and the number of taxpayers appear to have fluctuated greatly from year to year. Staple foodstuffs were bought from Africans for as much as thirty-five francs per sack by at least one European firm about 1910 during the beginning of the mining boom in Elisabethville. In 1915 the average price was estimated to be as low as seven to eight francs per sack, then the next year it was said to have climbed to twenty francs. The number of African taxpayers in Katanga, calculated by use of a simple average of district tax rates, varied from 63,930 in 1912 to 114,497 in 1915 (see unnumbered table below).

Year	African Taxpayers, Katanga
1912	62,930
1913	82,584
1914	67,048
1915	114,497
1916	102,952
1917	113,666

Source— Data from E. Coulon to Directeur du Bourse de Travail du Katanga, July 13, 1916, copy enclosed in a letter from Coulon to A. van Iseghem, July 19, 1916, in van Iseghem papers below; *Bulletin Agricole du Congo Belge* 9 (1918: 144–45); G. de Leener, *Le commerce au Katanga: influences belges et étrangères* (Brussels: Misch & Thron, 1911) p. 22; S. Milligan, Report on the Present Position of the Agricultural Industry and the Necessity or Otherwise of Encouraging Further European Settlement in Agricultural Areas (Livingstone: Government of Northern Rhodesia, 1931), p. 6; and Belgian Congo, *Rapport annuel* (various issues 1912–17).

African sales of commodities with an international market, such as ivory and rubber, also may have provided some opportunity for earning taxes without working for whites, but we have found no quantitative data on this, and qualitative information suggests such opportunites were not of major importance (Comité Spécial du Katanga, *Comité Spécial du Katanga 1900–1950*, p. 52).

15. Minimum mine wages for Rhodesian and other labourers from British governed colonies were set at fifteen francs per 'ticket' of thirty days of work in 1911. Wages for Congolese Africans were considerably lower. In 1913 the cost to employers was fourteen francs per worker for thirty days of work for Congolese workers and twenty-five francs for workers from British areas for the same work. These figures include, besides wages, an amount for rations, housing, a blanket, and provisions for the return journey home. If such non-wage costs to employers were the same per worker for Congolese and non-Congolese Africans, the non-Congolese received almost four times as much as their Congolese counterparts. Wages appear to have continued at the 1911 rate until 1919 when a new minimum wage contract was negotiated for Rhodesian workers, but we have been unable to confirm that the differential for Congolese labourers remained the same. In 1912 taxes were twelve francs per year for the three districts for which we have information. By 1916 taxes were twelve francs per year in some districts and half that in others; thus assuming, as our evidence suggests, that wages to Congolese were four francs per month in 1911 and continued at that level until 1919, the Congolese labourers would have had to work forty-five to ninety days per year to pay their taxes, depending on their home district.

Tax per Adult Male (in Francs)

Year	Haut-Luapula	Tanganyika-Moëro	Lomami	Lulua
1912	12.00	12.00	—	12.00
1916	12.00	12.00	6.00	6.00
1917	12.00	12.00	6.00	6.00
1918	—	—	—	—
1919	12.15	12.15	6.15	6.15
1920	12.45	12.45	6.45	6.45
1921	12.45	12.45	6.45	6.45
1925	20.60	12.45	8.45	8.45

Source—Data from Zambia Archives A/1/1/13; Bourse de Travail du Katanga, *Rapport annuel* (1913), pp. 7–8; *Comité Régional* 7 (April 1925): 156; and Belgian Congo *Rapport annuel* (various issues 1915–16, 1918–20).

16. During the outbreak of influenza in 1918, about half of the African labourers of Elisabethville reportedly deserted, and a similar proportion —45 per cent—deserted in the last three months of 1912, apparently also in reaction to outbreaks of disease (see *Mouvement geographique* [May 18, 1913], p. 240, and Belgian Congo, *Rapport annuel* [1918]. p. 101. There is also evidence that concern about disease made labour recruitment difficult in West Africa. Elliot Skinner cites reports of early observers there that at the beginning of colonial rule in Upper Volta recruiting was difficult because of knowledge in villages of the high death rate

among wage labourers, and he notes that the Mossi, the principal tribe of the country, were 'appalled at the death rate of migrants, and said 'Nansara toumde di Mossé ("white man's work eats [kills] people")' (Skinner, see n. 10 above).

17. A. de Bauw to Comité Local Bourse de Travail du Katanga. February 13, 1918, in Territorial Archives, Ministere de l'Intérieur, Lubumbashi, A9, 'Recrutement'.

18. An exception, perhaps, were the labourers from the Luapula tribe of Northern Rhodesia who came from an area where sleeping sickness was endemic and apparently migrated willingly to the copper belt which was free of sleeping sickness but had other diseases not common in rural areas (see Beaufort to Sharpe, and Hole to Brodie, n. 8 above).

19. Thornhill (see n. 8 above), p. 160. Some of the employment opportunities outside the tribal economies, such as serving as porters, sometimes involved only occasional, and perhaps short, urban sojourns while in employment, but the death rate appears often to have been high in the early years whenever there was a concentration of labourers. The death rate of Katanga porters in an entirely rural setting between June 1917 and March 1918 was 24·2 per cent (A Pearson and R. Mouchet, *The Practical Hygiene of Native Compounds in Tropical Africa: Being Notes from the Experience of the First Eighteen Years of European Work in the Katanga* [London: Bailliere, Tindall, & Cox, 1932], p. 18).

20. For the spectrum of European attitudes, see Ferdinand Harfeld, *Mentalités Indigènes* (Paris: Plon, Nourrit & Cie., 1913), 25 n.; for the prejudices of an enlightened man, see Eugène Gelders to A. van Iseghem, July 24, 1914, Musée Royale de l'Afrique Centrale, André van Iseghem papers. On the difficulties of keeping a wife, see *Journal of Katanga*, July 10, 1915; G. van der Kerken, *Les sociétés bantoues du Congo Belge* (Brussels: E. Bruylant, 1920), 245 n.; and the report by Inspector of Industry, A. Boulty, of March 8, 1919, in Territorial Archives, Ministère de l'Intérieur, Lubumbashi, A110, 'Main d'oeuvre indigène, Tanganika-Moëro.'

21. On the composition of diets in the tribal economies of this area, see Miracle, *Maize in Tropical Africa* (see n. 3 above), pp. 157–66, 193–95. Palm oil was important only among workers coming from areas north of the copper belt. For information on rations see, Royaume de Belgique, Ministère des Colonies. Administration de l'Agriculture, *Rapport sur l'agriculture du Katanga en 1911 et 1912* (Brussels, 1912), p. 16.

22. On cheating by merchants see, Royaume de Belgique, Ministère des Colonies, *Renseignements de l'office colonial* (Brussels: Belgium, Office Colonial, 1911), p. 138. On African curfews see, *Journal Administratif du Katanga* (1911), p. 13; and idem, 1912, p. 87–88; and *Journal du Katanga*, February 20, 1915.

23. Union Minière du Haut Katanga, Service Medical, 'Rapport annuel' (1921, unpublished).

24. Union Minière du Haut Katanga, *Union Minière du Haut Katanga 1906–1956*, p. 220; and idem, Union Minière Haut Katanga, *Evolution des techniques et des activités sociales* (Brussels: L. Cuypers, 1957), p. 226.

25. By 1927 transportation had been sufficiently improved so that the Belgian administration abandoned porterage in most areas (Ordonnance no. 37 of December 3, 1925 and Ordonnance no. 25 of September 7, 1927). In 1928 the railroad from Katanga to Kasai was completed, and

Katanga was able to cut off food imports from the Rhodesias and rely largely on Kasai for provisions.
26. At the beginning of colonial rule all labourers had to walk to employment centres. According to a survey of labourers in the Northern Rhodesian portion of the copper belt published in 1954, only 20 per cent of workers travelled the entire distance to their employment on foot, and 70 per cent made the whole journey either by bus or train or a combination of the two (David Niddrie, 'The Road to Work,' *Rhodes-Livingstone Journal*, no. 15 (1954), p. 40.
27. Exactly when this practice started cannot be determined, but by 1959 it was common enough to be frequently mentioned by workers' wives interviewed in the copper belt market places (see Miracle, 'African Markets and Trade in the Copperbelt' [see n. 11 above], p. 711).

18

THE PRODUCTIVITY OF AFRICAN LABOUR*

P. de Briey

Over the last sixty to seventy years tropical Africa has undergone an economic revolution. Its 140 million inhabitants, who for centuries had been producing nothing more than the necessities for subsistence, have now begun living and producing with an eye to the outside world. In other words a market economy has taken the place of the subsistence economy. This change was essential for progress. In the absence of any currency some medium of exchange had to be found for the purposes of education, the treatment and cure of endemic and epidemic sickness, the opening of communications and the acquisition of a minimum of industrial equipment or simply for the purchase of goods from Western traders. Africa, however, had no other medium of exchange to offer than its own farm produce or the labour of its people. While the resulting exchange has taken place partly through the sale of produce and partly through the hire of labour, 'there is a marked tendency in most territories for one or the other of these two forms of commercialisation to dominate. Thus, for example, production for market plays by far the more important part in money earning in the indigenous agricultural economies in the Gold Coast, French West Africa, Nigeria and Uganda, while in Kenya, Northern Rhodesia and Southern Rhodesia wage employment completely overshadows cash cropping.'[1]

Thus a market economy made its appearance in Africa. The process was and still is extremely slow. Even now, in tropical Africa as a whole, the major proportion (approximately 70 per cent) of the resources of cultivated land and of labour (approxi-

*Reprinted by permission from the *International Labour Review*, Vol. 72, 1955. (Supplement.)

mately 60 per cent) of the indigenous agricultural economies is still engaged in subsistence production.[2] Yet the development of a market economy is essential for any improvement in the standard of living of the people. In view of the rising population and the progressive erosion of the soil, to quote only the most obvious factors, there is a need to expand resources and acquire equipment, and this would be difficult in a subsistence economy. At the present stage of development the need for fresh changes is becoming evident. It is clear that transport facilities will have to be improved if there is to be any increase in the export trade. Productivity will also have to be raised to ensure a flow of goods to foreign markets, meet the needs of workers employed in non-indigenous undertakings, and maintain the standard of living of the producers themselves. New sources of production will also have to be discovered, and the reserves of labour must be used more effectively than in the past, possibly by finding work for them in industry instead of on the land.

It is not possible to go into the details of these developments here; one of them, however—the raising of labour productivity—is well worth studying by itself, since opinions on the subject are extremely varied.

If the output of unskilled labour in industry were to be taken as a yardstick, the picture of the African worker's standards of productivity would undoubtedly be gloomy. It is unanimously recognised that the output of unskilled African workers is extremely low in almost all the undertakings that employ them. An attempt to measure the productivity of labour in a factory in Durban (Union of South Africa) showed that the output of the average unskilled migrant worker was only 29 per cent of the figure taken as the optimum.[3] The report of the commission of inquiry set up to investigate the protection of secondary industries in Southern Rhodesia produced statistical evidence to show that output per head of local workers was considerably lower than in any other Commonwealth country.[4] A report published in 1946 expressed a similar opinion of labour in British East Africa (Kenya, Uganda and Tanganyika). It stated: 'The dominant problem throughout East Africa is the deplorably low standard of efficiency of the worker'[5]—a view confirmed as far as Kenya is concerned by the report of the Committee on African Wages published in 1954. The Governor-General of the Belgian Congo, speaking before the Government Council in July 1949, was also sharply critical of the low output of workers in this territory.[6] An inquiry held in Duala (Cameroons under French administration) found that—

> As compared with a White worker's output, that of a Negro varies between one-third and one-seventh or one-eighth, depending on the employer and the trade (or within a given trade). The usual proportion is about one-quarter. In other words, it takes a Negro four days to do what a White does in one. And this opinion was confirmed by all the employers that we talked to.[7]

The output of the African wage earner is only one determining factor in the productivity of the population as a whole. Since his output is low, his wage is low—enough, perhaps, for his own subsistence but quite inadequate to meet the requirements of a family. This low level of output among the wage-earning population ought to be offset by higher productivity among the independent farmers, the more so since the number of the latter has been much reduced by the movement into wage earning employment in non-indigenous undertakings. Those that remain must consequently produce enough to feed the absent workers, meet the needs of the traditional communities and maintain a flow of goods for exchange on foreign markets. In fact, however, the productivity of the independent farmer has fallen off in almost every part of Africa south of the Sahara.

This position is in no way exceptional. The work of Colin Maher and Humphrey[8] on Kenya, Clément,[9] Drachoussoff[10] and Malengreau[11] on the Belgian Congo, and Guilloteau[12] and Dumont[13] on French West Africa have shown that the exhaustion of the soil and the resulting drop in the incomes of African farmers are tending to become general. What is worse, it is clear that the native farmer is simply unable to increase his productivity, the limit to what he can do being governed by factors beyond his control. African farmers have neither the capital nor the technical knowledge, nor in some cases the cultivable land, to expand their output.

The result of this is that over large areas of tropical Africa output is inadequate, and low living standards and instability are prevalent among both the independent farmers and the African wage earners. The peoples of Africa are poor because they do not produce enough. In order to create wealth they must produce more, so that the surplus production can be used to buy more efficient tools, pay for the cost of education and vocational training, acquire fertilisers for their land, extend the expectation of life through medical care, etc. As it is, they have to eat most of their own output of food or use it to buy clothing and other basic consumer goods.

The position is by no means hopeless. In Africa as elsewhere, the productivity of men depends on a few major factors:

(1) the amount of labour in relation to the available land;
(2) the amount of labour in relation to the available capital;
(3) the methods of production;
(4) the state of the labour force from the standpoint of health, intelligence and character, and its skill and training.

The first three factors must be studied if the productivity of the independent farmers is to be raised. However, in the case of the wage earners, whose opportunities are governed in the main by the society in which they are brought up and the undertakings for which they work, the human factor is the only one that matters. Moreover, in such a thinly populated continent as Africa the importance of man himself is preponderant. The following pages are accordingly devoted to an analysis of the human factor in productivity.

The African Worker

The productivity of an undertaking does not depend entirely on the workers it employs, but it is evident that the human factor is decisive, since no job can be done without a practical and intelligent approach. It follows that in any analysis of the factors governing productivity, particular attention must be paid to the worker's physical and mental health.

In the first place the worker's fundamental aptitudes must be examined and also the kind of life he leads in his original environment, taking into account the attendant physical, climatic, social and moral circumstances. The next step is to try to understand what the transplantation to factory or city life means to him, and especially the importance he attaches to his conditions of employment (wages, accommodation and so on), industrial relations, basic education and vocational training. Lastly one must attempt to estimate the violence of the shock he suffers on embarking on a way of life entirely different in conception, pattern and tempo from anything he has previously experienced.

The aptitudes of African workers have been the subject of much study. Attempts have been made to test the average development of their intelligence,[14] but a comparison of the results obtained with those yielded by similar experiments on Europeans has produced no conclusive evidence, and the most recent writers on the subject do not hide their scepticism.

> It has indeed become abundantly clear in recent years that there is no present possibility of assessing the comparative general intelligence of Europeans and Africans in Africa; environmental differences are too many and too great, and have profound effects on traits (such as speed) and motives that influence the test achievement.[15]

The same author has been even more explicit in a recent booklet:

> It has become increasingly clear in recent years that no fundamental differences between different groups of Africans, or even between Africans and Europeans, have yet been demonstrated. It is possible that intrinsic differences do exist but, if so, they are probably quite slight and at present undiscoverable. . . . The manifest differences that do exist as between Europeans and Africans, and which have been described by many writers, can be well explained on the basis of experience, of environmental factors. The chief environmental factors that account for the observed diversities are climatic, infective, nutritional and cultural. Of these, the last is overwhelmingly important, and in general it can be said that the minds of men (unlike their bodies) are mainly products of their cultures.[16]

The African's vocational aptitudes, however, are also important. A number of interesting studies have been made in connection with short-course vocational training methods by an aptitude-testing mission working in Brazzaville in French Equatorial Africa, and Dakar in French West Africa. The head of the mission had recorded the following description of its findings:

> (1) In an initial experiment conducted in French Equatorial Africa, we found that the aptitudes (mechanical, verbal, mathematical, visual, etc.) that distinguish one European from another were by no means easy to discern in the young Africans we examined on recruitment.
> We then decided to measure their general level of intelligence, or rather their powers of adaptation. Judging by the success of the training courses, this proved to be an efficient method of selection. But the most interesting thing we found was that when we resumed our aptitude tests on the same subjects after four months' training, not only were the results more satisfactory, but the gifts of each subject had become normally apparent—which seems to confirm our

o

suspicion that aptitudes are impossible of measurement (at least by European standards) in the absence of any training similar to that given in the place of reference.

(2) In this experiment, and in the other experiments conducted later in French West Africa, the standard set for the tests was lower than is usual in France. The results obtained at the beginning of the training were also somewhat lower than those obtained in France with corresponding courses. Even so, it was only a few months before the progress charts caught up with those we had plotted for French workers, thus proving that the African's initial difficulties are neither inherent nor insuperable. . . .

So far everything goes to show that, given comparative equality of knowledge, the African worker's basic intellect is the same as that of his European counterpart—at least at the level we have studied.[17]

The African is closely bound up with his physical environment, and any assessment made of him must therefore take account of the climate in which he lives, the diseases he suffers from, the food he eats, and the social group from which he comes.

As regards climate, the view has been expressed that with freedom from malnutrition and infection, and when other circumstances are propitious, African society can rise to splendid heights, and that Africans themselves are basically well adapted to their climate.[18] Even if this view is considered over-optimistic, the African climate would not appear to be a major obstacle to the productivity of labour.

In a study of labour productivity in the Belgian Congo, Mr. Arthur Doucy has described the physical condition of workers from the Mayumbe, Tshuapa and Middle Kwilu districts on arrival from their tribal areas. He states:

(1) they all suffer from parasitic worms of the intestines;
(2) some suffer from parasitic worms of the blood;
(3) all have malaria;
(4) all have incipient yaws, for which they have received little or no treatment;
(5) most have or have had gonorrhoea;
(6) many have syphilis;
(7) some of these conditions reduce their haemoglobin level, which in many cases is as low as 65 per cent, i.e. a red blood count of 3 to 3½ million.[19]

This gloomy picture is unfortunately generally true, though the specific infections vary. Dr. Carothers, after mentioning the main diseases to which Africans are subject, adds: 'Few Africans are free from all of these, and it would be easy to find examples of persons infected concurrently with malaria, hookworm, bilharziasis, ascariasis, and taeniasis, with a haemoglobin level of about 30 per cent, and yet not complaining of ill health. "Normality" in the African, even from the standpoint of infection alone, is a rather meaningless abstraction.'[20] This description of the pathological conditions found among a high percentage of Africans has a parallel in the reports that have come in from various sources concerning the effects of the chronic malnutrition so common in many parts of Africa. The fact that many African communities are underfed has been placed on record on numerous occasions, notably in 1939 by the British Committee on Nutrition in the Colonial Empire,[21] and in 1949 by the Inter-African Conference on Food and Nutrition held at Dschang in the French Cameroons. Dr. Carothers also writes: 'In summary, African diets are lacking in a variety of constituents necessary for physical and mental health. These deficiencies are most widespread and prominent in regard to protein, vitamin A, and certain members of the vitamin B complex. The chief sufferers are the infants and young children, but no age is immune. The classical deficiency diseases are seldom seen, but the bulk of the population lives on the verge of their development, and in periods of stringency they promptly appear.'[22] The main deficiency diseases referred to are pellagra and malignant malnutrition, also known as 'kwashiorkor'.

The effects of chronic malnutrition have not been accurately assessed in Africa, but it appears certain that in vast areas where malnutrition is an everyday occurrence the inhabitants lack vitality and drive.

However far the low standard of productivity in Africa may be attributable to malnutrition and disease, it would be wrong to explain the inefficiency of the African industrial worker wholly in terms of his physical condition. The infections to which Africans are subject take a much stronger hold on them in the rural areas, where medical supervision is virtually non-existent and malnutrition is also more acute. On the other hand it would not be true to say that the African is generally incapable of sustained effort in his native environment. Many observers have testified to the contrary, among them Dr. Ombredane, who writes: 'It has often surprised me to see Negroes working from 8 o'clock in the morning until 2 in the afternoon without any break for rest or refreshment, in an effort to finish a hut or a piece of raffia work, a hatchet, a hoe, an ivory figure or a mask that they had started

making.'[23] Mr. Ryckmans quotes the case of men who think nothing of a 12-hour walk into the jungle to fetch well over a hun-
dredweight of brushwood.[24] Other illustrations can be found
in the back-breaking job of clearing farmland and in the many
other communal tasks that form a part of African village life. In
the case of the farming population, as was mentioned earlier, the
explanation of the low level of productivity lies in the inefficient
farming methods and the desertion of the villages by the men. In
the case of the wage-earning population, on the other hand, it
seems that some other explanation must be found.

It is natural to look first for a connection between the African
wage earner's indifference towards his job and the new setting in
which he finds himself, involving as it does the payment of a
wage as well as special housing, training, industrial relations and
so on.

To a European worker wages are the fundamental incentive to
work. It has often been said of the African worker that wages
offer no inducement and that less effort rather than more is likely
to be the result of higher pay. This bare statement will not stand
investigation. In a paper submitted to the Belgian Royal Colonial
Institute, Mr. R. van der Linden has shown how wage increases in
a Léopoldville shipyard between 1939 and 1950 were accompanied by an appreciable rise in productivity. What is true is that
many Africans with crops or cattle to look after in their villages
look for wage-paid employment with the sole idea of earning a
little extra money with which to pay their taxes or to buy some
article. If, having found a job, the wage is increased and they
succeed in saving the requisite amount more quickly, they see no
further point in working and either slacken off or try to leave.
What is taken to be a lack of logic, or as a sign of indifference or
laziness, is in fact the outward expression of a perfectly valid
piece of reasoning. Even so, before wages can play the same part
in the life of African workers as in the life of Europeans, money
and economic forces generally will have to acquire the same significance in the African's social group as in the Western world.
At the present time, Africans living in a subsistence economy can
still dispense with wages and not starve. This, however, raises the
problem of the African's relations with his social group—a point
to be considered later.

There is no need to emphasise how much a worker's output can
be affected by his housing. If an unstable worker is to settle, he
has to be given a chance of finding accommodation near his
workplace, and if he is to settle for any length of time some

arrangement must also be made to house his family. Some employers have recognised the benefits of a stable labour force and have arranged for suitable accommodation to be built for their employees. This, however, has not happened in the cities. In most cities the way the African population is huddled together in makeshift dwellings has to be seen to be believed.

However, while poor housing may discourage a worker from settling down, it should not be assumed that satisfactory housing will always have the opposite effect.

The value of training is self-evident. C. H. Northcott, writing of Africans in Kenya, states that men 'who knew nothing of mechanics and until they reached Nairobi had never seen a railway train, are met in the railway workshops with a display of mechanism so great that it bewilders even a well-educated European.'[25] The results achieved with training are in fact spectacular, but no worthwhile training can be given to a worker who stays only six months. Training presupposes a certain amount of stability; before a worker can be trained, moreover, he must be imbued with a desire to work.

It may be asked whether the problem can be solved by satisfactory labour-management relations. While an atmosphere of confidence and understanding can undoubtedly do much to encourage more effective and sincere co-operation on the part of African workers, it cannot guarantee success or higher output. There are certain over-riding factors influencing the conduct of the African worker, and even the best employer is powerless against them.

The analysis of the factors determining a worker's output leads to a fundamental question: Does the African want to work in an undertaking of the Western type? As one author has observed—

> Men of all races work only to achieve some end. If that end is unobtainable, or not valued very highly, they either work light-heartedly or not at all. The African in town is in just this position. His expenditure is limited almost entirely to consumable goods, the kind of bric-a-brac that a traveller picks up on his travels. With none of the tribal sanctions capable of operation, with few kinsmen in town to remind the worker of his obligations, and with no urban public opinion, there is nothing, either in his own social system or in that of the West, to inspire him to greater effort.[26]

The above quotation emphasises the solitude of the normal Negro worker. He has lost his attachment to the land, he no longer takes part in tribal consultations, he no longer shares in the labours, joys and sorrows of his village. The significance of this isolation is difficult to grasp without some knowledge of the African's normal way of life in his natural environment and as a member of his social group. Carothers writes—

> Life in Africa was highly insecure, but the individual did achieve some inner sense of personal security by adherence, and only by adherence, to the traditional rules—rules which received their sanction and most of their force from the 'will' of ancestors whose spirits were conceived as powerful and as maintaining their attachment to the land. There were fears, of course, and misfortunes were almost the order of the day, but even these were seldom without precedent, and for each of these there were prescribed behaviour patterns which satisfied the urge to action, so that the African achieved a measure of stability and, within his group and while at home was courteous, socially self-confident and, in effect, a social being. But this stability was maintained solely by the continuing support afforded by his culture and by the prompt suppression of initiative.[27]

Limits are placed on the freedom of the individual, for otherwise he would be lost to the community.[28] No culture is absolutely static, for a static culture cannot survive. The African tribal system, like every other, has an infinite capacity for adaptation. But the fact remains that for a man brought up under a system deeply rooted in tradition and so vitally dependent on a code of social behaviour, the change to an entirely different way of living is a great strain. As Carothers observes, change has become a familiar feature of modern Europe and America. For an African, however, the shock is incomparably more violent, and it is natural that when he suddenly finds himself confronted with a way of life in which he is left alone to face a multitude of unknown risks, against which his tribal culture can afford him no protection, his first sensation is one of insecurity. This is a point on which all observers are agreed. Mannoni states that when a Malgache finds his traditional chain of authority in danger, if not actually disrupted, he falls a prey to panic, insecurity and a sudden sense of insufficiency.[29] Balandier also notes that the formation of an urban proletariat has gone hand in hand with a rising sense of insecurity. In a report of Elisabethville prepared on 3 April 1950, Grévisse writes: 'The thought uppermost in the minds of the Bantu population of the towns is not a desire for individuality or freedom, as is often mistakenly believed; it is neither more nor less than a desire for some security.'[30] But the security an African requires is not of a mystical or instinctive kind; it is physical and economic. What he wants is a guarantee against starvation and an assurance that he can live and grow old in peace with his family.

> In Western civilisation, men work for money because of the security that it brings or because of the possessions and the prestige that a wealthy man can command. In African society men also sought security and prestige. These were likewise achieved only by hard work, although the concept of money did not enter into the situation. . . . The urban situation, however, demands that the African should work as hard as, or even harder than, he has ever done before but, at the same time, neither his work nor the money that he earns can provide him with the security or the prestige that he would like. The average urban African is unhealthy, badly housed, uneducated, and he lacks any security in town even if he happens to have been born there. . . . The bars to progress are very real to him and he knows that, under present conditions, town life in European employment can offer him little in the way of lucrative employment or future stability. Consciously or unconsciously, therefore, he refuses to cut himself completely adrift from his tribal kinsmen and his tribal background. This tendency to live and work in town while maintaining unproductive land in the reserves is referred to as the 'foot in both camps attitude' and is largely condemned on the grounds that a man who attempts to retain a foot-hold in both places cannot be efficient in either. There is considerable truth in this assertion . . . the actual situation is that the urban Africans are poised between two different ways of life or systems of belief. They see clearly enough that the kinship system of tribal days and the monetary system of the West are incompatible. They see the two systems in conflict and they want to come out on the winning side. At present, however, neither side can offer any long-term advantage. The monetary system of the West offers goods but no security. The kinship system offers few goods but some security. This security, however, is already somewhat suspect because of the break-up of the tribal order. On the other hand, the precarious state of those who are completely detribalised, who have no country home to retire to in their old age, or who have no knowledge of country life, is fully realised. And so the majority of men continue to sit on the fence and attempt to retain such rural security as is available together with as many of the material benefits of town life as they can obtain. . . . Little change can be expected in the low level of efficiency, however, because the motives that are fundamental in prompting a man to work—the desire for security and self-respect—cannot operate.[31]

At first sight it would appear that the way to raise productivity is to do away with the alternative—to assist the worker in severing his tribal ties and to settle him, together with his family, at or near a centre of employment. To quote Carothers: As things are, the chief incentive in the towns is to acquire money quickly with a view to a return to rural living. The ambition to improve one's skills and rise in urban industry cannot develop until the rural boats are burned; but I have no doubt that once these boats are burned and incentives are re-orientated these people will work as competently, and ultimately as creatively, as any other men.'[22]

This policy of stabilising African workers near a centre of employment has been adopted in the Belgian Congo for some years, and also, though more recently, in Kenya. The policy has been very clearly stated in the Report of the Committee on African Wages:

> Of a total of some 350,000 adult male African workers in employ-
> ment outside the reserves, it is estimated that more than half are
> of the migrant or 'target' type; that is to say, they are workers who
> have left the reserves for a specific purpose—for example, to earn
> sufficient money to pay tax, replenish a wardrobe or acquire a
> wife . . . and return to the reserves once that purpose has been
> achieved. Many of them spend no more than six months outside the
> reserves in any one year and, for all practical purposes, they may be
> regarded as temporary workers. . . . It is only by retaining his stake
> in the reserve, and by returning there at frequent intervals, that the
> African worker can ensure, for both himself and his family, the
> minimum requirements of sustenance, a house in which to live,
> and security for old age. It follows that, if we are to induce
> the African worker to sever his tribal ties, and convert him into an
> effective working unit, we must be prepared to offer him, in his new
> environment, advantages at least as favourable as those he already
> enjoys in the reserve. . . . They are—the payment of a wage sufficient
> to provide for the essential needs of the worker and his family;
> regular employment; a house in which the worker and his family can
> live; and security for the worker's old age. At a later stage—when we
> have reached our objective—consideration will also obviously have
> to be given to the problems arising from unemployment among a
> stabilised working population.[33]

These changes may be expected to yield positive results. In the Belgian Congo, undertakings that have been employing stabilised labour for some years have reported an appreciable improvement in efficiency. Even so, it would not appear that the problem has been solved. For more than ten years the Union Minière has made it a practice to employ stabilised African labour, but one of its advisers, Mr. Fischer, stated in a report to the General Assembly of the Belgian Colonial Congress on 6 June 1952 that a spirit of tribal solidarity still persists even among many of the more enlightened workers and that in the majority of cases money incentives are ineffective.

What, then, is lacking? One writer has observed that 'before wages can be fully operative as a factor in behaviour, they will have to find their proper place in a new pattern of society built up as a prolongation of the older order'.[34] As the same writer has observed elsewhere in connection with the new wage-earning population, it should be possible to resettle them, re-establish their bonds of solidarity, and rebuild an organic community entitled to protect their interests and providing them with the guarantees that their original community is no longer able to afford.[35]

It is interesting to see the progress being made in the British West African territories, which offer many useful pointers for the future, inasmuch as development, and especially the development of African urban society, has been more rapid there than elsewhere. In these territories, as in the rest of Africa, the rural population have left their homes and families and gone into the towns in search of work. Statistics show that between 1931 and 1950 the population of Lagos increased by 80 per cent as a result of an influx from every tribal group in the country.

> What has happened in consequence of this mingling of people and their shift from rural to urban pursuits is that a new social organisation has arisen. This is based on association, principally by occupation and by tribe, and it is taking responsibility for many of the duties traditionally performed by extended family and other kinship groups . . . Coleman reports similarly from Nigeria. There, too, these tribal associations have been organised spontaneously in the new urban centres. . . . 'They are the medium', says Coleman, 'for re-integrating the individual employed in an impersonal urban city by permitting him to have the essential feeling of belonging.' These Nigerian tribal associations also provide mutual aid and protection, including sustenance during unemployment, solicitude and financial assistance in case of illness, and the responsibility for funerals and the repatriation of the family of the deceased in the event of death. . . . The fact that many kinship groups are no longer economically self-sufficient impairs their solidarity for other social purposes, and the result is that occupational and other associations which cut across tribal and kinship lines have taken over many of the activities previously performed by the extended family, the lineage, and similar traditional organisations.[36]

It would seem at first sight that this immense and diversified effort on the part of Africans to build up an entirely new and integrated social structure for their own protection when the older traditional society is beginning to disintegrate corresponds to former developments in Europe. One immediately calls to mind the rapid growth of the trade unions, the co-operative movement and the mutual benefit societies that came with the Industrial Revolution. There are marked differences, however, between what happened in the West and what is now happening in Africa. In the West the changes sprang from a more or less conscious impulse and developed naturally out of the economic and social movements of the past. The political and social structure was disturbed and on occasion underwent far-reaching changes, but there was continuity. In many respects the peoples of the West emerged from the ordeal with an even greater sense of national solidarity than before, and the community at large was also strengthened by the access of new sections of the population to the responsibilities of government. Nothing of the kind has happened in Africa. There was no preparation for the brutal changes that the community has undergone since 1850, and the changes came through the intervention of a foreign people. The new arrivals were not in any way concerned with preserving the foundations of traditional African society, and the result was unquestionably a weakening of the social structure. In the closing years of the nineteenth century and the beginning of the twentieth, settlement ceased to be confined to small and isolated groups of Europeans (such as explorers, missionaries and merchants), and the formation of an organised and stable European colony using the commercial and industrial techniques of western Europe had a revolutionary effect on the indigenous population, to whom the advent of the European settlers revealed an alternative to farming and to the other traditional forms of tribal life. To the members of a strictly closed society such as then existed on the continent of Africa, the prospect of escape that was offered in this way could only serve to precipitate a crisis. The occupation of African territory by a foreign administration was also accompanied by interference in every aspect of their lives: religion, the organisation of society, feeding habits, farming methods, family relationships, the wisdom of the elders, the education of children—nothing remained intact. The African felt the ground shifting beneath his feet and suddenly perceived that the most stable elements in his experience had been shaken and were untrustworthy. Some of the officials sent out by the colonial Powers to administer and develop the new territories realised the extent to which the African community had been disturbed and tried to preserve as much of the political and social system as they could. Lord Lugard's 'dual mandate' has its counterpart in Galliéni's orders for Madagascar and Lyautey's instruction for Morocco. But however well inspired such efforts may be, there are limits to what they can achieve; it is not always possible to preserve a system that is no longer in touch with present-day requirements or with the most progressive sections of the population. In a large part of tropical Africa the social structure is disintegrating, if it has not already done so, and a new and improvised system of society cannot easily acquire the solidity and strength of one that is rooted in tradition. It may be argued that before doing away with the tribal basis of society an honest attempt should be made to give it new vitality and strength. Such an attempt, however, is not always possible. However poor and inadequate the new framework of society may be, it is always better than no framework at all. Consequently, where the traditional system seems to be declining, the possibility of re-modelling the whole of indigenous society has to be considered.

All these factors have a direct effect on productivity. Every human being lives, works and dies within the framework of society, and, should it ever be threatened with collapse, his life and work are influenced accordingly. For the African, the problem of security is two-fold—collective and individual. The reason why collective security is such an urgent problem is that the primitive society was based on a code of neighbourly assistance that constituted a permanent guarantee for every member of the group. The spontaneous associations that are being formed among the mass of the detribalised working population hold out a promise for the future. In the economic and cultural sphere the community development schemes and other similar ventures, and in the social sphere the mutual benefit societies, seem to have made a great impression, without having any specific political affinities, and should bring out the best leaders among the African population. The community principle behind these projects should make for consultation and so provide a safeguard against arbitrary action. Similarly the efforts made to eliminate racial opposition and discrimination and build up a homogeneous society could undoubtedly do much, with time, to reduce one element of tension that makes for insecurity among the African population.

The African has also a problem of individual security. The straitened circumstances of their families now force the younger generation to make a rapid choice. Their own existence and that of their dependants are in danger; for them this is a new situation, since the livelihood of their fathers and forefathers had always been assured by the communities in which they lived. If the African decides to go to work in a factory he encounters a new form of insecurity; wheras he naturally hopes to find the same neighbourliness and community spirit in his new surroundings that he was accustomed to find in his native village, he is suddenly confronted with antagonism.

> When a tribal Negro agrees to enter the employment of a foreign master, he does so, perhaps without realising it, on the very real assumption that the master will take the place hitherto occupied by his tribal chief, or rather by the tribe in its entirety as represented by the chief, i.e. that he will take him over as he is, and be responsible for every aspect of his life—in fact, be a kind of father and mother to him. If we may be permitted to use precise and rather abstract terms, the Negro looks upon his wages not as payment for work done but as a token of a social contract.[37]

Mannoni gives a somewhat similar description of how relationships of dependency are formed in Madagascar.[38]

This feeling of insecurity can be partly overcome by the worker's belonging to a union; this gives him a new and vital sense of comradeship but stresses still further the antagonism that he finds so painful.

A number of rural employers in one of the provinces in the Belgian Congo have decided, with the assent of the African labour they employ, to replace the contract of employment by a contract under which the worker no longer enters into a personal commitment but simply undertakes to do a job.[39] The agreement is concluded between the two parties more or less on a equal footing, and the African worker has no difficulty in finding many precedents for it in tribal law. This is also true of other contracts, such as the contract of supply and certain contracts between landlord and tenant. There are, of course, many types of industrial employment to which contracts of this kind are hardly suited. Even so, the contract of employment itself is flexible enough in many ways. The modern world has ceased to regard it as the token of a sale in the ordinary meaning of the term and has recognised that the employer is not freed of all obligations when he has paid for the work. He is obliged to take account of the worker as a person, and the majority of Western laws require him to pay a pension to aged workers, compensation to workers injured at their work and even special allowances to workers with large families. Recreation facilities are also organised. All this is evidence that labour is not a commodity, and we are therefore forced to recognise that the African's reaction is essentially the reaction of a human being against an abstract and rigid legal concept. Yet it should be possible to make the human factor play an even greater part in the contract of employment by increasing the number of joint councils of employers and workers and by making them competent to deal with certain private matters of immediate concern to the workers and their families.

There are many other ways of encouraging the African worker to settle down in a normal social system, e.g. by schemes for providing housing at low cost, by affording facilities whereby the worker can become the owner of a house or land, by stabilising workers and their families at or near their places of employment, by paying wages adequate to support a family, by encouraging co-operatives, indigenous handicrafts, basic education, vocational training, and so on. Many of these suggestions are now being followed up in Africa, but there are two aspects of the worker's social life that have not been given the attention they deserve. The first is the position of the aged worker. There can be no question of security for a worker who knows that he has nothing to expect in the way of provision for his old age in the urban or industrial centre where he works. His natural inclination will be to keep open some line of retreat to his traditional environment. He will not work well, will be content to draw a meagre wage and will choose his own time to leave his employment. A great deal consequently remains to be done to guarantee detribalised workers a pension and, if possible, a house, and perhaps the chance on increasing their resources from market gardening.

Equal importance attaches to the facilities for workers' upgrading. Mr. Cumper, in his analysis of productivity in Jamaica, considers that the low standard of efficiency of local labour is to some extent attributable to the rigid system of social stratification, which in practice prevents any worker from rising above the foreman level.[40]

Exactly the same is true of Africa. In the Union of South Africa and in Southern Rhodesia law, tradition and the pressure of European labour all combine to keep the African worker in the semi-skilled or unskilled grades. In Northern Rhodesia the position is the same, except that it has been brought about by the action of the European workers' unions. In British East and West Africa, the Belgian Congo and the French territories, the inadequate vocational facilities, the Negro's lack of general education and, in certain cases, the presence of European labour still keep the African in a position of inferiority from which he has little prospect of escaping. Yet no man can be expected to reach a high standard of efficiency when he is denied the chance of improving his situation by work. The efforts already made to generalise vocational training might be coupled with an endeavour to introduce the principles of Training Within Industry as recognised and applied in Europe and America.

A worker's productivity, after all, is no more than a particular manifestation of human behaviour and should be studied in the context of the whole man. The African has had a very violent shock and has suffered considerably as a result. In a closed society where all precautions had been taken to safeguard the individual against all the hazards of life, a revolution has suddenly exposed him to a variety of hazards for which he is wholly unprepared. He cannot be expected to behave as if nothing had happened. The African of today has no assured future ahead of him and finds it impossible to pin his faith either in the values of the Western world, to which in any event he has hardly any access, or in the values of his former world, whose foundations have been shaken.

We are now in a position to see what is involved in raising the productivity of the African worker. Essentially it means restoring his self-confidence, and this will not be easy—the task of building up a feeling of security from nothing is beyond the powers of any human agency. Psychological adjustment must come first. However, much can be done to make adjustment easier. A number of possibilities have been mentioned in this article, and there are others. To seek out these possibilities, try them out and make them known is one of the most important duties of those who are helping to shape the destiny of Africa.

NOTES

1. United Nations: *Enlargement of the Exchange Economy in Tropical Africa*, Document E/2557, ST/ECA/23 (New York, 1954), p. 4.
2. *Ibid.*, p. 3.
3. University of Natal, Department of Economics: *The African Factory Worker* (Cape Town, Oxford University Press, 1950), p. 99.
4. Quoted by B. Gussman in 'Industrial Efficiency and the Urban African' (*Africa*, Vol. XXIII, No. 2, April 1953, p. 135).
5. Colonial Office, United Kingdom: *Labour Conditions in East Africa*. Report by Major G. St. J. Orde Browne (London, H.M. Stationery Office, 1946), p. 15.

6. *Bulletin du Centre d'étude des problèmes sociaux indigènes* (C.E.P.S.I.) (Elisabethville), 1949, No. 10, p. 96.
7. J. Guilbot: *Petite étude sur la main-d'oeuvre à Douala* (Yaoundé, 1947), pp. 50–51.
8. N. Humphrey: *The Kikuyu Lands* (1945), quoted in *East Africa and Rhodesia* (London), 25 Sep. 1947, p. 57.
9. J. Clément: 'Etude relative au paysannat indigène', in *Contribution à l'étude du problème de l'économie rurale indigène au Congo belge*, special issue of *Bulletin agricole du Congo belge* (Brussels), Vol. XLIII, 1952.
10. V. Drachoussoff: 'Essai sur l'agriculture indigène au Bas-Congo', *Bulletin agricole du Congo belge*, Vol. XXXVIII, No. 4, Dec. 1947, pp. 855–856.
11. G. Malengreau: 'Les lotissements agricoles au Congo belge', in *Contribution à l'étude du problème de l'économie rurale indigène au Congo belge, op. cit.*
12. J. Guilloteau: 'La dégradation des sols tropicaux', in *Record of the XXVth Meeting held in Brussels on the 28th, 29th and 30th November 1949* (Brussels, International Institute of Political and Social Sciences (Comparative Civilisations), 1950).
13. R. Dumont: 'Etude de quelques économies agraires au Sénégal et en Casamance', in *L'agronomie tropicale*, Vol. VI, Nos. 5 and 6, May-June 1951, pp. 232–233.
14. S. Biesheuvel: *African Intelligence* (Johannesburg, 1943).
15. J. C. Carothers: *The African Mind in Health and Disease*, Monograph Series, No. 17 (Geneva, World Health Organisation, 1953), pp. 90–91.
16. Idem: *The Psychology of Mau Mau* (Nairobi, Government Printer, 1954), p. 2.
17. R. Durand: 'La formation professionnelle et la psychologie des noirs', in *Problèmes d'Afrique centrale*, No. 24, 2nd quarter 1954, pp. 105–106. For an account of similar experiments in the Belgian Congo, which gave similar results, see A. Ombredane: 'Principes pour une étude psychologique des noirs du Congo belge', in *L'Année psychologique*, 1951, p. 539.
18. *The African Mind in Health and Disease, op. cit.*, pp. 170–171.
19. Institut royal colonial belge: *Bulletin des séances*, XXV-1954–2 (Brussels, 1954), p. 785.
20. *The African Mind in Health and Disease, op. cit.*, pp. 32–33.
21. Economic Advisory Council, Committee on Nutrition in the Colonial Empire: *First Report*, Parts I and II, Cmd. 6050 and 6051 (London, H.M. Stationery Office, 1939).
22. *The African Mind in Health and Disease, op. cit.*, pp. 40–41.
23. A. Ombredane, *op cit.*, p. 532.
24. P. Ryckmans: *Dominer pour servir* (Brussels, L'Edition universelle, 1948).
25. *African Labour Efficiency Survey, op. cit.*, p. 120.
26. B. Gussman: 'Industrial Efficiency and the Urban African', *loc. cit.*
27. *The Psychology of Mau Mau, op. cit.*, pp. 2–3.
28. Rev. P. Charles: 'Travail et psychologie africaine', in *Les missions et le prolétariat* (Brussels, Desclée de Brouwer, 1954), p. 169.
29. O. Mannoni: *Psychologie de la colonisation* (Paris, Editions du seuil, 1950), pp. 32–33.

208   AN ECONOMIC HISTORY OF AFRICA

30. Quoted by E. Toussaint in 'Rendement de la main-d'oeuvre indigène' (*Bulletin trimestrial du Centre d'étude des problèmes sociaux indigènes* (*C.E.P.S.I.*)), 1953, No. 21, p. xvi.
31. B. Gussman, *op cit.*, pp. 141–143.
32. *The Psychology of Mau Mau, op. cit.*, p. 24.
33. Colony and Protectorate of Kenya: *Report of the Committee on African Wages* (Nairobi, Government Printer, 1954), pp. 13, 15 and 16.
34. Rev. P. Charles: 'Problèmes de travail et réalités africaines', in *Bulletin bimestriel de la Société belge d'études et d'expansion*, No. 152, Aug. 1952, p. 585.
35. 'Travail et psychologie africaine', *loc. cit.*, p. 170.
36. Kenneth Little: 'The Study of "Social Change" in British West Africa', in *Africa*, Vol. XXIII, No. 4, Oct. 1953, pp. 277–279.
37. 'Travail et psychologie africaine', *loc. cit.*, p. 173.
38. O. Mannoni, *op cit.*, pp. 31–33.
39. Even if the idea of the employers was merely to evade their responsibilities under the legislation governing contracts of employment the fact is interesting, since it shows that African workers prefer a situation that safeguards their independence even if it is less well paid.
40. G. E. Cumper: 'Two Studies in Jamaican Productivity', in *Social and Economic Studies* (Institute of Social and Economic Research, Jamaica), Vol. 1, No. 2, June 1953, p. 34.

19

MORAL EFFECTS OF WAGE-EARNING AND THE AFRICANS*

G. St. J. Orde Brown

The influence of the wage-earning habit is by no means as generally beneficial as it is physically; while employment under good conditions should prove to be of real advantage as far as health is concerned, there are many dangers connected with it from an ethical standpoint, and the welfare of the community may be gravely affected thereby.

Considering first the case of the worker himself, it is clear that he is exposed to numerous influences which will be entirely strange to him, from the moment that he leaves his village. The journey to work will itself be a novel experience for one accustomed to consider it unsafe to venture far from home, away from the protection of tribal law, among other tribes for whom the life of a stranger has little sanctity. Normal life must be to a great extent interrupted, and the tribal authorities satisfied about all social obligations before they will acquiesce in the venture; the complicated system of family loans and obligations in which the African lives must be dealt with to guard against distraint or other action during the worker's absence elsewhere; the family must be provided for, and some one must be found to act as guardian of home interests. If the journey is a long one, there will be the alarming possibilities of robbery, attack, or illness on the way, against which the only insurance is the solidarity of the party setting out.

On arrival at the place of employment, the recruit will have to face a formidable array of regulations and formalities; he will probably have been medically examined before, but this may

*Reprinted by permission from G. St. J. Orde Browne, *The African Labourer*, Frank Cass, 1967.

P   209

be repeated. He will then be allotted quarters in the labour lines, where he and his friends form a tiny unit in the crowd of natives of other tribes. The routine of the life must be learnt, and a measure of discipline and method acquired by a man who has never previously had to trouble himself about time or date. Strange food will be issued to him, very likely of a kind that will disagree with him at first, while cooking in a method that will ensure the observance of tribal requirements is probably impossible. Various other infringements of tradition are inevitable, and the novice lives in a state of anxiety about the result, until he loses faith in the ancestral beliefs. Female society will be limited and undesirable, while the new-comer must make acquaintance with a standard of life in sexual matters which is entirely opposed to normal Bantu views. Opportunities will be ample for the purchase of all sorts of striking novelties, mostly useless and some pernicious; secondhand clothes of quite unsuitable European type will replace healthy nudity, and an occasional chance may occur to acquire a taste for the black man's outstanding peril, European liquor. Housing is probably of a type quite unlike any native dwelling, while illness or disease leads to detention in a sinister building where the patient is separated from his friends and made to submit to a strange diet and treatment, while the knowledge that the white doctors are addicted to cutting up people both dead and alive forms a persistent nightmare.

Some occurrence may render him unclean or bring him under other tribal ban, removable only under the auspices of the qualified native authority; the latter will of course not be available, so the burden must be borne or resort must be had to some unorthodox local practitioner. The victim, however, soon learns that the dire effects which he has always believed would follow any infringement of tribal law do not in practice occur, so he grows to despise them and the elders who have in the past interpreted them for him.

African adaptability will probably enable him to settle down in the new surroundings without too much discomfort, and intercourse with strangers will give him a broader outlook; things which shocked him on first arrival will soon become familiar and normal. The community spirit which so largely dominates the African's behaviour will have been broken down by contact with the wider world, and the old rules for guidance will no longer receive respect.

Such an experience must greatly change the worker, and he will return to his village home with a very different outlook; he has acquired an attitude of scepticism towards ritual observances, and has perforce braved the spiritual terrors held over the heads of infringers of tribal custom. His respect for the elders of the community will have been greatly weakened, and he is likely to become a social rebel disliked and suspected by the more conservative and steadier element of society.

Accident may bring him into conflict with tribal law; he may find his hard-earned wages impounded to pay his share of a family fine, when his loyalty to the established system will be severely strained. His property or family may have suffered during his absence, and his appeal to the village heads will be prejudiced by their dislike of his subversive opinions; his wife may be in the house of another man, and his efforts at redress may meet only with the reply that he should not have been away for so long.

There is also the possibility that he may have returned infected with venereal disease, with obviously disastrous effects on his family life.

It is not suggested that these results are likely to occur in every case, or that they cannot be largely reduced; they are, however, summarised as an indication of the disturbing nature of the forces to which the novice is likely to be exposed.

The effect in the villages will be equally pronounced. A primitive and self-contained community will be exposed to an influx of returning travellers who have experienced entirely novel methods of life; new ideas will be imported, and old observances and codes will be criticised; tribal law and authority, formerly unquestioned, will be disputed or ignored.

It cannot be expected that the elders, accustomed to be regarded as the exponents of the ancient and infallible rules, will not resent such an attitude; the subversive element will be regarded with extreme hostility, as being disruptive of all moral standards, and the offenders will be subjected to marked disapproval. The fact that tribal law derives its authority so largely from the support of supernatural penalties for infringement renders it very vulnerable to the attacks of the sceptic, and the community is thus divided into two hostile elements with irreconcilable views. The elders will be alarmed and shocked at the result produced by foreign adventure on their young men, and will accordingly become steady and determined opponents of the wage-seeking habit.

The position of the women will also be affected, for, apart from the possibility of actual infection, disputes are sure to arise as a result of the long absence of the husbands, while the laxer morals of the returned workers will tend to corrupt their families; a life of prostitution, virtually unknown to primitive Bantu society, will become a possibility. According to European ideas, the standard of many primitive tribes is low; there is, however, reason for believing that they regard paid prostitution as something entirely alien and shameful, and that a woman attempting to live such a life in the uncontaminated African community would receive very summary treatment. Once, however, the laxer attitude of the labour compound is introduced, either by the men or by wives who have accompanied their husbands to work, there is a general tendency for the old standard to be broken down, and genuine marriage is replaced by a temporary union that may lack even a nominal sanction. Where Islam is influential, the easy divorce permitted by it will prove far more attractive than the observance of the old Bantu family obligations in such transactions.

In any case, it is obvious that the herding together of large numbers of men with but little female society must produce undesirable results, and unnatural practices are a constant menace.

The greater contentment and better health of the married worker are so generally recognised that many employers are to be found who will go far in concessions for the benefit of the man who wishes to come accompanied by his wife; travelling expenses are paid, additional rations are issued, and special housing accommodation is provided, in varying degrees, and in some instances an appreciable proportion of the workers will be found to have their wives with them. In such cases, these will of course be greatly benefited, and the potential evils of the compound will be largely reduced.

The employer will naturally aim at retaining such people on his property; the longer the husband remains, the better his knowledge of his work, and the less the proportionate cost of bringing the family there in the first instance; so every encouragement is given to such cases to remain on. Here, however, the tribal influence is in opposition; the party will naturally tend to be homesick after a time, while there will also be anxiety about interests left behind, so that sooner or later the family will be found on their return journey. They may perhaps have had enough of alien adventure, and may drop back into village life permanently, or they may stay for a while and then feel a call for the more entertaining life of the wage-earner. Occasionally they will settle permanently on the place of employment, and cut themselves adrift finally from tribal life.

This last type will be found chiefly among the more skilled

and higher-paid employees of the large companies, or as 'squatters' on farms, or, again, as doubtfully desirable additions to a floating urban population; wherever they are, they present a difficult problem to the administrator. Divorced from the old tribal traditions and restraints, they no longer have a mass of public opinion to guide and control their actions; it is unlikely that they will have become genuine converts to some other faith, though very possibly they are nominal Christians or Mahometans. For practical purposes, however, they are without any real standard of behaviour, and obey only such police or company regulations as may be effectively enforced. The ease with which such people may drift into the criminal classes, or the fertile ground which they will provide for inflammatory political propaganda, must be obvious.

In the villages, such developments are quite realised by the elders, in so far as they recognise the possibility that a man who leaves accompanied by his wife may never return; their traditional anxiety to preserve and extend the tribe therefore renders them hostile to the departure of that woman, and it will generally be found that the native authorities are openly or secretly exerting their influence to discourage this, even when they may be quite favourable to the exodus of the men who may be expected to bring back additional wealth to the village. Congestion in native reserves will of course reverse this attitude and act as an incentive to migration.

It is possible that the usual attitude of the tribal authorities towards the departure of women with their husbands is not really so well advised, even from their point of view, as they imagine. The presumption is that the work-seeker who has left his family behind him will feel this as a tie, and may thus be relied upon to return eventually. In practice, however, it may well occur that he forms a union with a woman of the neighbourhood in which he is employed, who is naturally strongly opposed to joining another tribe of which she knows nothing, and the man has thus an incentive to remain away permanently. If, however, he has been accompanied by his tribal wife, the couple will retain old habits and associations to a greater degree, and a return to their original home is far likelier. It would thus seem that the practice of wives accompanying their husbands tends to ensure the return of a greater proportion of the men, even though in a few cases the couple may be permanently lost to the tribe. There is thus considerable difficulty in the way of the realisation of the object of some companies—the establishment of a small community of

workers accompanied by their families, and living under much
the same social conditions as those of the uncontaminated tribe.
While this may in itself be probably the most salutary solution
of the problem, it must involve the steady depletion of the home
population, and will therefore meet with strong opposition from
those interested in the welfare of the tribe. So a definite conflict
arises between the interests of the migrant worker and those of
the village community which he is leaving; inevitable progress
and the consequent displacement of population seem likely to
perpetuate this divergence, and the satisfactory settlement of the
difficulty presents one of the greatest of the problems connected
with African labour.

The widespread adoption in varying degrees of a system of
administration which will utilise the tribal organisation in its
method of government makes increasingly important the influence
of the returning worker upon the position and power of the native
authority; it will obviously be futile to endeavour to strengthen
and develop this authority while at the same time permitting the
growth of an element which is constantly tending to weaken
and discredit it. To the sympathetic European administrator, a
chief may appear a fine and capable personality with the interests
of his people genuinely at heart; to the home-coming wage-
earner he may seem merely an ignorant and inexperienced old
man engaged in a struggle to preserve obsolete and irritating
restrictions. The degree to which this is likely to occur will, of
course, depend largely on the difference in outlook and breadth
of view between the native authority and his young critic. There
would therefore seem much to be said in favour of the efforts
made by some governments to furnish the future native rulers with
a considerable measure of education and experience, so that they
will be in a position to retain the respect of their more progressive and enterprising followers.

Capital: Some Aspects of Saving and Investment

PART FIVE

Capital: Some Aspects of Saving and Investment

20

SAVING AND INVESTMENT BY AFRICANS*

W. O. Jones

One of the most commonly offered explanations of why a people do not save, that their incomes are so low as to allow no margin over the minimum required for subsistence, has two possible meanings. If by minimum required for subsistence is meant an amount barely large enough to permit survival, then the general proposition is equivalent to saying that a decline in income would result in starvation and death. If on the other hand minimum requirements for subsistence are defined in terms of what a population conceives to be tolerable, then the general proposition is that the desire for consumption goods is so high as to consume all current production. Put in these absolute terms it seems most unlikely that the proposition is true of any human population. For it implies complete improvidence, complete failure to provide for periods when game may be scarce and crops may be short. In absolute terms, indeed, it implies consumption of all crops at time of harvest. It would also mean a society without tools, without homes, even without clothing, all of which depend on deferment of consumption in order to come into being and all of which furnish consumption satisfactions over a period of months or years. Not to save at all means not to survive.

The extreme form of the proposition that income is at the subsistence level leads to absurd conclusions. But we are not much better off if we try to define minimum consumption in more realistic fashion. A wide range exists, for example, between a minimum cost diet that will barely support life and diets enjoyed by even the poorest human populations. If we attempt to specify a minimum cost diet capable of supporting an individual in 'full vigour', new difficulties arise because of the various ways

*Reprinted by permission from W. O. Jones, *Economic Man in Africa*, Stanford University, Food Research Institute Studies, 1960, pp. 126–32.

in which that condition may be defined. It is in fact almost impossible to arrive at a definition of subsistence minimum that is useful and that will be generally accepted.

This is not to say, however, that subjective appraisal of levels of consumption, and of capacity for saving of income above some sort of base consumption level, are without value. When consumption records can be obtained they will give indications of 'nonessential' consumption and of the extent to which it might be possible to divert income from consumption without harmful consequences. They may also indicate what level of consumption a population considers as normal or adequate, and make it possible to identify individuals or groups who have incomes sufficiently greater than this normal to permit savings. Another reason given for inability to save, that the claims of the family or lineage are so strong as to compel any individual whose income rises above the modal minimum to share the surplus for consumption by relatives, can only be tested by examining what in fact happens when incomes are at different levels.

Reports of some quantitative studies of income and expenditure in East and West African communities since World War II suggest that there is a large variation in individual and family income, that many Africans have incomes large enough to permit savings of some sort, and that a few with relatively large incomes are able to preserve a substantial part of their income from the rapacity of their kinfolk. These studies also provide information about the kinds of things people buy, thereby providing some indication of the rationality of African consumption.

A 1954 survey in the town of Akuse, which is about 60 miles northeast of Accra, reports details of income and spending of 163 families classified according to their total monthly expenditures (4). Highest and lowest expenditures by individual families were not reported, but average incomes of each of the ten expenditure groups into which the sample was divided ranged from 174s. (20 families) to 1,100s. (9 families) per month, or from 55s. to 217s. per person per month. Expenditures for home consumption averaged 42 per cent of gross income but varied from 26 to 51 per cent depending primarily on how much of gross income came from resale of purchased goods. Net savings deposits averaged 6·6 per cent of gross income and were reported by 8 of the 10 classes. Cash savings amounted to 4 per cent of gross income for the entire sample but were more than 15 per cent in one of the wealthier classes. Other saving could not be determined because it was included in the general category of remittances paid and received. Savings were said to have been unusually high because the survey was conducted in September and families were beginning to save for Christmas.

The Akuse sample was drawn from all families in the community. It has been more customary to collect information only from the families of wage earners and to exclude families with incomes above a certain level. In the 1951 study of budgets of unskilled labourers in Jinja, Uganda, for example, it was found that ten men in the sample of 120 were receiving extra income from the sale of beer, giving them a total income almost three times as large as that of the rest of the sample. These ten men accordingly were excluded from the survey (7). Such studies show much lower savings. In Takoradi-Seckondi net savings deposits of labourers were less than one per cent of gross receipts, according to a 1955 survey of families with wage incomes of £5-£15 a month (5). A similar survey of budgets of unskilled labourers in Jinja, Uganda, in 1952, however, showed net savings of 16·6 per cent of income, with the lower income group saving about 4 per cent of income, and the higher income group, one-fourth of the sample, saving 36 per cent of income (8). The very high figure reported for the second group results in part from the fact that these labourers grew an unreported amount of food for their own consumption and this was not included in income.

Surveys of cocoa-producing farmers in Ghana and Nigeria report much higher absolute savings per family than do the urban surveys, and also greater variation of income. The study of Galletti, Baldwin, and Dina, referred to earlier, reports income in great detail for 187 families in western Nigeria. Net business receipts of these families in 1951/52 ranged from less than £20 to more than £2,000, with 8 per cent of the families receiving 38 per cent of all income (Chart 1). Income from farming was slightly less concentrated: 9 per cent of the families received 28·8 per cent of all net farm income. Savings amounted to no less than 40 per cent of disposable cash income (2 p. 461). Galletti and his associates also provide statistics relating non-business expenditures and expenditures on food to net receipts. As receipts rose, expenditure on food rose to a level of a bit less then £100 per year, but not above that (Chart 2). Total non-business (domestic) expenditures rose more persistently than expenditure on food, but consumed an increasingly smaller part of net receipts.

In southwestern Ghana, a budget survey of 1,000 cocoa-growing families in the Oda-Swedru-Asamankese Area in 1955/56

CHART 1.

Nigerian Cocoa Farmers: Distribution of Cash Receipts from
Farming and All Business Receipts, by Households, 1951-5*

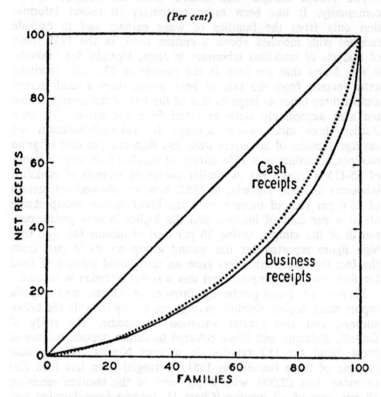

(Per cent)

*Based on R. Galletti, K. D. S. Baldwin, and I. O. Dina, *Nigerian
Cocoa Farmers . . .* (Nigeria Cocoa Mkt. Bd., London, 1956), pp. 452, 458.

reports gross earned incomes ranging from under 1,000s. to over
15,000s. a year. Net income in the lowest class averaged 689s.,
that in the highest 13,365s. Domestic expenditure ranged from
816s. in the lowest class to 3,565s. in the highest (3).

Some information about size of cocoa holdings in Ghana and
Nigeria is summarised in Chart 3. Lines plotting cumulative per
cent of farmers against cumulative per cent of area or production
are grouped fairly closely; in general it can be said that large

CHART 2.

Nigerian Cocoa Farmers: Net Receipts, Nonbusiness Expenses, and
Value of Food Consumed, per Household, 1951–52*

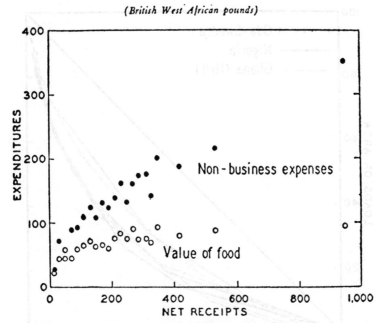

(British West African pounds)

*Based on R. Galletti, K. D. S. Baldwin, and I. O. Dina, *Nigerian
Cocoa Farmers* . . . (Nigeria Cocoa Mkt. Bd., London, 1956), p. 473.

farms making up 10 per cent of all farms account for from 30
to 40 per cent of acreage and output and the 5 per cent of farms
that are largest account for from 21 to 27 per cent of acreage
and output. Information from the Ivory Coast shows similar
variation in size of coffee farms (32, p. 218):

	Per cent of all farms with area less than			
District	2 ha.	5 ha.	10 ha.	25 ha.
1	60	85	95	100
2	36	73	91	99
3	17	41	67	91
4	30	70	95	94·5
5	54	88	96	100
6	32	66	86	92

Property distribution in 54 Tonga households and 60 Ngoni

CHART 3.

Size of Cocoa Holdings, Nigeria and Ghana, 1950's*

(Per cent)

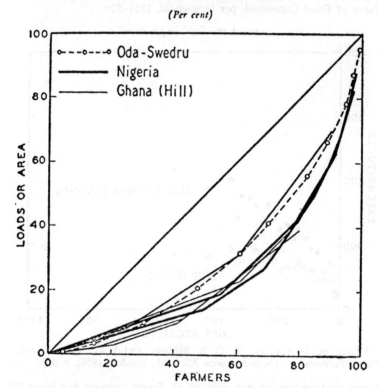

Sources: Nigeria, area, Cocoa Survey Study, and six villages in economic survey from R. Galletti, K. D. S. Baldwin, and I. O. Dina, *Nigerian Cocoa Farmers . . .* (Nigeria Cocoa Mkt. Bd., London, 1956), p. 150; Ghana (Hill), loads, seven villages, from Polly Hill, *The Gold Coast Cocoa Farmer: A Preliminary Survey* (London, 1956), pp. 89–90; Oda-Swedru, loads, from Ghana, Off. Govt. Stat., *Survey of Population and Budgets of Cocoa Producing Families in Oda-Swedru-Asamankese Area: 1955–56* (Stat. and Econ. Papers, No. 6, July 1958), pp. 70–71.

households in Northern Rhodesia, as reported by Phyllis Deane, also fail to confirm the leveling effect of tribalism on accumulation of wealth (Chart 4). The general distribution is not much more equal than those shown in Chart 3, resembling most closely the distribution of income from cocoa in the Oda-Swedru-Asaman-

CHART 4.

Value of Household Goods Owned by 54 Tonga Families, 60 Ngoni
Families, 1947, and Value of Durable Goods Owned by 187 Nigeria
Families, 1951–52*

(Per cent)

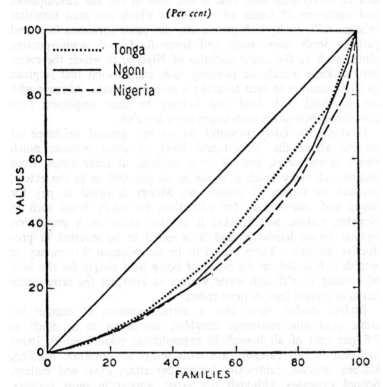

Sources: Tonga and Ngoni from Phyllis Deane, *Colonial Social
Accounting* (Cambridge, England, 1953), p. 194; Nigeria from R. Galletti
K. D. S. Baldwin, and I. O. Dina, *Nigerian Cocoa Farmers . . .* (Nigeria
Cocoa Mkt. Bd., London, 1956), p. 165.

kese Area of Ghana. Although the value of household goods
owned by the Tonga and Ngoni (less than £50 for the wealthiest
household) is much less than the value of durable goods owned
by the Nigeria cocoa-producing families studied by Galletti and
his associates (up to more than £2,300 per family), the two dis-
tributions are much the same.

In the urban budget studies and in the surveys of cocoa producers, loans and borrowing figure prominently. Africans make use of a variety of credit arrangements, many of them of local or traditional origin. They include the 'pledging' of cocoa farms in lieu of mortgaging land that is not held in fee, the development and operation of farms on shares, in which one man furnishes labour, skill, tools, and provisions, the other furnishes land and perhaps lends some tools and some food, and money-pooling clubs, such as the *esusu* societies of Nigeria, to which the members make a weekly or monthly cash contribution that is given to each member in turn to make a major purchase. Africans who are provided with food and lodging by their employers may contribute their entire cash wages to such a club.

Evidence is fairly plentiful as to the general existence of income above the 'subsistence' level, of some incomes much above modal level, and of some savings, at some times, from incomes of every level; it is not at all plentiful as to the extent, amount, or nature of investment. Money is saved to pay for feasts and ceremonials, for education, for costly items such as bicycles, radios, and trucks; it is also saved as a precaution against future hardship; and it is saved to be invested in productive activities. There seems to be no evidence that money or wealth is hoarded, in the sense of being held simply for the sake of holding it, although some writers so interpret the large cattle herds of certain East African tribes.

Budget studies show that a certain amount of current income goes into consumer durables, amounting to as much as 7·5 per cent of all household expenditures (Oda-Swedru). Items included in this category are such things as furniture, bedding, kitchen utensils, tableware, lamps, carpeting, axes, and cutlery. School expenses, although not large, appear in most budgets. Bicycles and sewing machines, to be used both for pleasure and profit, are familiar African investments. But investments more clearly productive in nature must also represent a substantial fraction of some of the larger incomes. The large fleets of trucks that carry goods and passengers throughout West Africa are African-owned, as are many of the trucks supplying such cities as Leopoldville and Brazzaville in Central Africa. Perhaps the largest single type of investment, however, is in the form of cocoa, coffee, and banana plantations. Galletti and his associates estimate that in 1951/52 the cost of clearing and planting one acre of cocoa amounted to between £50 and £75. This is a permanent investment that will yield little or no return for the first 4 to 8 years, but that can be expected to yield well for 15 years or more thereafter.

Examination of detailed records of expenditure by families in Dar es Salaam, Jinja, Kampala, Mbale, Akuse, Accra, Kumasi, Sekondi-Takoradi, Western Nigeria, and the Oda-Swedru district of Ghana supplies no evidence that Africans are irrational in consumption habits. The items for which money is spent are just those same reasonable necessities and amenities that the European of similar position might buy. Food bulks large, accounting for at least half of most family expenditures. Clothing, rent, fuel, and light account for another 15 per cent, alcoholic beverages and tobacco around 10 per cent. Expenditures on clothing probably increase with income and may be as little as 10 per cent (Jinja, 1951) or as much as 23 per cent (Oda-Swedru). The items going to make up each major subtotal are not at all peculiar nor particularly African. Examination of imports of consumer goods by the African countries is just as unrewarding to the searcher after peculiar and irrational wants. Imports are today, as they have been for centuries, made up almost entirely of goods that the African does not produce and that he wants for the same reasons European and American consumers want them; cloth, manufactured goods, beverages, some foodstuffs, machinery and equipment, petroleum products, chemicals, bicycles, automobiles, and radios figure large in the imports of most countries. A pressing problem over most of tropical Africa is the providing of useful and wanted goods in greater diversity at prices Africans can pay. Walter Elkan speaks of a 'discontinuity in the price range of the things men want to buy' and holds it responsible for much behaviour that appears strange in western eyes (1). As the supply of goods increases, and costs of transporting and merchandising them decline, we can expect to see economic desires operating even more forcefully, among more people, to stimulate production and efficiency.

REFERENCES

(1) Walter Elkan, 'Incentives in East Africa,' *Colonial Review* (London), December 1956, p. 241.
(2) R. Galletti, K. D. S. Baldwin, and I. O. Dina, *Nigerian Cocoa Farmers* . . . (Nigeria Cocoa Mkt. Bd., London, 1956).
(3) Ghana, Off. Govt. Stat., *Survey of Population and Budgets of Cocoa Producing Families in Oda-Swedru-Asamankese Area: 1955–56* (Stat. and Econ. Papers, No. 6, July 1958).

(4) Gold Coast, Off. Govt. Stat., *1954 Akuse Survey of Household Budgets* (Stat. and Econ. Papers, No. 3, June 1955).
(5) ———, *Sekondi-Takoradi Survey of Population and Household Budgets, 1955* (Stat. and Econ. Papers, No. 4, March 1956).
(6) Jean Tricart, 'Le Café en Côte d'Ivoire,' *Les Cahiers d'Outre-Mer* (Bordeaux), July-Sept. 1957.
(7) Uganda, E. Afr. Stat. Dept., *The Pattern of Income, Expenditure and Consumption of African Unskilled Labourers in Jinja, November 1951* (August 1952), p. 3.
(8) ———, *The Pattern . . . in Jinja, 1952* (May 1953).

21

CAPITAL INVESTMENT IN
SUB-SAHARAN AFRICA*

Sir Alan Pim

The Public Debt is a part of the general question of capital investment in Africa which has recently been the subject of a careful investigation by Dr. Frankel. He has classified the foreign capital invested between 1870 and 1936 under the heads of (*a*) public and private listed capital including government loans and grants, and other capital issues as listed on stock exchanges or in the financial press; and (*b*) non-listed capital including that brought in by settlers. The figures given by him for the amounts of the capital investments from abroad in the African tropical territories between 1870 and 1936 will be found in the Appendix.[1] Investments in Southern Rhodesia and Bechuanaland cannot, however, be separated from those in Northern Rhodesia, nor investments in Tanganyika from those in Zanzibar, and the figures for these territories are therefore included in the statement. The corresponding figures for the Union of South Africa, including Basutoland and Swaziland, are public listed capital £225,000,000, private listed capital £251,000,000, and non-listed £48,000,000, giving a total investment of £524,000,000, as compared with £543,000,000 in the whole of Central Africa.

The most striking features of these statistics are (1) the preponderance of capital investments in British territories over those in foreign territories; it may be noted incidentally that British territories have a larger proportion of the total African trade than their proportion of the invested capital; (2) the concentration of the private listed capital in the mineral regions; and (3) the very high proportion of public as compared with private capital in

*Reprinted by permission of Oxford University Press from Sir Alan Pim, *The Financial and Economic History of African Tropical Territories*, 1940.

the predominantly agricultural dependencies. In the Belgian Congo, on the contrary, the proportion is low mainly as the result of the systems of concessions and guarantees which have characterised their methods of development. Investments in railways represent more than half the public listed capital, and in some territories the proportion is considerably higher. The figures for Nigeria represent a special type of investment, as most of the private listed capital has been invested through the trading companies, and has been largely accumulated out of the profits of trade. The capital of the companies controlled by the United Africa Company alone is estimated by Frankel at £25,000,000. The estimates for non-listed capital are necessarily speculative and a conservative estimate[2] has been taken for the private listed and non-listed capital invested in Kenya. Dr. Salvadori has expressed the opinion that probably £20,000,000 has been invested from abroad in agriculture, and the official report that about £4,000,000 was brought in during 1920–1 tends to support a higher total estimate.

The direction and character of capital investment[3] has much wider and more far-reaching effects in Africa than in other parts of the world where it is applied under conditions of free competition. In the early stages capital was necessary for the development of trade, and for establishing a framework of communications and an administrative and military organisation. In the era of the concession companies, which were for the most part in non-British territories, the investments were for the purpose of exploiting readily accessible national wealth, and not of organising constructive activities. These companies, in fact, destroyed the real economic resources. When views of a more far-seeing character began to influence policy, governments which could not, or would not, provide the necessary finances, revived the device of Chartered Companies, not as before on the basis of private monopolies, but with special privileges relating to land, minerals, and other natural resources, and with powers of taxation coupled with administrative obligations. Vague general expectations combined with patriotic sentiment enabled them to continue for some time raising money from the public, but when the prospects of speedy results faded, and the limitations on the powers of capital were realised, it became increasingly difficult to raise the necessary funds and the Chartered Companies were obliged to relinquish their task. The German companies in particular had a short life for this reason. Even the Niger Company, though it was financially successful owing to its extensive trade, could hardly have continued to bear the burden of administering and developing its vast territories.

Subsequently the main investments have been in territories with extensive mineral wealth where industry was able to use large masses of unskilled native labour under European supervision. Where these resources, or other natural products, were lacking, development depended on the introduction of new agricultural products and new economic methods, either through the establishment of European plantations, or by the creation of systems of peasant production. These processes involved heavy capital expenditure on communications and public works, which had to be paid for by the expansion of exports, an expansion which was only possible if an increasing supply of labour could be made available. Investments were, moreover, largely made on the assumption that labour would continue to be available at low rates of pay, and strong vested interests were thus created for the maintenance of these rates. Where the demand for labour began to exceed the supply these interests pressed for the provision of the necessary labour by the use of direct or indirect compulsion. Investment in Africa has thus been bound up with very wide political and sociological issues and has profoundly affected every aspect of native life.

Judged by the standards of other countries,[4] and even of other parts of Africa, investments in tropical Africa are still on a very modest scale. Even in the Union of South Africa the foreign capital invested represents only £55·8[5] per head of the population, and in the Rhodesias £38·4 per head. In the Belgian Congo it is at the rate of £13 per head, in Kenya and Uganda £6·8, but in Nigeria it is only £3·9 per head, and in French West Africa £2·1. The estimates of population are very uncertain, but these figures indicate the slow progress which has been made in developing income-creating opportunities by the application of capital from abroad. They do not include the accumulations of private funds from local sources for commerce, industry, or agriculture. The value of the trade resulting from the application of capital differs considerably according to the character of the products. In some territories the chief products (e.g. palm products) are produced under primitive conditions involving little preliminary expenditure except on public works, communications, and commerical facilities, and the resulting proportion of the total African trade is greater than the proportion of total investments. British West Africa[6] for example has 9·6 per cent of the invested capital and 12·4 per cent of the trade, and French

West Africa has 2·5 per cent of the capital and 5·9 per cent of the trade.

Capital, however, requires the co-operation of the other factors of production, and, as Professor Frankel remarks,[7] 'the greatest social and economic fact in the modern penetration of Africa is the universal dependence on black labour'. In the tropics more especially, at whatever altitude, non-native enterprise is in a far more fundamental way dependent on native labour than it is in South Africa. The number of natives employed as wage-earners in the African tropical territories is given as follows in *An African Survey*. In 1936 Northern Rhodesia had 53,000 employed internally, and 51,000 in other territories, though the latter figure is certainly an understatement. In 1935 Nyasaland had 120,000 employed outside the territory, in addition to those in local employment. In 1936 Tanganyika had 252,000 employed, Kenya 183,000, Uganda 51,000 excluding the cotton pickers, Nigeria 227,000, and the British Cameroons 18,000. In 1934 the Gold Coast had 12,000 in general employment and 24,000 in the mines, the latter figure rising to 35,000 in 1936; Sierra Leone had 9,500 employed in the mines in 1935. In the same year French West Africa had 179,000 in employment, and the French Cameroons 54,000, but the number in French Equatorial Africa is unknown. In 1936 the Belgian Congo had 409,000, and Ruanda-Urundi 43,000. These figures are subject to considerable uncertainties and largely represent non-permanent labour. The mines of the Belgian Congo are distinguished by a definite policy of developing a separate class of industrial labour and of providing the social services required by such a community.

NOTES

1. Frankel, *Capital Investment in Africa*, Table 28.
2. *Ibid.*, p. 163.
3. Frankel, Chapter I, sections III and IV, deal with these subjects.
4. Although the comparison is not accurate, the order of magnitude of these figures may be compared with the estimates made by Sir Josiah Stamp of the capital per head of population in the more important countries on the outbreak of war in 1914. His estimate for the United States was £424, for the United Kingdom £318, France £313, Germany £244, Italy £128, Russia £85, Denmark £90, and Japan £44. (See the *Encyclopaedia Britannica*, article 'Wealth, National'.)
5. Frankel, p. 170.
6. Frankel, p. 209.
7. *Ibid.*, p. 8.
8. *An African Survey*, p. 607.

APPENDIX

Capital Invested from Abroad in Individual Territories, 1870–1936

British Territories

	Public listed capital £000	Private listed capital £000	Total listed £000	Non-listed capital £000	Total capital £000
Nigeria	34,721	36,790[a]	71,511[a]	3,576	75,087
Gold Coast	13,462	20,160	33,622	1,681	35,303
Sierra Leone	2,454	750	3,204	160	3,364
Gambia	234	—	234	12	246
Sundry West African		2,730	2,730	—	2,730
Kenya and Uganda	31,542	8,583	40,125	6,019	46,144
Tanganyika	31,211 ⎫	15,841	47,181[b]	4,718	51,899
Zanzibar	129 ⎭				
Nyasaland	10,298[c]	1,000	11,298	848	12,146
Bechuanaland	886 ⎫				
Southern Rhodesia	35,993 ⎬[d]	53,484	93,094	9,309	102,403
Northern Rhodesia	2,731 ⎭				
Total British Territories	£163,661	£139,338	£302,999	£26,323	£329,322

French

Equatorial Africa	15,248	5,000	20,248	1,012	21,260
West Africa	16,477	12,500	28,977	1,449	30,426
Togo and Cameroons	11,306	6,431	17,737[e]	887	18,624
Total French Territories	£43,031	£23,931	£66,962	£3,348	£70,310

Belgian

Belgian Congo including Ruanda-Urundi	35,846	100,670	136,516	6,821	143,337
Grand total	£242,538	£263,939	£506,477	£36,492	£542,969[f]

(a) Includes capital invested not only in Nigeria, but in other West African Territories by such companies as the African and Eastern Trading Corporation and the United Africa Company.

(b) Includes £33,574,000 invested in German East Africa.

(c) Includes approximately £4,000,000 of private railway capital including the Trans-Zambesi Railway.

(d) Includes £25,900,000 invested in the Rhodesian Railway system which extends into Bechuanaland and Portuguese East Africa. Also £837,000 raised abroad by Public Utility Companies.

(e) Includes £15,827,000 invested in German Togoland and the Cameroons. The post-war figures are for the French Mandates only.

(f) It is interesting to compare the figures in this statement with the liberal provision made by Italy for the development of its new Empire of Ethiopia as set out by Quaranta in his recent book. In addition to an annual subvention of about £10,000,000 a grant of £133,000,000 has been made as a first provision for a programme of development. Of this sum £5,500,000 is for military works, £2,200,000 for white settlement, and the balance for 10,704 kilometres of roads, public buildings, maritime and hydraulic works, medical services, mining development, and telegraphs and telephones.

22

SOME ASPECTS OF INVESTMENT AND ECONOMIC DEVELOPMENT IN THE CONTINENT OF AFRICA*[1]

S. Herbert Frankel

Human societies necessarily picture the future in terms of the habit patterns of expectation formed by their past experience. It is therefore not surprising that the European colonising powers, as I endeavoured to show in my book on Capital Investment in Africa,[1] originally thought of their task of pacifying and opening up the continent very much in terms of investment in railways, roads, and communications which, it was hoped, would, as was the case in America, pave the way for the migration into an 'empty' continent of European peoples who would 'naturally' proceed to develop its resources. The construction of a basic framework of communications was in any case an inescapable burden. It was necessary for strategic and administrative reasons; without it the African continent would have remained as closed to the world economy as it had been south of the Sahara almost since the dawn of history.

Most of this basic framework of modern administration and economic intercourse had to be paid for by investment from abroad in the form of government grants, loans, military expenditures, and the like. Private investors did not, and could not have been expected to, undertake the task since the individual net product was insufficient, and was never expected to be other than insufficient, to meet the current yield expectations of investors.

It is significant that of the total capital invested in Africa from 1870 to 1936 nearly one-half was supplied by governments or public authorities. Of the remainder a large part has been connected with mining and exploration activities, especially gold-

*Reprinted by permission from *Africa*, Vol. XXII, No. 1, 1952.

mining, and therefore in directions where the expected individual net product to private enterprise was assumed to be considerable, or at any rate speculatively attractive.[2]

The construction of the modern economic framework did not, however, for political, economic, and climatic reasons, bring with it the expected large migration of European peoples with the social and psychological heritage of modern industrialism. On the contrary, the foundation of all modern economic development was provided by the psychologically, socially, and economically unadjusted labour of its indigenous peoples.

This led to the development of a peculiar pattern of economic production, the characteristic feature of which is the employment of a relatively very large proportion of unskilled, undifferentiated, indigenous labour which tends to be increasingly divorced from employment on the land, and even from residence on it, with a consequent continuous increase in urbanisation. Mining enterprises in Africa typify the pattern of production which characterises economic evolution in Africa under the impact of investment from abroad, and in them is exposed in an extreme form the general dilemma which the modern world at present faces in African economic development.

As is well known, whenever the agencies utilising capital from abroad, be they government or private, have to make direct or indirect provision for servicing the debts so incurred or for providing the foreign investor with a sufficient yield on equity capital to ensure that further supplies of it will be made available, the development of industries exploiting mineral and other natural resources for export is inevitable. This in effect means that the economy, having undertaken the capital investment to provide the basic modern economic framework to which I have referred, must, unless there is very considerable migration which provides the whole range of the required complementary labour and skill from abroad, detach labour from the indigenous social pattern of tribal economic organisation. It will perforce have to use it in those directions which will yield exports to meet the external payments obligations, as well as to pay for imports not covered by investment from abroad. Indeed it will need to detach labour from the indigenous economic structure even for carrying out the original capital construction of the framework, and it will be forced in general to engage in these types of production which will be expected to yield immediately the greatest individual net product. This is inescapable unless capital is made so 'cheap', i.e. is available for such long periods of time, in such amounts, and on such easy terms of debt service, that it is possible to use it for very long-run improvements in order to establish the modern pattern of economic activity. I have in mind improvements which will develop the efficiency or productivity of labour itself—using the term in its widest sense to include organisational, managerial, or entrepreneurial ability. I also have in mind improvements to 'land and natural resources', for example, new or more suitable types of plant and animal life, soil conservation, water supplies, and the like.

To illustrate this I would ask you, momentarily, to enter with me into the realm of fancy. Let us imagine that capital were to be supplied from abroad as a free good in unlimited quantities. That would, of course, mean that as far as the indigenous peoples were concerned they could (if we make the far-reaching assumption that they wished to do so) proceed unhampered to adopt western industrial civilisation and to remould it nearer to their hearts' desires in the course of its transplantation to Africa. They could devote their time to acquiring proficiency in new pursuits, to evolving new methods of agriculture and industry, to planning and building modern cities, and to preparing themselves, their children, and their children's children for their chosen new way of life. They would be able to take *unlimited* time in realising the new heaven on earth—since meanwhile they could be fed. housed, educated, and generally equipped for it by unlimited supplies of food and other consumer's necessities, as these and the machinery and equipment needed for construction purposes would be paid for by the gifts of Fairy Godmother 'Dame Capital', who might possibly reside in Washington in the Headquarters of the 'Point Four' Administration. We cannot be certain that they would necessarily use her gifts in these directions. It might well happen, if history were to repeat itself, that while the less popular 'Dame Necessity', the Mother of Invention, was busy looking over her shoulder they might prefer to sit for too long under the shadow of the proverbial African palm-tree, in deep contemplation of the past which alone they know.

But let us proceed. The moral of this fanciful story is, of course, that the line between capital and the whole 'heritage of improvement' is not and never can be a hard and fast one. As Cannan pointed out,[3] capital is not the whole of that man-made heritage. In common usage the term capital was, in the past, generally applied to purchasable and saleable private, and more recently to 'public', property. It used to exclude things not openly sold for and bought with money. This use of the term suffers from serious disadvantages into which I do not wish to enter here, except to say that when there is a *change* from one type of economic and social organisation and *way of life* to another, society may require resources to enable it to support itself during the process of transition and while it is engaged on acquiring the new social heritage. Resources so utilised are as much 'capital' as are machinery or factory buildings or other kinds of 'saleable' property. Such resources might consist of food imports to enable a part of the society in question to devote itself to scientific research and experimentation, to study, to teaching, or to acquiring new skills in administration or industry.

Unfortunately in the real world financial Fairy Godmothers are rare. Consequently the *immediately possible* pattern of economic activity involves the employment of that type of labour and those natural resources which are at hand, or can be very soon brought into combination, in order to yield a sufficient and not long-deferred net product. The need to resort to such combinations of the factors as are immediately possible has grave consequences because there results from such combinations a particular pattern of economic activity which tends to perpetuate itself and to become ever more rigidly established. It creates its own vested interests and makes difficult the establishment of other forms of the productive combination of resources. Indeed, it may lead to the establishment of legal and social sanctions specifically designed to prevent any change which will alter the production pattern itself.

Such sanctions already permeate the whole of the South African economy. They have as their object the perpetuation of supplies of labour of that undifferentiated and unskilled type on which the 'modern' economic pattern of production was first erected. Many examples of this process, both in Africa and elsewhere, readily spring to mind. Thus in British Guiana it was, in an earlier period, actually a criminal offence to grow rice at a time when it was being imported from as far as India and Burma to feed the Indian immigrants, because it was feared that rice-growing would lead to the deflection of labour from the sugar plantations.[4]

This tendency lies at the root of the dilemma of African development to which I have referred. For in all African territories the development of modern methods of economic organisation is in greater or lesser degree accompanied by increasingly rapid disintegration of the indigenous economic and social structure. However primitive those indigenous institutions may now appear to western eyes, they did in fact provide the individuals composing the indigenous society with that sense of psychological and economic security without which life loses its meaning.

Now of course all economic development involves a process of disintegration of previous patterns of economic cohesion. But whereas in the highly industrialised countries of Europe and America we have come to take for granted—far too readily, I fear—this process of disintegration and subsequent reintegration of the 'factors of production' into new and 'better' combinations (assuming the 'right' decisions of policy by the economic élite, whether composed of private or public entrepreneurial agencies), in Africa we take any such process for granted at our peril. For in Africa as we have seen, the factors of production cannot be assumed to be ready for recombination. They are highly specific to a particular way of life and work which had previously achieved an equilibrium within a narrowly circumscribed ecological and human environment; they are not as a rule capable of successful recombination into a variety of new patterns of production. On the contrary, they tend to be recombined into patterns of activity which may give rise to grave problems of social and economic instability, and may eventually involve comparatively heavy social and economic costs, just because there is no time for their necessarily slow preparation for stable integration into a new economic and social whole.

This time period of preparation is, of course, again but another name for the supply of the necessary subsistence or capital fund on which the community can draw in its transition from the old to the new. Without the expenditure of 'capital' on its improvement most African labour can only be used at present for its physical brawn. It cannot be utilised in any other economic capacity. But such capital expenditure, for example on re-education and relocation, involves vast changes in 'consumer habits'. The whole way of life of the people concerned is affected —their diet, the 'protective' clothing they require, the housing suited to their new urban conditions, and a large range of other needs which must be met for physiological and psychological reasons to ensure the social health and economic efficiency of the transplanted community.

Now in the first round of development the new society is not burdened with all these social or capital costs because broadly speaking the modern sectors of the economy make use of migrant labour, i.e. of labour not fully detached from its indigenous economic structure. But such a system of migrant labour finally leads to the undermining of the rural economy which serves as its base, owing to the progressive deterioration of the whole social and economic life of the indigenous structure as it is drained of its able-bodied and more enterprising members. Thus the labour force becomes progressively detribalised until finally the modern sector of the economy has to provide for the whole social and capital cost of maintaining a large and relatively un-skilled urban proletariat. If urbanisation and the destruction of the rural economy is rapid the process may even destroy a con-siderable part of the previous 'subsistence' production and of the man-made improvements in the indigenous economy. That sub-sistence production is, of course, bound in any case to be in-adequate to supply the food and other agricultural requirements of the new urban population. Consequently the economy comes to be faced with the need for developing new patterns of agricultural production and has to shoulder the burden of the additional capital costs thereof; it may indeed have to save the land itself from erosion and other forms of deterioration. In this connexion it must always be remembered that the indigenous rural economy has not the knowledge, skill, or capital to initiate these changes itself—even if the physical labour resources which remain on the land are sufficient for the purpose.

The short-fall in food production can be made good by imports which, unless paid for by greater exports (which would of course lead to an even more rapid disintegration), would have to be financed by capital from abroad. Yet even this latter alternative is, apart from the capital costs involved, not at all as simple a process as might appear to be the case. It, too, requires con-siderable changes in food-habits, tastes, and distributive organi-sation which may require a long time to bring about.

It is on account of the increasing rapidity of the process of disintegration to which I have referred that there have been grow-ing demands in all African territories for greater expenditures on 'Welfare'. A very large part of these expenditures simply reflect the unavoidable social capital costs of change which have to be borne, either equally or unequally, within the community, unless the human suffering which change involves can be mitigated by gifts or not too burdensome capital investment from abroad.

It remains to consider how the psychology of investment from the standpoint of those supplying capital from abroad has been affected by the vast changes that have taken place in Europe since the turn of the century. It is well to remember that the climate of opinion in which the great speculative investments in Africa took place when Europe was the world's banker has suffered a sea change. Gone are the days when the opening up of Africa could be looked upon as a natural part of Europe's economic and financial expansion. Gone is the easy belief that given only communications, order, and 'good' government Africa's natural resources would automatically yield an adequate return to those supplying equity capital for their development. The supply of risk capital is at a premium in Europe itself. The complex financial structure, with its far-reaching personal links and experience, built up by a generation of venturesome European investors in relation to Africa, has not yet been created in other capital markets on which Africa might draw. It may indeed never again be built on the pattern of the past.

Nor is the continuous supply of capital by the governments of European powers, or their agencies, more certain. Quite apart from the fact that the available supplies of such capital are by no means permanently assured, there are new factors of importance which have only become apparent recently. Firstly, there is the fact that much of the capital now needed in Africa is for purposes other than the construction of that economic framework to which I have earlier referred. To an increasing extent it has become necessary for governments to endeavour to finance enterprises which in one form or another could previously be left to private enterprise. But the institutions and experience for this new kind of investment are still lacking.

Secondly, is the fact that European colonial powers no longer exercise sovereignty to the same extent as previously, so that the automatic existence of legal and constitutional safeguards for private persons or for governments themselves in relation to investment in African territories previously under their rule can no longer be taken for granted. African nationalism carries with it all and perhaps even more than the usual dangers which foreign governments of nationals have to fear from the unpredictable policies of sovereign nation states.

Thirdly, the very social and economic disruption to which we have referred is making the future course of economic development in Africa and its political repercussions more uncertain. Latent tensions are being released which may affect not only the productivity of capital itself but the willingness of external investors—public or private—to become involved in them.

Thus one can sum up by saying that the problem of economic development in Africa has in fact ceased to be, if it ever was, a narrow economic question. By this I wish to convey that it is no longer merely a question of encouraging capital investment and economic development in specific directions in response either to the expected economic opportunities for particular types of enterprise; nor is it a question of undertaking particular developments in accordance with the strategic or political requirements of the outside world. It is a question of incorporating Africa into the world economy at a rate and in a manner which will not endanger the peace and political stability of Africa itself.

Africa has become a problem of world statesmanship: the 'White Man's Burden' has become the burden of the free world in much more than metaphorical terms. For as long as we can foresee, Africa itself will not be able to provide even a small fraction of the economic and technical framework required to make it a more effective part of the work and life of the outside world. Much patient and persistent effort will be required to create new international, financial, economic, and administrative institutions for the development of the productivity of its peoples.

It is also clear that capital investment in and by itself is not the answer to Africa's economic problems, and that the process of investment especially cannot be thought of in merely abstract terms or in terms of broad statistical aggregates. Far greater attention has to be devoted to the particular institutional manner in which it is supplied and used so as to ensure that it will meet the need which perhaps dominates all else—the need to fashion new economic structures which will prove to be socially stable. This really means that Africa's need is for more capital of a kind which cannot yield, and should not be expected to yield, immediate net returns.

Whether such capital can in fact be supplied in sufficient amounts, and, if so, how it can be effectively mobilised for, and effectively applied in, a continent so ill equipped with complementary human factors of production, and in the face of such great ecological and environmental difficulties, we do not yet know. In that ignorance lies the challenge of Africa to the freely creative world.

NOTES

1. *Capital Investment in Africa. Its Course and Effects*, Oxford University Press, 1938.
2. In all speculations the individual winners are, fortunately or unfortunately, usually unaware of the extent of the losses of those who are unsuccessful. The over-all yield to the capital invested in mining enterprise in Africa illustrates this very forcibly. Africa has in one sense profited much from the over-optimism usually displayed by gamblers.
3. 'Capital and the Heritage of Improvement', *Economica*, London, Nov. 1934.
4. See G. B. Masefield, *A Short History of Agriculture in the British Colonies*, Oxford University Press, 1950.

23

FOREIGN INVESTMENT AND TECHNOLOGICAL DIFFUSION: THE CASE OF BRITISH COLONIAL AFRICA*

T. R. De Gregori

Although the term *economic development* is appropriate to describe events in developed countries, currently it is most frequently used in connection with the attempts of less developed nations to raise their standard of living. Implicit in the latter is the transfer of technology (skills, knowledge, and tools) from the *haves* to the *have nots*. The character of this technological transfer (that is, private investment, bank loans, gifts, and so on) is the subject of much theoretical and ideological controversy. This process of technological borrowing has deep historical roots and has been the subject of economic inquiry for almost two hundred years. Both the technological diffusion and the inquiry concerning it warrant brief outlining for the light that they can cast upon contemporary problems.

It has been generally assumed by writers on technological diffusion that poorer countries need a net transfer of financial resources (that is, import surpluses) to augment domestic savings and to initiate development. In international trade theory and texts on the subject, this transfer was manifested in a four-stage model: Stage I, import surpluses as foreign capital is being invested; Stage II, export surpluses, repatriation of foreign capital; Stage III, export surpluses, investment abroad; Stage IV, import surpluses financed by receipts from prior investments in Stage III. In the following investigation only occasionally did the data fit this model. On closer analysis the four-stage theory is of questionable relevance, even where the facts seem to fit the model.

The four-stage model is of more than just historical interest.

*Reprinted by permission from the *Journal of Economic Issues*, Vol. 2, No. 4, 1968.

For, as we shall see below, it is an intricate part of a larger body of economic theory concerning economic development. Much of contemporary writing by economists and other assumes the need for foreign capital as an initator of development, both in the past and in the present. If, as we contend, the diffusion of science and technology has been the major factor in stimulating economic advancement in less developed areas, then it is possible if not probable that the current emphasis on saving and foreign investment is misplaced. 'Non-economic' factors loom large in the transfer of technology and they are not always complementary to the so-called 'economic' factors. An economic policy that encourages domestic saving and foreign investment is frequently aligned with a political and social oligarchy that restricts the utilisation of modern technology. Unless development economists are willing to borrow and incorporate insights from other social sciences, their theories cannot be operational or predictive for economic transformations that involve cultural and political resistances to technological and social change. These aspects of the economic development problem will also be discussed while we explore the alterations of current opinion necessary to engender operational hypotheses.

Technological diffusion is as old as man. One group evolves a tool tradition that is borrowed and modified by another. Thus, from the early Stone Age, tools and techniques diffused over wide areas, and groups that were behind borrowed or on occasion saw new possibilities for combinations of tools, thereby surpassing the lender. Not only is the relation of tools to particular problems and environments relevant, but equally important is the relationship of tools to human beings and the social institutions they created. The question as to why one group or another borrowed or failed to borrow a technology cannot always be explained in terms of environment, and therefore the human factor in social institutions has to be considered.

The process of technological diffusion is well-known to social scientists and is an increasingly important element in most historical writing. However, there is a hiatus in economic literature when dealing with the diffusion of technology from Western Europe and the United States since the advent of capitalist institutions. Technological diffusion becomes a secondary consideration to that of the diffusion of patterns of ownership—that is, capital movements and foreign investment. In early periods, alien technology did, at times, entail foreign ownership; generally, though, this would be in the form of a conquest or a migration of people and not private foreign investment. In the long run, however, the critical factor was not the movement of capital or goods, but of ideas; in other words, ideas that could be incorporated with other knowledge in a continuing process of production and technological development. Thus, for England and Northern Europe, alien technology was basically a 'free good,' and we can speak of their 'indebtedness' to Asia and the Mediterranean civilisations in a purely metaphorical sense. This 'free good' can be characterised not only in terms of the immediately preceding centres of inventive activity but also in terms of the entire mainstream of technological evolution from earliest times. Technological progress is cumulative; without these earlier inventions the later ones would have been impossible. The question that follows here is whether technological diffusion is valid as an explanation or partial explanation of economic change with respect to capitalist industrial countries and less developed nations. Secondly, given the extraordinarily high level of indebtedness throughout the under-developed world (a cause of much concern to economists), it is clear that the character of the social and political aspects of technological borrowing has altered.[1] How has economic theory explained this transformation? What is the relevance of this explanation to contemporary economic development?

From the era of Ricardo to very recent times, economic theory has placed emphasis on the role of capital in economic advancement. Some theorists outside the main currents did place heavy emphasis on Technology, but with a few exceptions, such as Marshall, most economists mentioned technology but did not assign a significant role to it. Capital was generally understood to mean money; what else could be accumulated by saving? Quite obviously, economists had other things in mind when they talked about capital—that is, machinery, skills, and knowledge—but the very structure of their theories prevented these factors from playing an influential role in the analysis of economic change.

As the English ownership of overseas assets became an important agent in the trade balances in the mid-nineteenth century, economists were accommodating and providing an explanation. From Adam Smith onward, economists had posited a declining rate of profit as accompanying an increasing degree of prosperity. When applied to international trade, this meant that profits were higher in less developed areas, and consequently, profit-seeking investors would seek these great profits unless they were offset by political or other risk factors. In trade this meant that the developed country would initially export more than it imported, with the balance representing the movement of goods paid for by investors and destined for less developed areas. These assets would, under the right conditions, stimulate development and earn profits, all or part of which could be repatriated, thus beginning a reversal of the flow of goods. Part of the profits could be reinvested so that theoretically (and in actuality) an underdeveloped country could export more than it imported, and at the same time, foreign ownership of domestic assets could be growing. This was a convenient theory for the time, as England was enjoying import surpluses that were in part paid for by repatriated profits (while foreign investments continued their rapid growth), the other part being payments for services such as shipping.[2] One critic at least has questioned the notion that there is always an initial outflow of goods from developed countries for a significantly sustained period of time, and if his criticism is correct, the theory would lack empirical foundation.[3]

If we look at sub-Saharan Africa from its early maritime contact with Europe until the mid-to-late nineteenth century, there is little that could be defined as foreign investment, other than a few trade forts and different scattered European enclaves. There were commercial relationships, of course, with the slave trade unfortunately playing a dominant role throughout this period. Modern scholarship correctly recognises that African middlemen not only were guilty of participation in the slave trade but were in fact essential to it. Equally, we ought to recognise another endeavour in which Africans were playing an active role throughout these centuries: that of borrowing elements of Western technology. Around the trade forts and, later, mission stations some Africans were learning to read; others were learning skills, such as carpentry and cooperage. Africans yielded up a variety of cultigens to the rest of the world and in turn borrowed and learned the techniques of planting and processing such crops as maize, manioc, and cocoa. Much of this borrowing was primarily due to the initiative of the Africans.[4] In other cases it was a joint endeavour as Europeans consciously brought tools, skills, and ideas and sought to adapt them to local needs. Of course, prior to maritime contact, Europeans and Africans had long traditions of culture contact and technological diffusion with other areas, both as lenders and borrowers. Africa on the eve of colonisation was a very different place from the Africa of four centuries earlier, and the main agencies for the beneficial aspects of this change were the initiative of the Africans and the well-established process of culture contact and borrowing technology.

In the areas of Africa destined to be under suzerainty, we are fortunate to have some rudimentary foreign trade statistics while European presence (consequently, what little investment there was) was limited to the coast. In compiling these (and allowing for error as much as possible), I found the following pattern or tendency: those countries that were poor in potential and therefore received very little foreign investment (that is, Somaliland and Nyasaland) tended toward early and sustained import surpluses. In this respect, the theory of foreign investment seems to explain best those economies where such investment was small. Poorer regions in what later became federated territories also tended toward early import surpluses (that is, Northern Nigeria, Natal, and Orange Free State). Peasant economies, such as Nigeria (see Table 1), or Ghana (see Table 2), and possibly Southwest Africa (see Table 3), tended to develop sustained export surpluses after an early period of alternating surplus-deficits or small surpluses.[5] Here, then, we have an outflow of goods that, unless a consistent bias to the data can be shown, cannot be explained in terms of an earlier goods contribution.

In other peasant economies, such as Uganda and Tanzania (see Table 4), there may have been initial import surpluses, but early in the game a pattern of export surpluses emerged. In fact, the pattern for these two countries is persisting into the present, while in other countries, such as Nigeria and Ghana, the pattern was reversed in the mid-1950s with the spending for development of accumulated funds. These accumulated funds were a source of some controversy in British economic journals of the 1940s and 1950s. They were kept in London and consisted of marketing board surpluses and sterling cover for colonial currency (frequently 100 per cent or more) and in effect constituted low- or no-interest loans from the colonies to the United Kingdom. Further, the African colonies were earning badly needed dollars that they were yielding to the mother country, while branch banks were remitting surplus savings to the metropolitan head office. The total amount of these funds was substantial (for Ghana alone, it was £190-£200 million at the time of independence) and constituted a flow of funds in a direction contrary to traditional theory and to the rhetoric of the postwar period.[6]

In the Cape Colony there is a consistent import surplus from the early 1800s (possibly paid for with the invisible export of services to ships that stopped en route to and from the Orient)

TABLE 1

Lagos (Colony of Southern Nigeria)   (Part 1, pp. 347–348)

	Imports	Exports
1868–1872	£ 383,255	£ 545,433
1873–1877	431,686	552,964
1878–1882	436,281	569,865
1883–1887	473,871	582,436
1888–1892	515,877	571,161
1893–1897	796,278	885,962
1898–1902	874,689	986,094
1903–1907	2,118,782	2,170,087
1908–1912	5,443,258	4,872,762

Territory Administered by the Royal Niger Company   (Part 2, p. 348)

1887–1893 (7 yrs.)	154,371	297,615

Protectorate of Southern Nigeria   (Part 3, p. 349)

1892–1896	760,608	862,425
1897–1901	902,167	958,227
1902–1905 (4 yrs.)	1,571,309	1,529,085

Protectorate of Northern Nigeria   (Part 4, pp. 349 and 350)

1901–1904 (4 yrs.)	271,705	99,600
1905–1906 not available		
1907–1912 (6 yrs.)	934,666	519,963

Nigeria 1913–1923   (Part 5, p. 350)

1913–1918 (6 yrs.)	6,784,485	7,334,026
1919–1923	13,494,206	12,705,501

Nigeria 1924–1957   (Part 6, pp. 351–352)

(data below in £1,000s)

1924–1927 (4 yrs.)	13,288	15,945
1928–1932	11,059	13,612
1933–1937	8,992	12,746
1938–1942	7,973	12,016
1943–1947	19,134	25,094
1948–1952	71,425	99,428
1952–1957	132,683	134,963

TABLE 2

Ghana (Gold Coast) 1856–1894		(Part 1, pp. 352–353)
	Imports	Exports
1856–1861	£ 122,730	£ 129,061
1862–1867 not available		
1868–1872	223,578	297,910
1873–1874 not available		
1875–1879	371,045	400,310
1880–1884	407,654	405,306
1885–1889	415,930	414,570
1890–1894	650,993	704,634
Ghana (Gold Coast) 1895–1923		(Part 2, p. 354)
1895–1898 (4 yrs.)	958,272	880,177
1899–1903	1,720,486	862,409
1904–1908	1,988,501	2,029,886
1909–1913	3,720,464	3,776,128
1914–1918	4,322,065	5,508,133
1919–1923	9,421,294	9,477,525

The figures for the years before 1900 include specie imports and exports, having the net effect of exaggerating imports. Further, during this period, there was frequent warfare in Ashanti, necessitating military imports. Conversely, for some of the early years, imports are F.O.B.

Ghana (Gold Coast) 1924–1957		(Part 3, pp. 355–356)
	(data below in £1,000s)	
1924–1927 (4 yrs.)	9,144	12,603
1928–1932	7,844	10,328
1933–1937	7,248	10,721
1938–1942	7,342	12,579
1943–1947	12,418	17,407
1948–1952	50,495	71,521
1953–1957	83,535	95,722

TABLE 3

Southwest Africa 1924–1954		(Part 2, p. 372)
	(data below in £1,000s)	
	Imports	Exports
1924–1929 (6 yrs.)	£ 2,478	£ 3,228
1930–1934	1,463	1,651
1935–1939	2,115	3,250
1940–1944 not available		
1945–1949	8,805	10,939
1950–1954	19,672	31,560

TABLE 4

Tanganyika 1924–1957		(Part 1, p. 384)
	(data below in £1,000s)	
	Imports	Exports
1924–1927 (4 yrs.)	£ 2,938	£ 3,068
1928–1932	3,275	3,036
1933–1937	2,912	3,885
1938–1942	3,967	5,606
1943–1947	7,767	8,681
1948–1952	27,729	30,091
1953–1957	35,814	40,148

until just immediately prior to the gold and diamond discoveries (see Table 5). Here, and to a degree, elsewhere, foreign investment can be identified from the beginning with export surpluses, not import surpluses. This was certainly the case in neighbouring Transvaal. In the other mineral countries, such as Zambia (as well as the Congo), there was a substantial goods inflow for about three to five years in the 1920s and then, there were consistent and extremely large export surpluses thereafter (see Table 6). Without a doubt, here was a capital contribution; but as the

TABLE 5

Cape Colony 1860–1909		(p. 365)
	Imports	Exports
1860–1864	£ 2,561,846	£ 2,165,365
1865–1869	2,073,252	2,371,541
1870–1874	4,002,930	4,648,092
1875–1879	5,936,230	5,625,099
1880–1884	7,596,288	7,742,134
1885–1889	5,546,140	7,788,303
1890–1894	10,017,987	11,917,037
1895–1899	16,294,329	20,171,390
1900–1904	25,254,743	16,944,130
1905–1909	16,360,299	41,581,433

The Cape Colony imports for 1900–1904 reflect the movement of military supplies by the British in fighting the Boer War.

Transvaal 1902–1909		(Part 2, p. 368)
1902–1905 (4 yrs.)	16,983,923	15,242,917
1906–1909 (4 yrs.)	17,325,132	31,481,819

TABLE 6

Northern Rhodesia 1906–1923		(Part 1, p. 375)
	Imports	Exports
1906–1913 (8 yrs.)	£ 207,011	£ 120,578
1914–1918	298,136	224,173
1919–1923	578,099	533,073
Northern Rhodesia 1924–1953		(Part 2, p. 376)
	(data below in £1,000s)	
1924–1928	£ 1,610	£ 591
1929–1933	3,565	1,868
1934–1938	2,489	7,500
1939–1943	5,480	12,173
1944–1948	9,745	17,334
1949–1953	35,589	65,544
Federation of Rhodesia and Nyasaland 1954–1963		(p. 379)
	(data below in £1,000s)	
1954–1958	£ 151,644	£ 165,497
1959–1963	147,927	210,286

investor would say, this capital was very productive, which is an economic euphemism for saying that the profits were very high. Unfortunately, this euphemism implies a productive contribution that 'created' these profits, apart from any governing social and political relationship. Ownership and authorship are confounded, the Africans being the losers. As to the technology involved, it certainly was not a free good. But who deserved the payoff for the technological contribution? Michael Faraday and all those involved in the development of electricity, which created a great demand for copper, or those individuals in western United States and Australia who developed the flotation process, which converted Zambian copper ores into a resource? It was this latter knowledge, not capital, that was critical (and remains so) and which, coupled with political power, meant that Europeans reaped large portions of the benefits of these developments. Economists have a *post hoc* explanation of these profits, a quasi-rent for monopoly power. Even with later political independence, lack of this knowledge factor limits the new government's options and ability to benefit from its resources.

In some white settler areas (Kenya, for example) import surpluses predominate, but account must be taken for remittances brought by settlers. Thus, from our evidence, traditional foreign

S

investment theory is verified only in three categories: (a) the poorer peasant economies that have experienced the least development; (a) *some* white settler territories; (c) *some* mining economies. The first category needs no further elaboration, since foreign investment theory purports to explain development and not the lack of it. There is little comfort in these countries for traditional economic theorists, because these countries as a group have not done as well as those peasant economies that were not the beneficiaries of import surpluses. Categories (b) and (c) do provide evidence for established international trade theory, but they also provide sufficient contrary evidence to cast doubt upon the theory. Thus, while it is quite clear that a white settler territory such as Kenya has experienced early and sustained import surpluses, in Rhodesia export surpluses began in 1905 and have continued to the present with few exceptions (see Table 7). In the mining territories only Zambia (and the Congo) has a clear definable stage of import surpluses for investment—during the 1920s. (In the Congo, considering that the earlier flow of financial resources had been outward, the 'necessity' for an inflow of funds in the 1920s can be attributed to the structure of political control and not necessarily to economic backwardness.)[7] Further, in Zambia (and the Congo) the investment period is so short and the payoff so large that foreign investment seems more a rationalisation and less a theory. In other mining areas, such as Cape Colony and Transvaal, foreign investment in these enterprises can be identified with years of export surpluses, and not with the expected import surpluses.[8]

To some, the above presentation might appear to be an exploitation theory; the reader would not be entirely remiss in

TABLE 7

Southern Rhodesia 1924–1953		(Part 2, p. 374)
(data below in £1,000s)		
	Imports	Exports
1924–1928	£ 6,167	£ 6,617
1929–1933	6,232	6,478
1934–1938	7,289	8,991
1939–1943	9,154	14,682
1944–1948	24,061	21,561
1949–1953	72,985	52,290

Post-World War II figures are strongly influenced by large immigration and settler remittances.

drawing that conclusion. However, this would skirt an essential point, namely, that it is the author's conviction that if economic development has taken place, and if it is contrary to various theories, so much the worse for the theories. In essence, the period of colonial control witnessed a continuation and intensification of the earlier process of the diffusion of technology. That price charges for this development were often exorbitantly high can justify using the term exploitation. It must be remembered, however, that in this context exploitation, as distinguished from plunder, is more effective, is possible only where economic development is taking place. Elsewhere I have argued that colonialism created a broad framework in which diffusion of technology and knowledge could occur as well as creating some institutions and practices which restrict technological development. This has been particularly true in the development of, or failure to develop, an urban labour force with technological habits of thought.[9] Unravelling these difficulties and seeing the many potentials and barriers to development require a broader spectrum of analysis than traditional economic theory can provide. It is fortunate that many development economists are beginning to broaden their horizons, for our concepts of foreign investment are certainly in need of decolonisation.

Other aspects of our economic thinking are equally outmoded. These matters would be of primary concern to economists were it not for the fact that other social scientists and intelligent laymen use (and misuse) economic terminology. There is a sense in which the factors of production of classical economics—land, labour, capital, and, later, enterprise—were not born of the analysis of the productive process but, rather, were an imputation of the productive contribution for socially determined forms of income, rent, wages, interest, and profit. This schema has run into difficulties as the categories are not always clear; factors other than land give rise to rent (called quasi-rent), and factors such as labour partake of properties of capital. More recently, the whole concept of capital, which is the basis for justifying foreign investment as necessary for economic development, is undergoing change. In the last ten years, numerous journals and books have published empirical studies on rates of saving and levels of capital formation in economic growth. In general, the studies found that some countries have accelerated their rate of growth without a corresponding change in their rate of saving. Further, capital is found to account for only a small part of economic growth. As for foreign capital investment, other than some dubious claims for the United States and England, the countries that are now industrial did industrialise with their own resources, and some did so very rapidly.[10] Unfortunately, rather than raise fundamental questions, most of these authors have preferred to redefine their terms or create new ones to eliminate these discrepancies. Thus, to some writers, capital essentially incorporates all agents of production not included in the other factors. With this verbal legerdemain the theory can never be proved wrong, since anything contributing to development—that is, technology, skills, foreign exchange, and so on—is part of capital. Nor can the theory be operational, because it does not tell us how we can create this generalised capital; it merely tells us what to call it after we have recognised it.

In regard to our above discussion of the lack of foreign trade data supporting traditional theory, a modern theorist would claim that the small number of Europeans in Africa in the nineteenth century made a human capital contribution. While not denying the importance of these individuals for the diffusion of technology, it is merely a supposition to attribute all subsequent export surpluses to their contribution, particularly since some of them (primarily missionaries) were not the beneficiaries of the profit expatriation. Again, with intangible human capital, one can impute the magnitude necessary to verify a theory presumed to be true. Verifying old truths can be profitable academically, since it saves one's colleagues the necessity of rethinking and redefining issues, but it does not contribute to the solution of the problems of our time.

Finally, the postwar period has clearly shown us that capital or foreign investment alone cannot engender development. In Europe, where one had the skills, knowledge, organisation, and so on, foreign aid provided a catalyst for economic recovery. In some countries large sums of money and considerable technical assistance have been rendered, with few tangible accomplishments to show for it. While some of the aid has found its way into the pockets of venal and corrupt officials, the cause of failure has been the social and political difficulties involved in economic transformation. In recognition of these difficulties, economists now speak of 'absorptive capacity', which is useful but unfortunately is more a term than an explanation. Again, it must be emphasised that economic development theory to be successful must be an integral part of an integrated social analysis if it is to be successful. For the need is not to determine the absorptive capacity of an economy (though that is important), but to expand it. The need, in short, is to involve people in a behavioural change, using new tools, thinking new ideas, and doing new things. This behavioural change is necessary both in developed and underdeveloped countries and for the social scientists in all these countries.

We have to view economic change as one aspect of a broader human and cultural change. The individuals involved in the process of development have a cultural heritage and must be seen as active agents in their own betterment. Nineteenth-century investors and investment theory not only assumed the passive acquiescence of the native, but in many cases, investors went so far as to use military power to guarantee it. Not only are such attitudes and practices intolerable in the present world, they are also contrary to what we know about the process of technological and cultural borrowing. Today most African countries are independent; they seek to be free and economically well-off; the least the social sciences can do is to evolve operationally and developmentally oriented concepts consistent with these aspirations.

NOTES

1. See, for example, Dragoslav Avramovic, *et al. Economic Growth and External Debt*, Baltimore, 1965.
2. According to a recent official British government publication, the *British Record*, Great Britain has had export surpluses in the visible balance of trade only in seven of the last 175 years: 1797, 1802, 1816, 1821, 1822, 1956, and 1958. Trade invisibles have traditionally more than made up this gap and even in the recent years, if overseas military expenditures are excluded, continue to do so. *British Record*, No. 14, November 27, 1967, p. 2.
3. See Wendell Gordon, 'Foreign Investments,' special issue of *University of Houston Business Review*, Vol. 9, Fall 1962. In my book, *Technology and the Economic Development of the Tropical African Frontier*, Cleveland, 1968, I present foreign trade and other data on the flow of funds in British Colonial Africa, which are the bases for the essay here.
4. See, for example, Polly Hill, *The Migrant Cocoa Farmers of Southern Ghana*, Cambridge, England, 1963.
5. The data that were used to compute the five-year averages in the accompanying tables are derived from the British Parliamentary Papers, *Statistical Abstracts*. The complete tables with yearly figures are found in De Gregori, *African Frontier*, pp. 273–78, and each table indicates the specific issues of the *Statistical Abstracts* used to compile the tables. Difficulties and shortcomings of the data are noted with each table and are also discussed in De Gregori, *Ibid.* In some cases discontinuities in the series necessitated using 4, 6, 7 averages; these are all noted in parentheses. All data are C.I.F. imports and F.O.B. exports except as noted in Tables 6 and 7, where trade figures are F.O.R.

6. For a more detailed analysis of these flows, see Chapters 8 and 9, De Gregori, *African Frontier*.
7. See R. L. Buell, *The Native Problem in Africa*, New York, 1928, Vol. II, pp. 432–434, 442–450, reprinted by Frank Cass, 1965.
8. See Table 5.
9. See De Gregori, *African Frontier*, Chapter 5.
10. For example, see Robert Solow, 'Technical Change and the Aggregate Production Function,' *The Review of Economics and Statistics*, Vol. XXXIX, No. 3, August 1957, pp. 312–320; Moses Abramovitz, 'Resource and Output Trends in the U.S. Since 1870,' *American Economic Review, Papers and Proceedings*, Vol. XLVI, No. 2, May 1956, pp. 5-23; and Simon Kuznets, *Modern Economic Growth*, New Haven, 1966, pp. 72–85. For a review of these and similar studies, see De Gregori, pp. 313–316.

INDEX

absorptive capacity, 252
Accra, 225
advances system, 166
African labour, 5
African traders, 143
African worker, 192
aggregate supply curve for labour, see labour supply curve
agricultural revolution, xii
Anglo-American Corporation of South Africa, 65
Angola, x, 44, 72, 73, 75, 81, 83, 85; head tax in, 82; her imports, 78, 79; mineral discoveries in, 83
Angolan uprising, 73
Anti-slavery Committee of the League of Nations, 170
Ashanti, 165
assimilados, 74
assimilation policy, 73, 83
Association of West African Merchants (AWAM), 145
association theory, 22

backward-sloping labour-supply functions (also backward-bending supply curves), xi, 176, 178, 181
Baldwin, Robert E., x
Bancroft copper mine, 65
Barotseland, 62, 68n
Basutoland, 162
Bathurst, 40
Bauer, P. T., xii
Bechuanaland, 44, 227
Beira and Mashonaland Railway, 69n
Belgian Congo, vii, 6n, 23, 24, 42, 43, 44, 45, 80, 118, 160, 162, 168, 170, 174, 176, 179, 190, 191, 194, 200, 204, 228, 229, 230, 248, 250
Belgian Royal Colonial Institute, 196
Belgium, 5, 6
Bell, Sir Hesketh, 47, 48
Benguela Railway, 43, 80

Benue River, 40
Berlin Act of 1885, 220
Berlin Conference of 1884–5, vii
Bismarck, Otto von, 14, 15
black pod, 118
Brazza, Savorgnan de, 52; his mission, 56
Brazzaville, 56, 193, 224
bride payments, 62
British Cameroons, 230
British colonial methods, 14, 20
British Committee on Nutrition in the Colonial Empire, 195
British Empire, 29, 30, 31
British South Africa Company, 42, 60, 65
British West Africa, 48, 229
Broken Hill, 43, 60, 69n; production of lead and zinc at, 61
Buganda, 140
Bulawayo, 43
Bwana M'Kubwa (also Bwana Makubwa), 61, 64, 69n

Cabinda, 81
Cabora Bassa Dam in Mozambique, 81
Chad, 54
Cannan, Edwin, 235
Cape Colony, 245, 250
capital, 9, 233, 234, 235, 239; foreign, 242; investment, 227, 228, 231; non-listed, 227; private listed, 227, 228; public listed, 227, 228; social, 238
capital-intensive methods of production, 161
capital-using methods of production see capital-intensive methods of production
cash cropping, 189
cash crops, viii, 138; compulsory growing of, 167
cattle industry, 62
Chamberlain, Joseph, ix, 7, 8, 9, 10, 11, 17
Chambishi copper mine, 66
chartered companies, 14, 15, 228

255

For Product Safety Concerns and Information please contact our
EU representative GPSR@taylorandfrancis.com Taylor & Francis
Verlag GmbH, Kaufingerstraße 24, 80331 München, Germany